Garfield
life to
the fullest

BY JIM DAVIS

Ballantine Books • New York

2017 Ballantine Books Trade Paperback Edition

Copyright © 1999, 2017 by PAWS, Inc. All rights reserved.
"GARFIELD" and the GARFIELD characters are trademarks of PAWS, Inc.

Published in the United States by Ballantine Books, an imprint of Random House,
a division of Penguin Random House LLC, New York.

BALLANTINE and the HOUSE colophon are registered trademarks of Penguin Random House LLC.

Originally published in slightly different form in the United States by Ballantine Books,
an imprint of Random House, a division of Penguin Random House LLC, in 1999.

ISBN 978-0-425-28564-0
Ebook ISBN 978-0-425-28565-7

Printed in China on acid-free paper

randomhousebooks.com

9 8 7 6 5 4 3 2 1

First Colorized Edition

THINGS GARFIELD WOULD NEVER SAY...

Do you think these jeans make my butt look big?

Odie— I love ya, man!

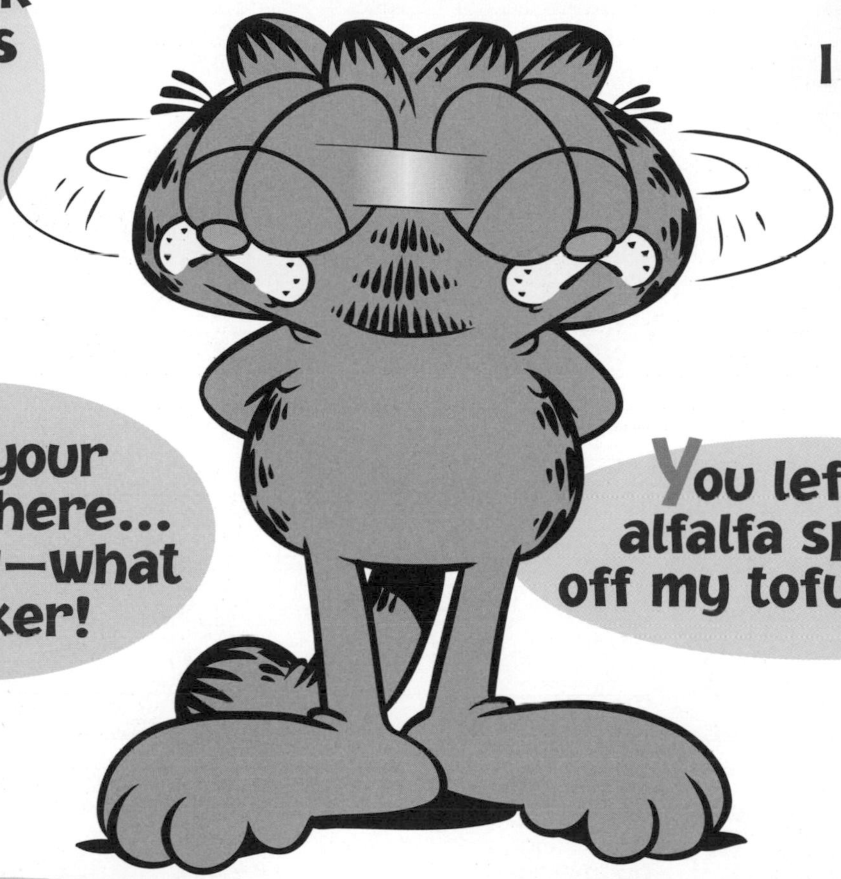

Jon, your date's here... and wow—what a looker!

You left the alfalfa sprouts off my tofu burger.

Cats...dogs... spiders...can't we all just get along?

Anyone wanna go "halvsies" on that last piece of double-fudge banana cheesecake?

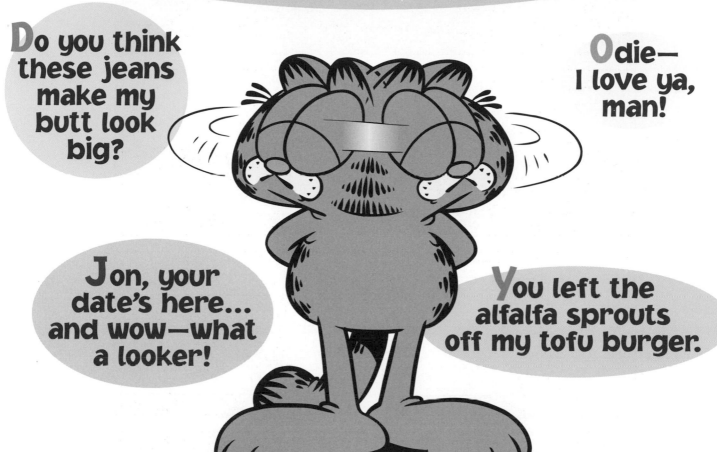

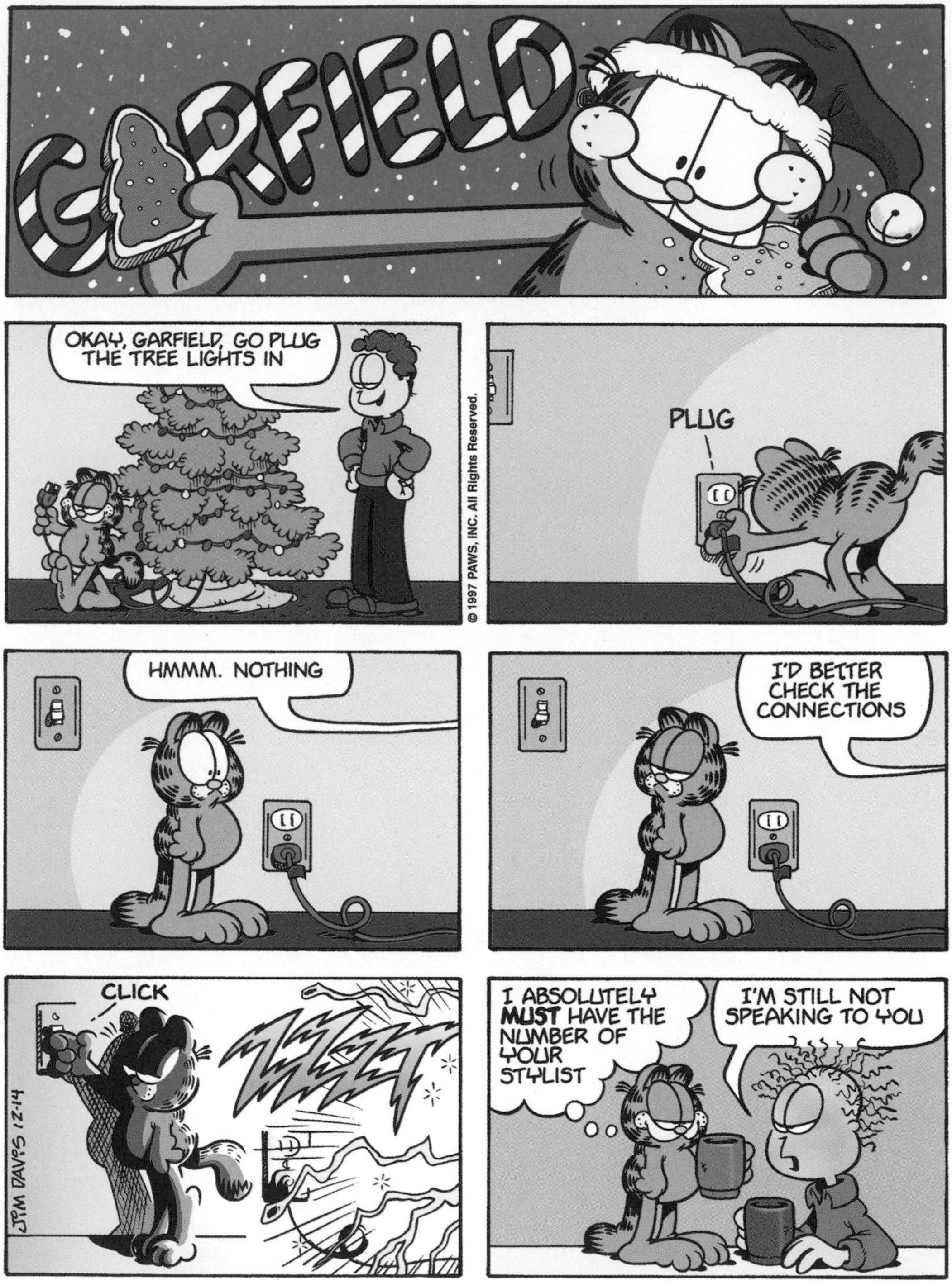
GARFIELD
OKAY, GARFIELD, GO PLUG THE TREE LIGHTS IN
© 1997 PAWS, INC. All Rights Reserved.
PLUG
HMMM. NOTHING
I'D BETTER CHECK THE CONNECTIONS
CLICK
I ABSOLUTELY MUST HAVE THE NUMBER OF YOUR STYLIST
I'M STILL NOT SPEAKING TO YOU

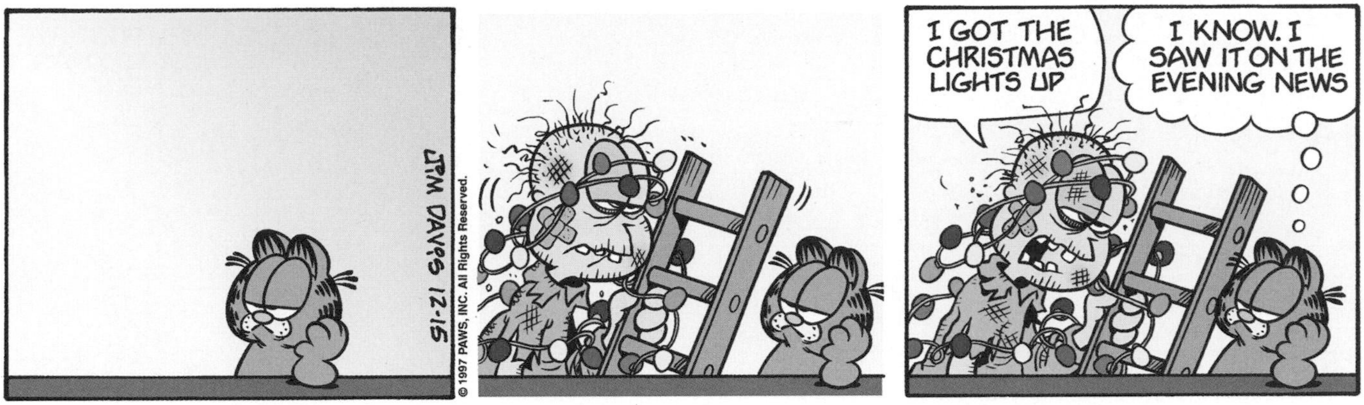
JIM DAVIS 12-15
© 1997 PAWS, INC. All Rights Reserved.
I GOT THE CHRISTMAS LIGHTS UP
I KNOW. I SAW IT ON THE EVENING NEWS

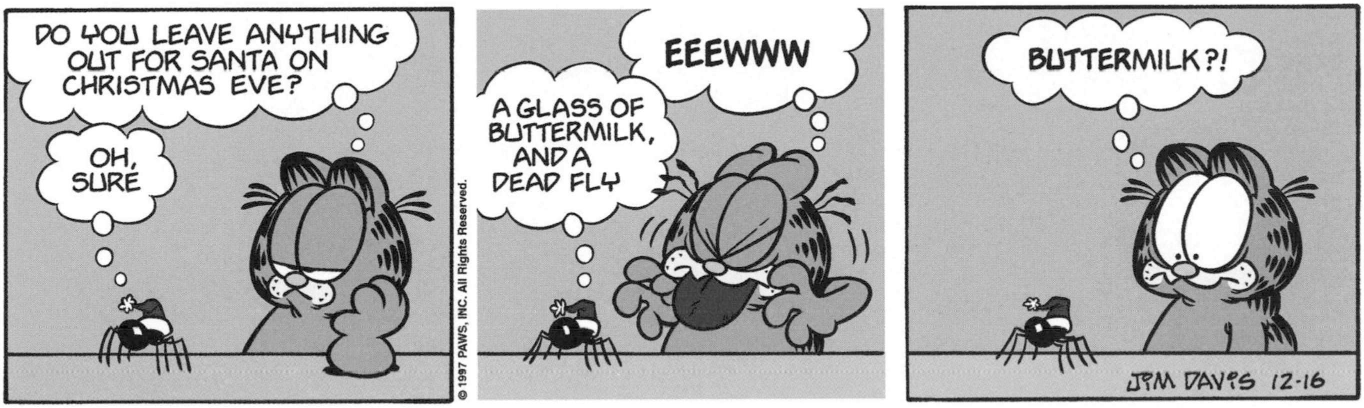
DO YOU LEAVE ANYTHING OUT FOR SANTA ON CHRISTMAS EVE?
OH, SURE
© 1997 PAWS, INC. All Rights Reserved.
A GLASS OF BUTTERMILK, AND A DEAD FLY
EEEWWW
BUTTERMILK?!
JIM DAVIS 12-16

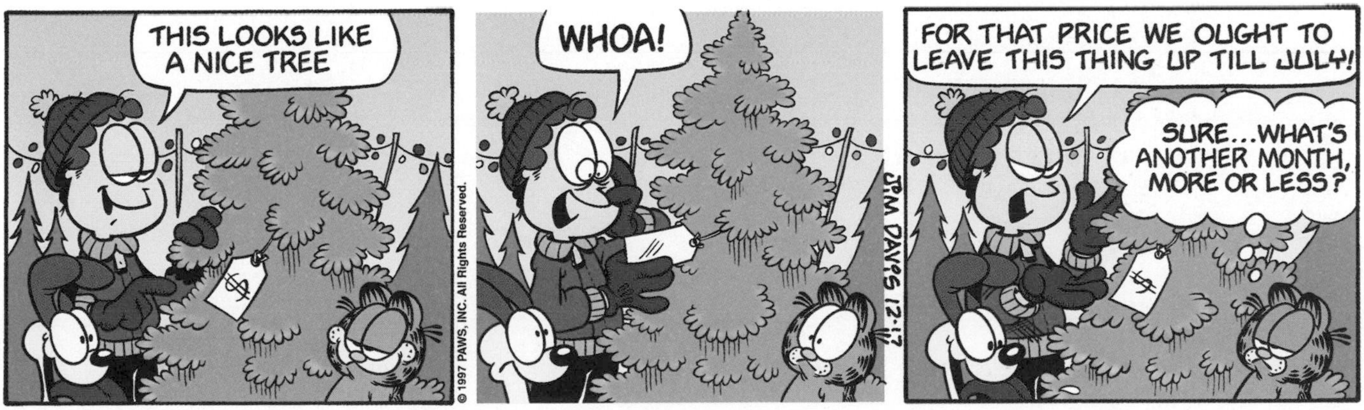
THIS LOOKS LIKE A NICE TREE
© 1997 PAWS, INC. All Rights Reserved.
WHOA!
JIM DAVIS 12-17
FOR THAT PRICE WE OUGHT TO LEAVE THIS THING UP TILL JULY!
SURE...WHAT'S ANOTHER MONTH, MORE OR LESS?

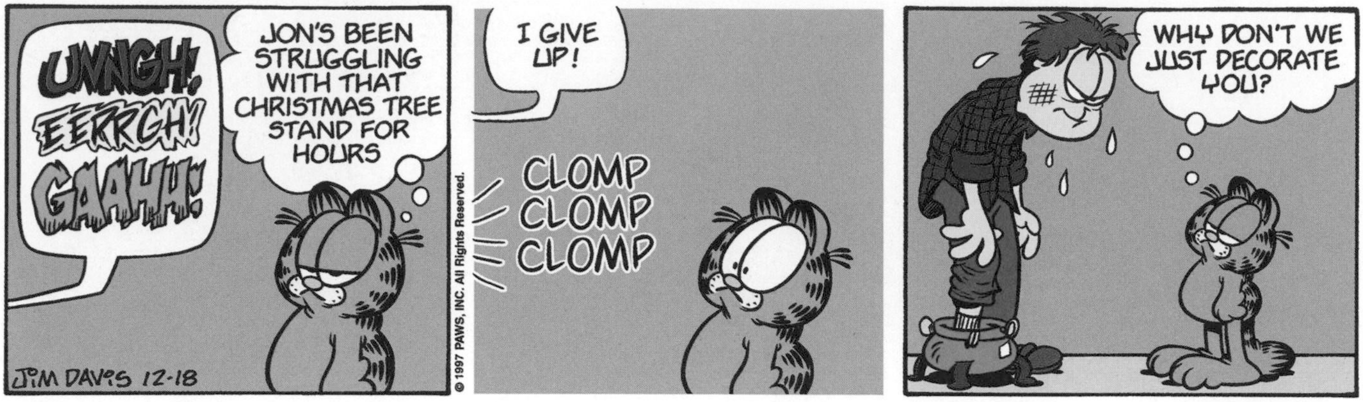
UNNGH! EERRGH! GAAHH!
JON'S BEEN STRUGGLING WITH THAT CHRISTMAS TREE STAND FOR HOURS
JIM DAVIS 12-18
© 1997 PAWS, INC. All Rights Reserved.
I GIVE UP!
CLOMP CLOMP CLOMP
WHY DON'T WE JUST DECORATE YOU?

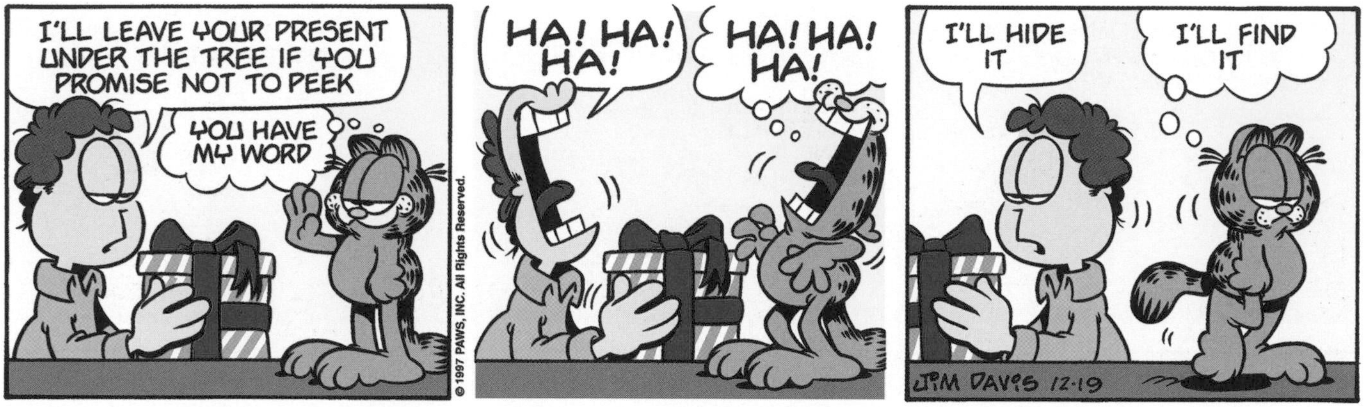
I'LL LEAVE YOUR PRESENT UNDER THE TREE IF YOU PROMISE NOT TO PEEK
YOU HAVE MY WORD
© 1997 PAWS, INC. All Rights Reserved.
HA! HA! HA!
HA! HA! HA!
I'LL HIDE IT
I'LL FIND IT
JIM DAVIS 12-19

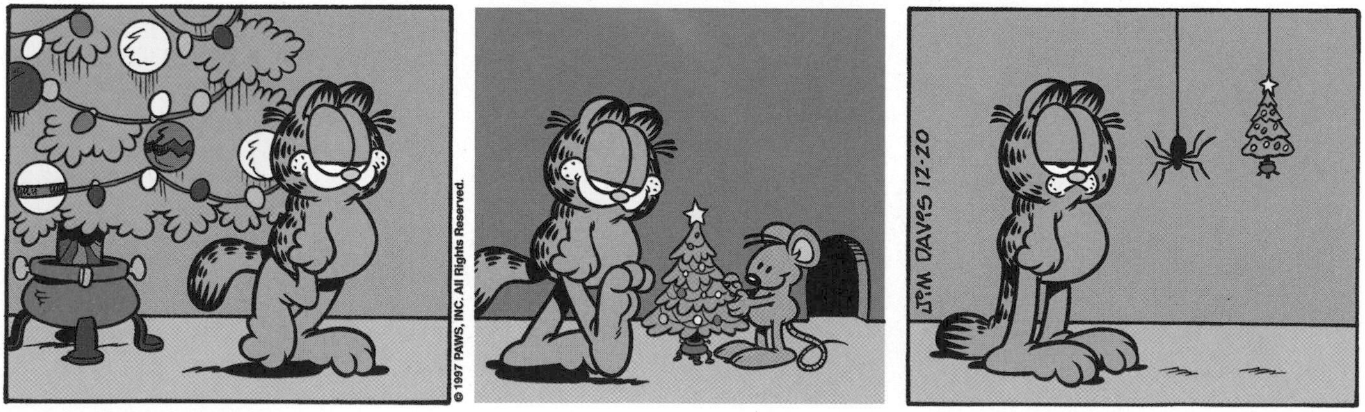
© 1997 PAWS, INC. All Rights Reserved.
JIM DAVIS 12-20

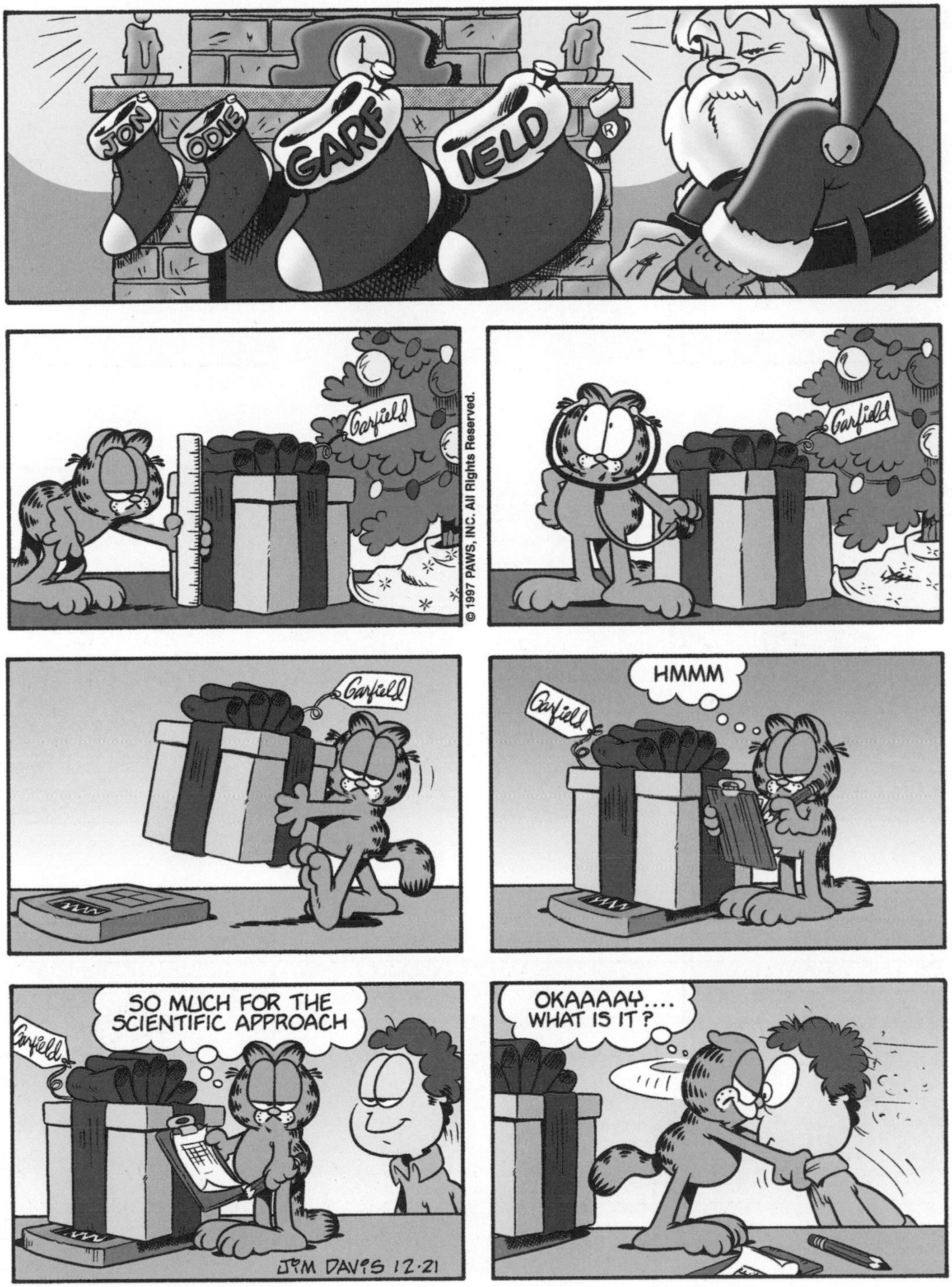
JON
ODIE
GARF
IELD
Garfield
© 1997 PAWS, INC. All Rights Reserved.
HMMM
SO MUCH FOR THE SCIENTIFIC APPROACH
JIM DAVIS 12·21
OKAAAAY.... WHAT IS IT?

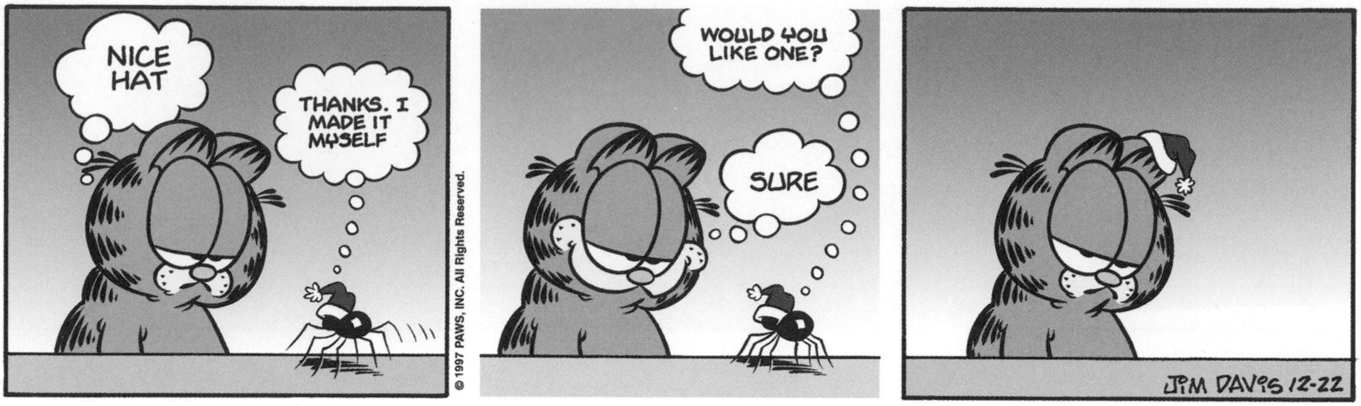
NICE HAT
THANKS. I MADE IT MYSELF
© 1997 PAWS, INC. All Rights Reserved.
WOULD YOU LIKE ONE?
SURE
JIM DAVIS 12-22

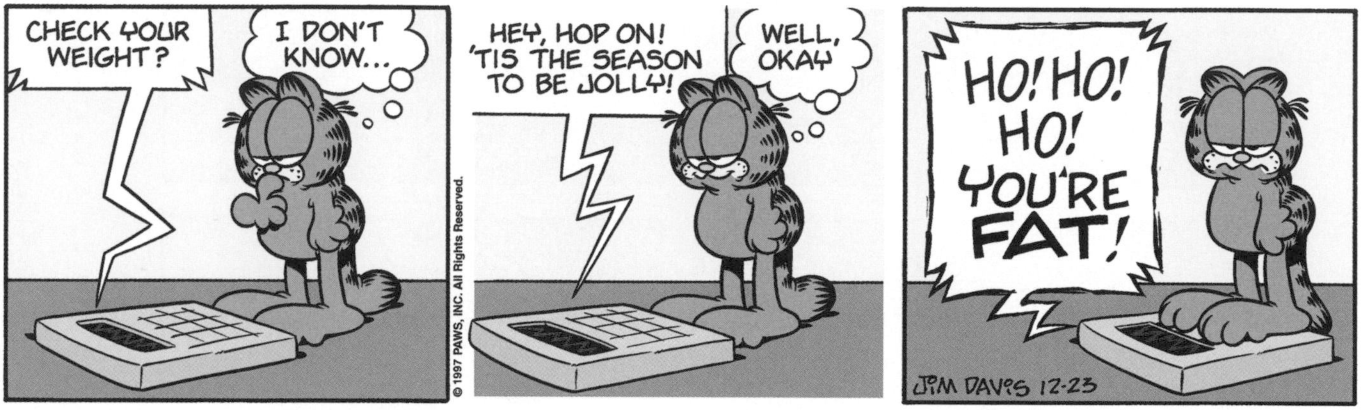
CHECK YOUR WEIGHT?
I DON'T KNOW...
© 1997 PAWS, INC. All Rights Reserved.
HEY, HOP ON! 'TIS THE SEASON TO BE JOLLY!
WELL, OKAY
HO! HO! HO! YOU'RE FAT!
JIM DAVIS 12-23

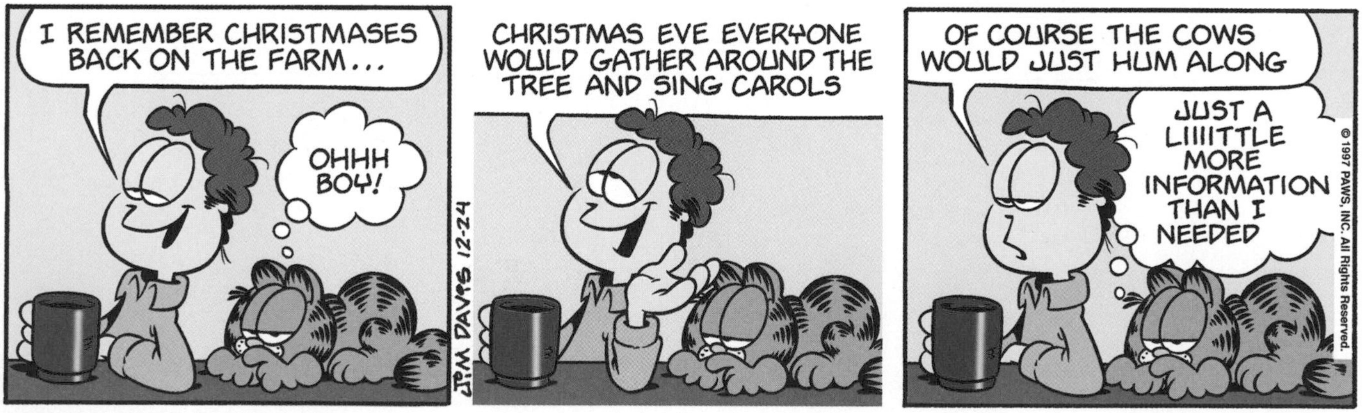
I REMEMBER CHRISTMASES BACK ON THE FARM...
OHHH BOY!
JIM DAVIS 12-24
CHRISTMAS EVE EVERYONE WOULD GATHER AROUND THE TREE AND SING CAROLS
OF COURSE THE COWS WOULD JUST HUM ALONG
JUST A LIIIITTLE MORE INFORMATION THAN I NEEDED
© 1997 PAWS, INC. All Rights Reserved.

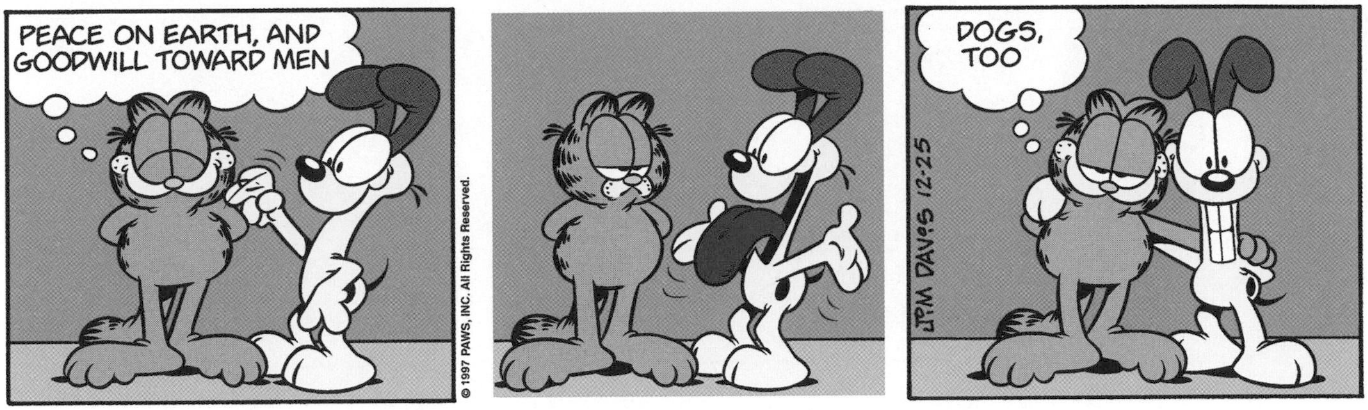
PEACE ON EARTH, AND GOODWILL TOWARD MEN
DOGS, TOO
JIM DAVIS 12-25

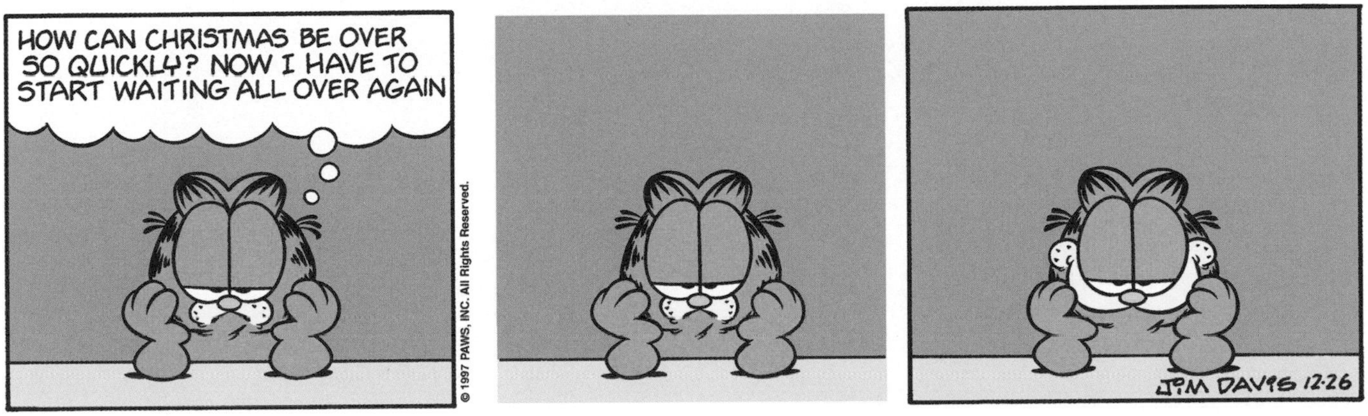
HOW CAN CHRISTMAS BE OVER SO QUICKLY? NOW I HAVE TO START WAITING ALL OVER AGAIN
JIM DAVIS 12-26

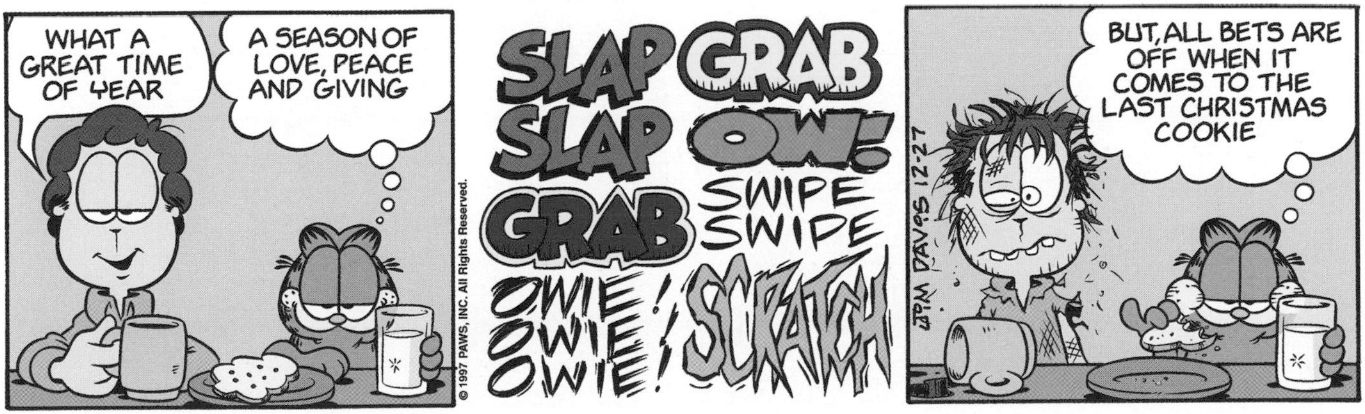
WHAT A GREAT TIME OF YEAR
A SEASON OF LOVE, PEACE AND GIVING
SLAP GRAB
SLAP OW!
GRAB SWIPE SWIPE
OWIE! OWIE! OWIE!
SCRATCH
BUT, ALL BETS ARE OFF WHEN IT COMES TO THE LAST CHRISTMAS COOKIE
JIM DAVIS 12-27

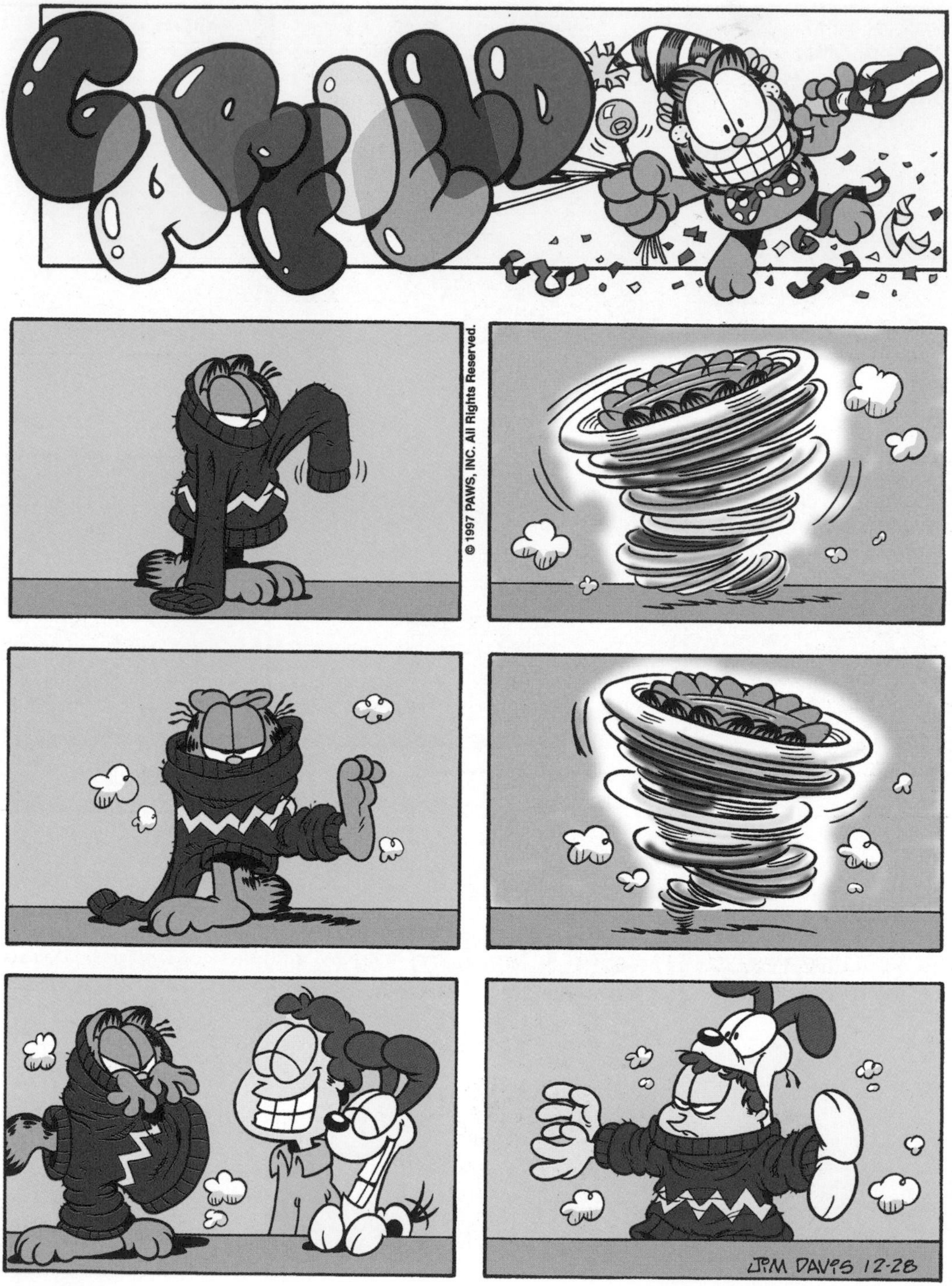
GARFIELD
© 1997 PAWS, INC. All Rights Reserved.
JIM DAVIS 12-28

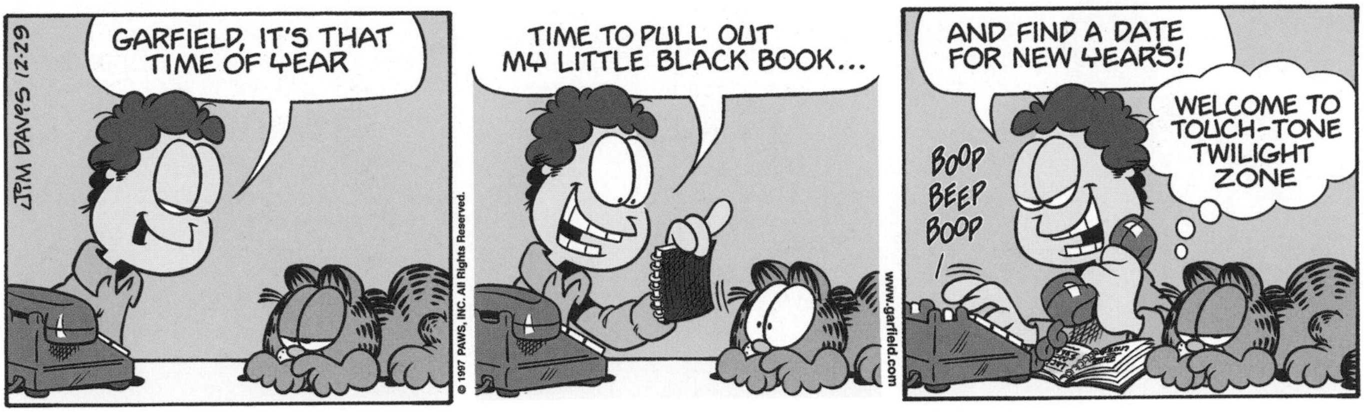
JIM DAVIS 12-29
GARFIELD, IT'S THAT TIME OF YEAR
© 1997 PAWS, INC. All Rights Reserved.
TIME TO PULL OUT MY LITTLE BLACK BOOK...
www.garfield.com
AND FIND A DATE FOR NEW YEAR'S!
BOOP BEEP BOOP
WELCOME TO TOUCH-TONE TWILIGHT ZONE

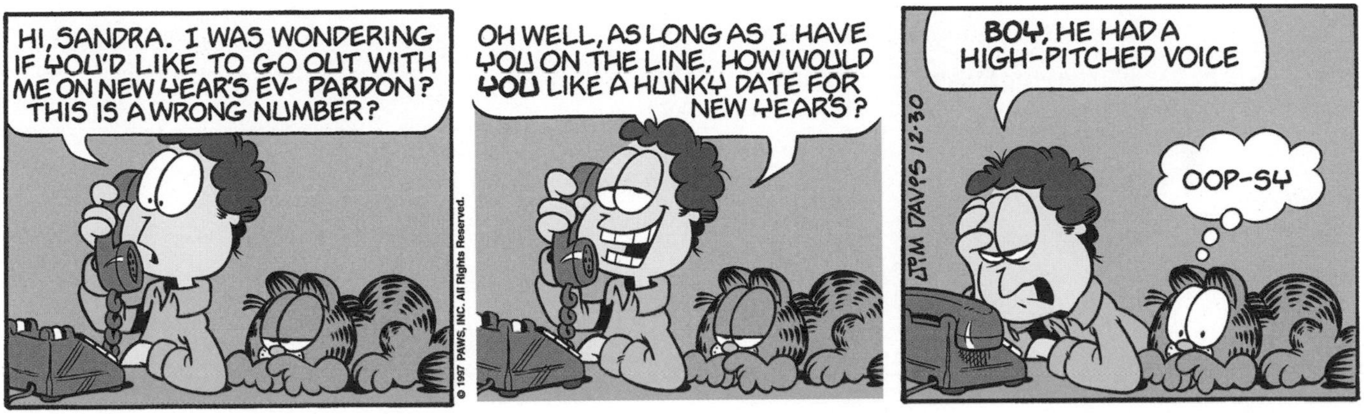
HI, SANDRA. I WAS WONDERING IF YOU'D LIKE TO GO OUT WITH ME ON NEW YEAR'S EV- PARDON? THIS IS A WRONG NUMBER?
© 1997 PAWS, INC. All Rights Reserved.
OH WELL, AS LONG AS I HAVE YOU ON THE LINE, HOW WOULD YOU LIKE A HUNKY DATE FOR NEW YEAR'S?
JIM DAVIS 12-30
BOY, HE HAD A HIGH-PITCHED VOICE
OOP-SY

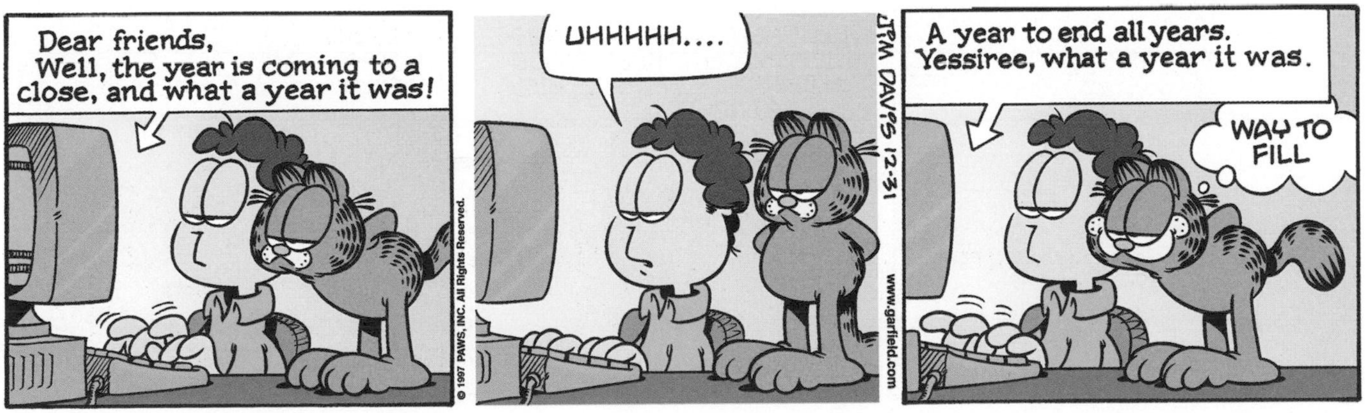
Dear friends,
Well, the year is coming to a close, and what a year it was!
© 1997 PAWS, INC. All Rights Reserved.
UHHHHH....
JIM DAVIS 12-31
www.garfield.com
A year to end all years. Yessiree, what a year it was.
WAY TO FILL

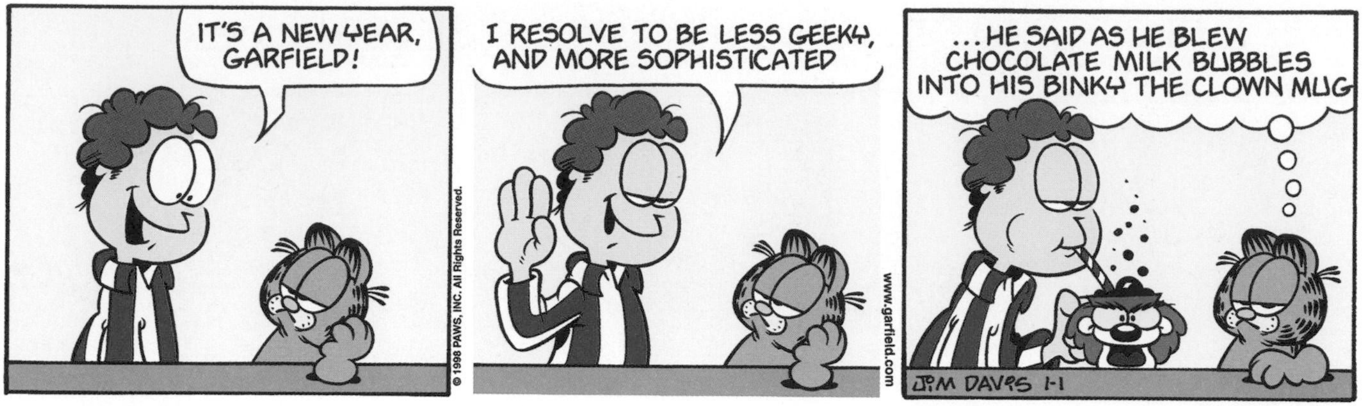
IT'S A NEW YEAR, GARFIELD!
I RESOLVE TO BE LESS GEEKY, AND MORE SOPHISTICATED
...HE SAID AS HE BLEW CHOCOLATE MILK BUBBLES INTO HIS BINKY THE CLOWN MUG
© 1998 PAWS, INC. All Rights Reserved.
www.garfield.com
JIM DAVIS 1-1

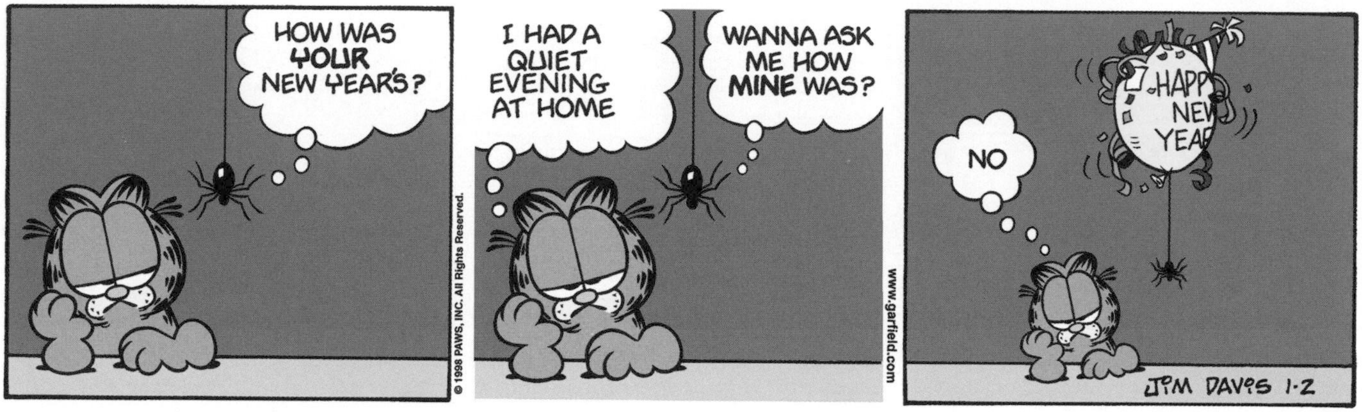
HOW WAS **YOUR** NEW YEAR'S?
I HAD A QUIET EVENING AT HOME
WANNA ASK ME HOW **MINE** WAS?
NO
HAPPY NEW YEAR
© 1998 PAWS, INC. All Rights Reserved.
www.garfield.com
JIM DAVIS 1-2

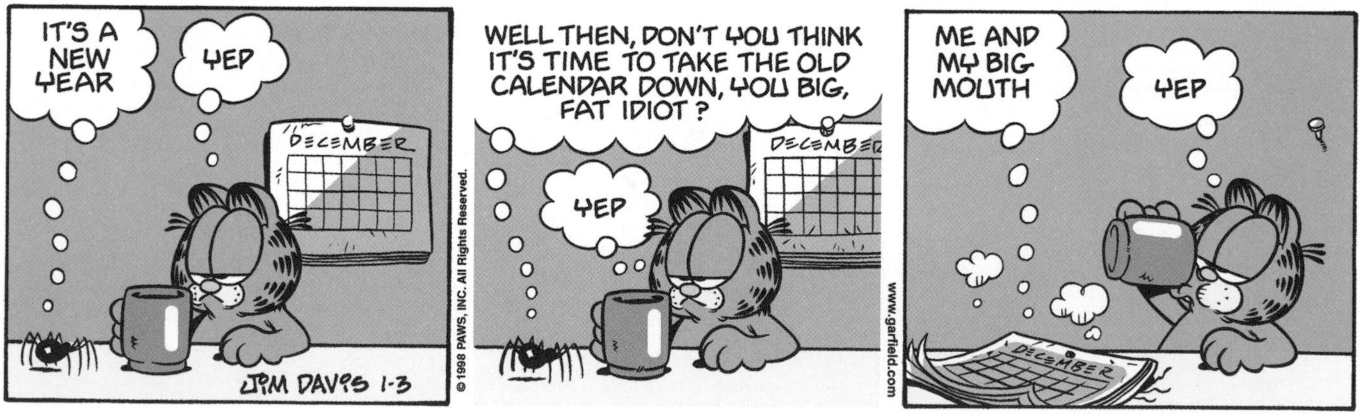
IT'S A NEW YEAR
YEP
DECEMBER
WELL THEN, DON'T YOU THINK IT'S TIME TO TAKE THE OLD CALENDAR DOWN, YOU BIG, FAT IDIOT?
YEP
ME AND MY BIG MOUTH
YEP
DECEMBER
© 1998 PAWS, INC. All Rights Reserved.
www.garfield.com
JIM DAVIS 1-3

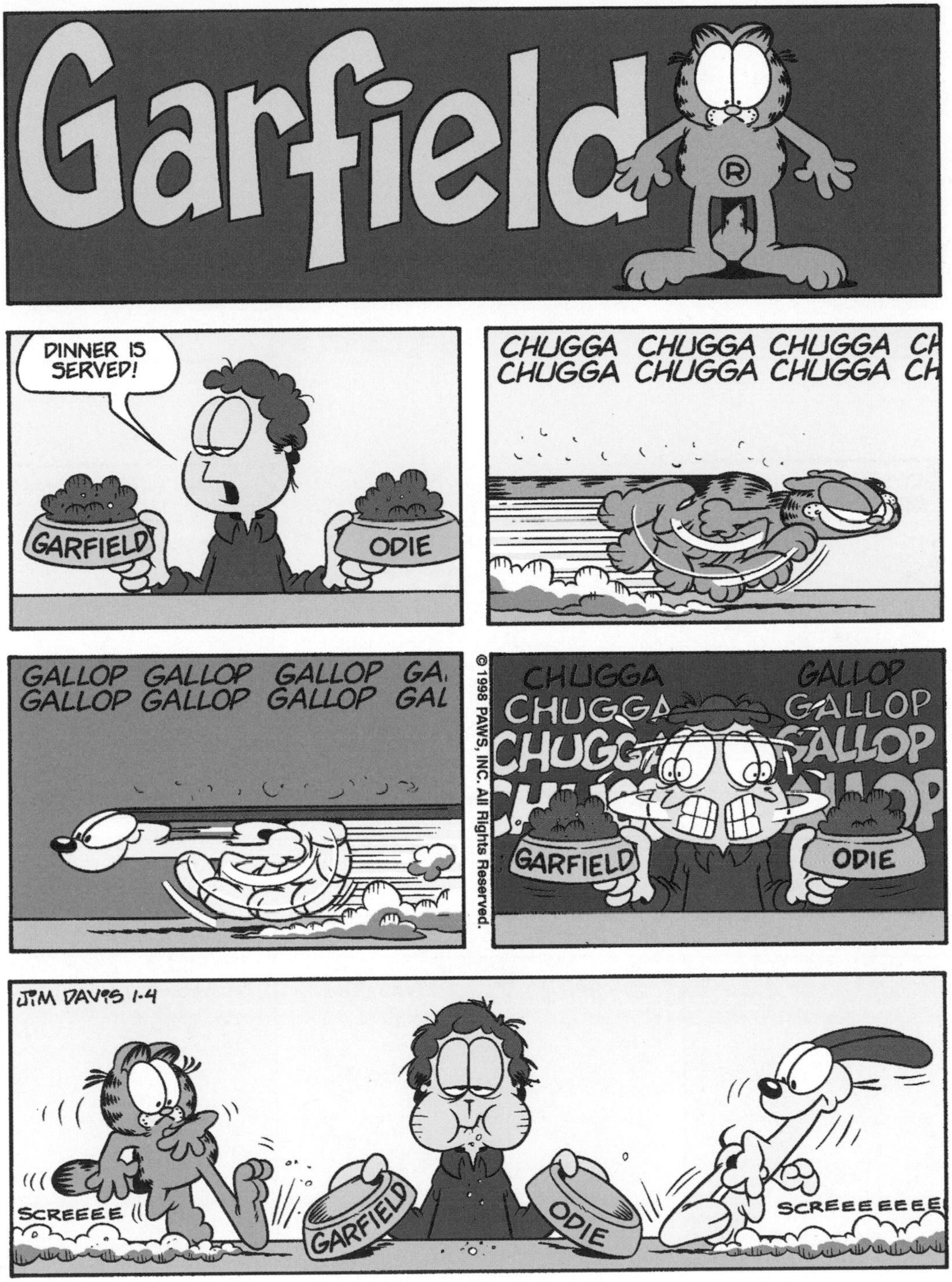
Garfield
DINNER IS SERVED!
GARFIELD
ODIE
CHUGGA CHUGGA CHUGGA CH
CHUGGA CHUGGA CHUGGA CH
GALLOP GALLOP GALLOP GA
GALLOP GALLOP GALLOP GAL
© 1998 PAWS, INC. All Rights Reserved.
CHUGGA
CHUGGA
GALLOP
GALLOP
GARFIELD
ODIE
JIM DAVIS 1-4
SCREEEE
GARFIELD
ODIE
SCREEEEEEE

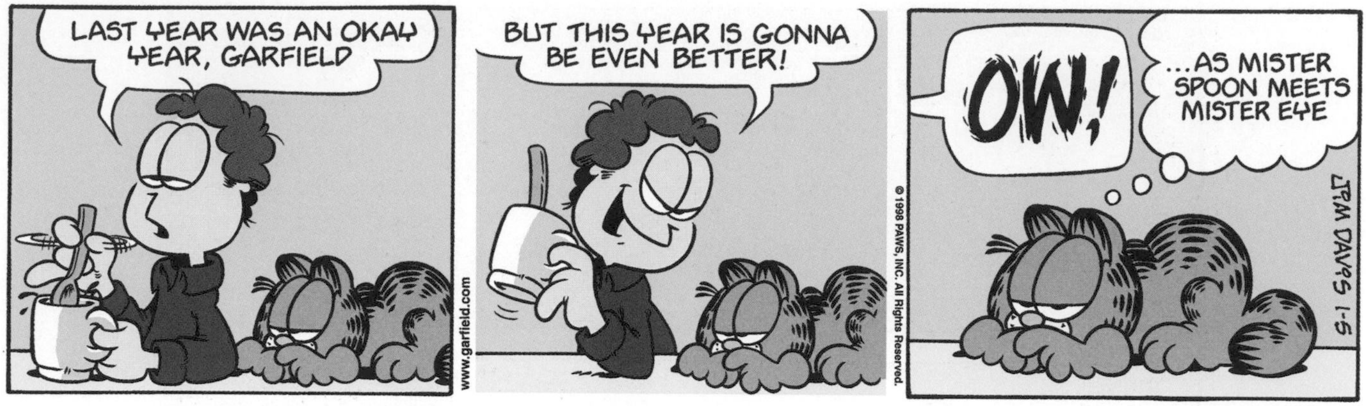
LAST YEAR WAS AN OKAY YEAR, GARFIELD
www.garfield.com
BUT THIS YEAR IS GONNA BE EVEN BETTER!
© 1998 PAWS, INC. All Rights Reserved.
OW!
...AS MISTER SPOON MEETS MISTER EYE
JIM DAVIS 1-5

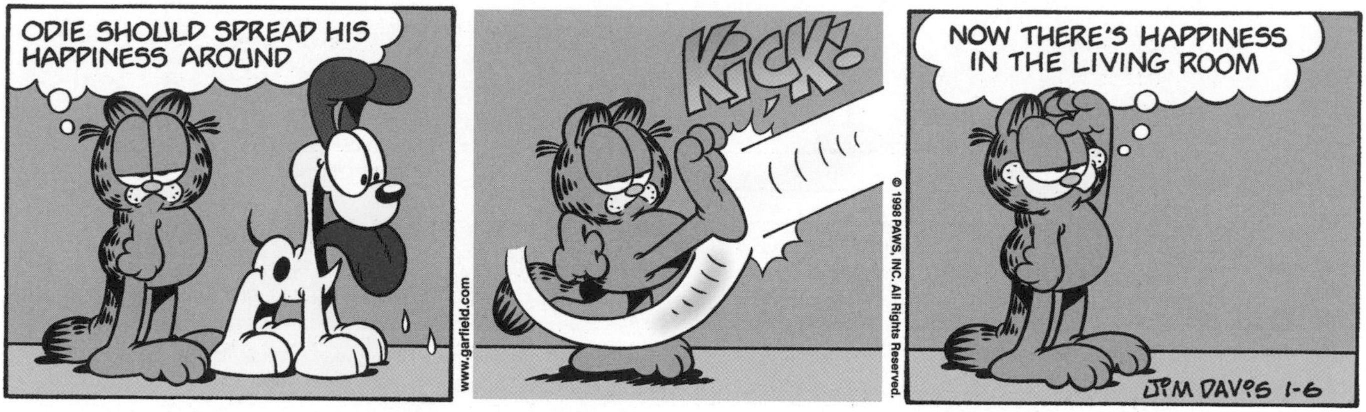
ODIE SHOULD SPREAD HIS HAPPINESS AROUND
www.garfield.com
KICK!
© 1998 PAWS, INC. All Rights Reserved.
NOW THERE'S HAPPINESS IN THE LIVING ROOM
JIM DAVIS 1-6

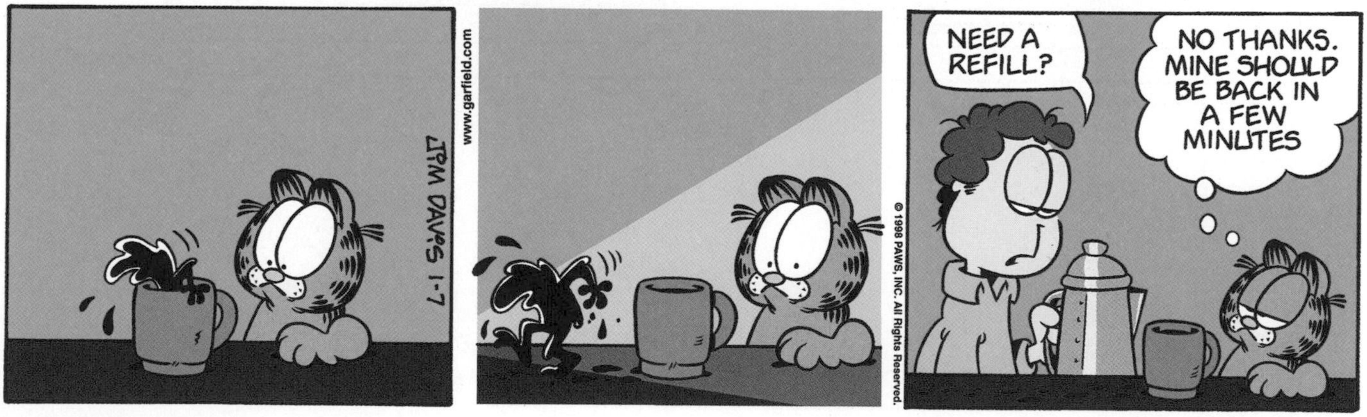
JIM DAVIS 1-7
www.garfield.com
© 1998 PAWS, INC. All Rights Reserved.
NEED A REFILL?
NO THANKS. MINE SHOULD BE BACK IN A FEW MINUTES

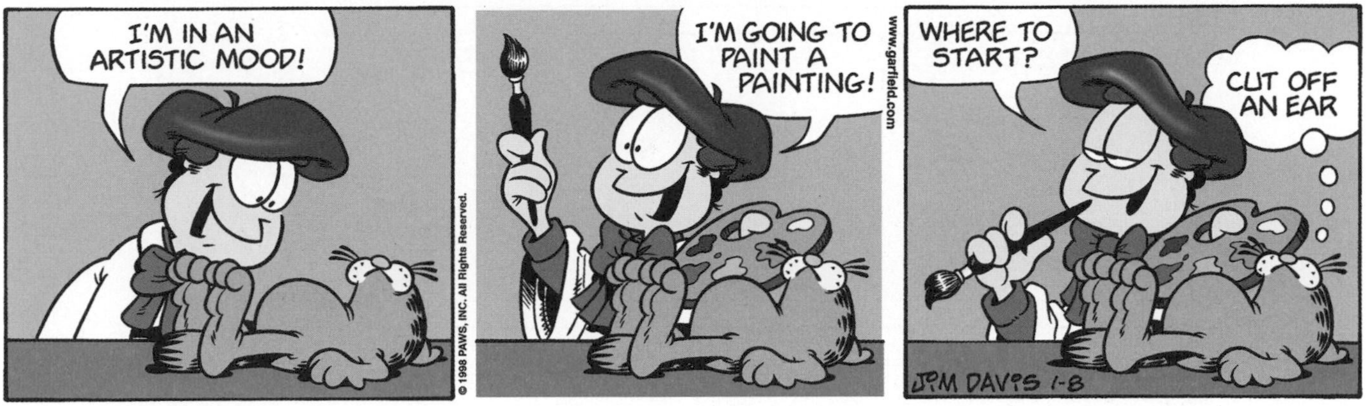
I'M IN AN ARTISTIC MOOD!
I'M GOING TO PAINT A PAINTING!
WHERE TO START?
CUT OFF AN EAR
© 1998 PAWS, INC. All Rights Reserved.
www.garfield.com
JIM DAVIS 1-8

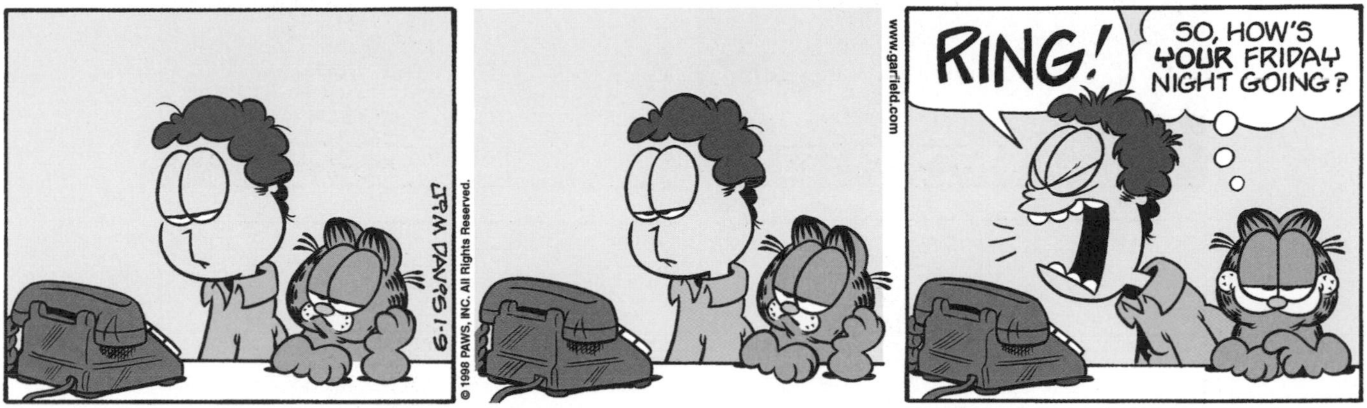
RING!
SO, HOW'S **YOUR** FRIDAY NIGHT GOING?
© 1998 PAWS, INC. All Rights Reserved.
www.garfield.com
JIM DAVIS 1-9

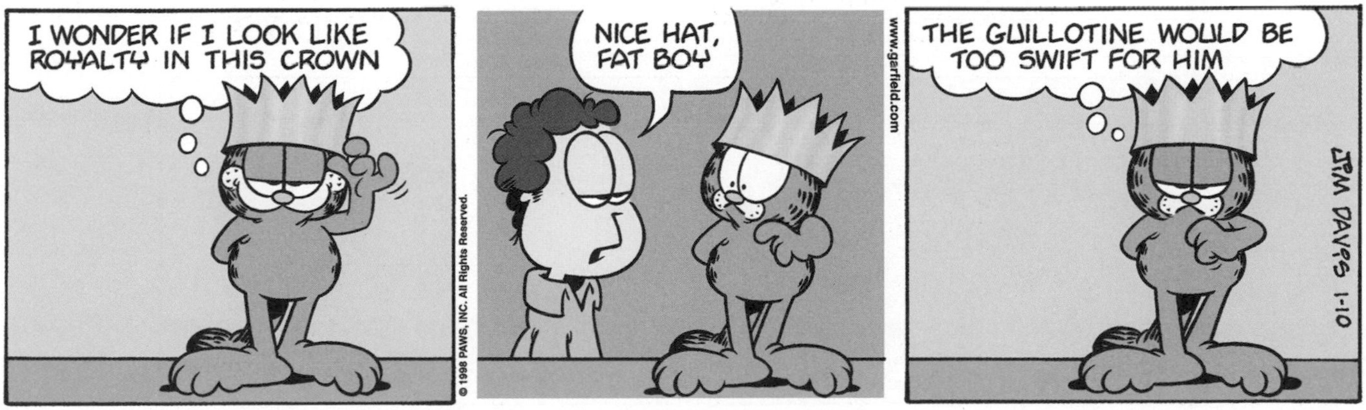
I WONDER IF I LOOK LIKE ROYALTY IN THIS CROWN
NICE HAT, FAT BOY
THE GUILLOTINE WOULD BE TOO SWIFT FOR HIM
© 1998 PAWS, INC. All Rights Reserved.
www.garfield.com
JIM DAVIS 1-10

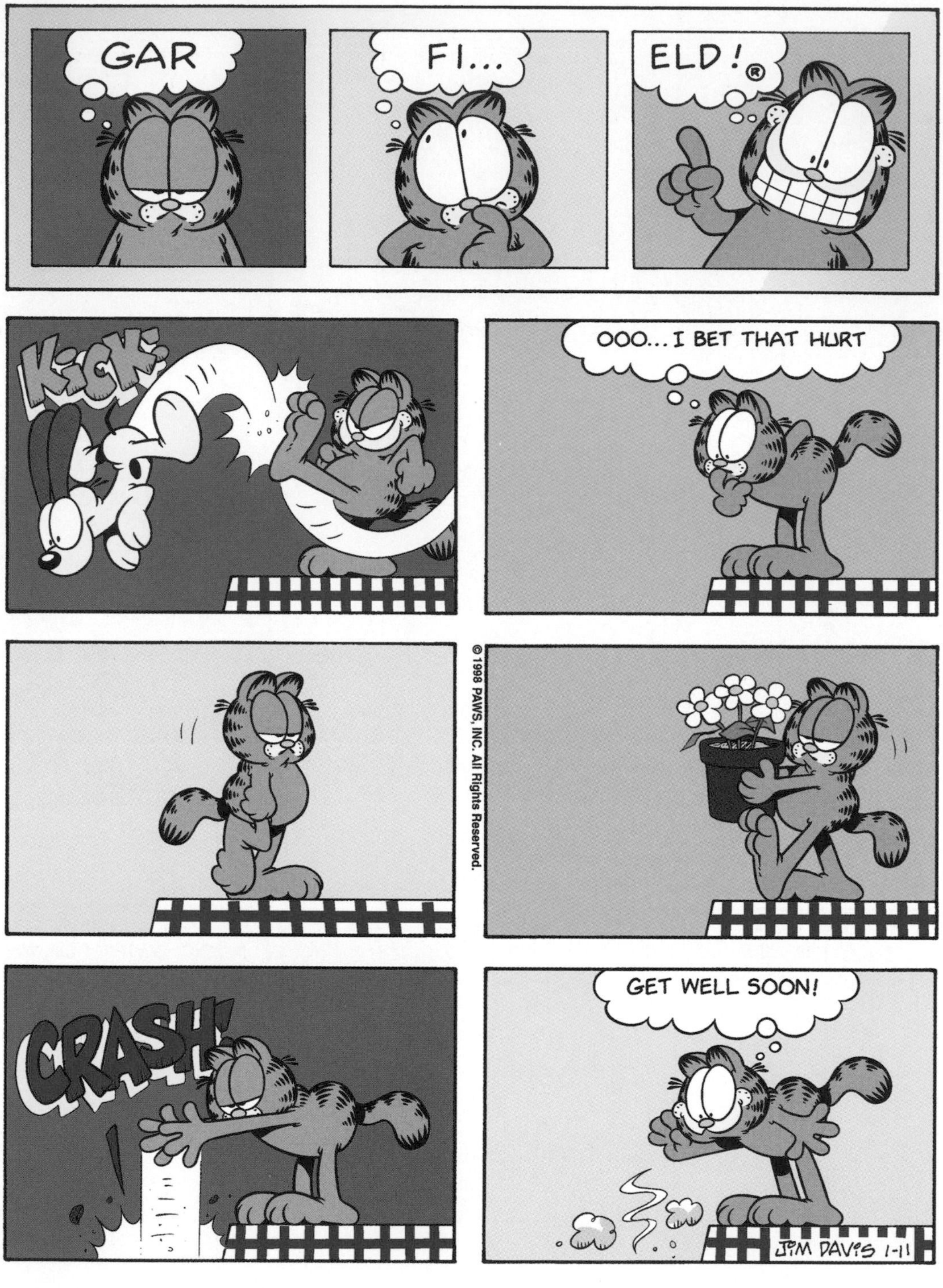
GAR
FI...
ELD!®
KICK!
OOO... I BET THAT HURT
CRASH!
GET WELL SOON!
JIM DAVIS 1-11

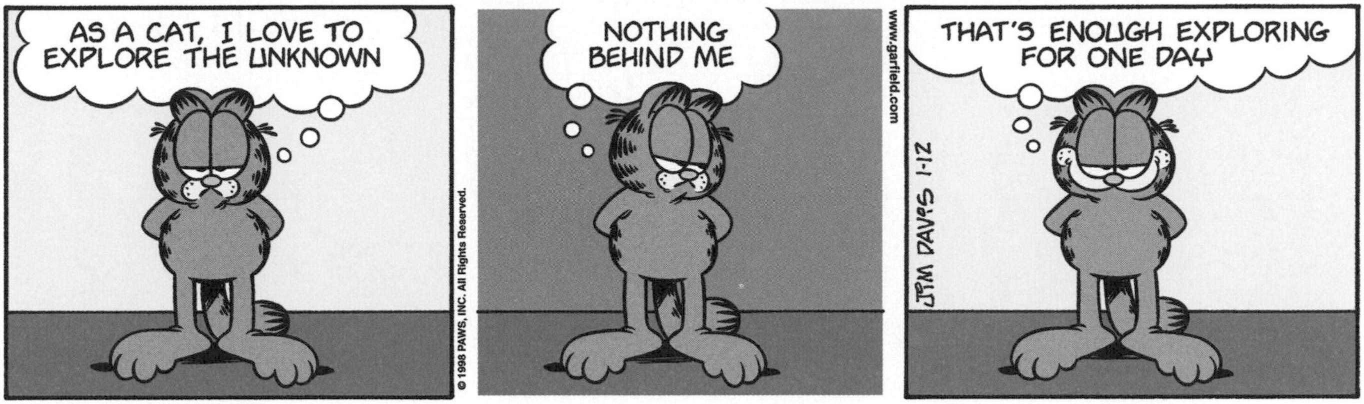
AS A CAT, I LOVE TO EXPLORE THE UNKNOWN
© 1998 PAWS, INC. All Rights Reserved.
NOTHING BEHIND ME
www.garfield.com
THAT'S ENOUGH EXPLORING FOR ONE DAY
JIM DAVIS 1-12

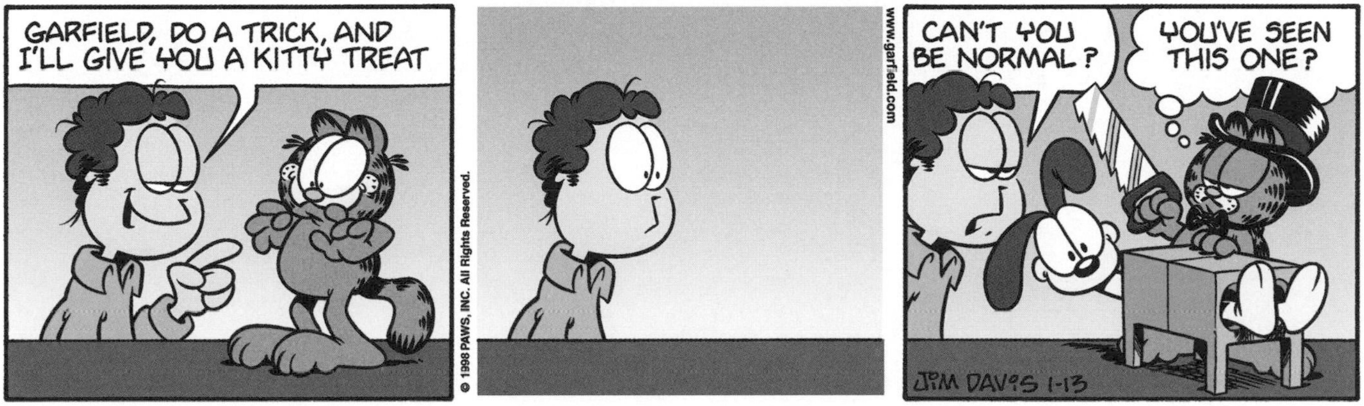
GARFIELD, DO A TRICK, AND I'LL GIVE YOU A KITTY TREAT
© 1998 PAWS, INC. All Rights Reserved.
www.garfield.com
CAN'T YOU BE NORMAL?
YOU'VE SEEN THIS ONE?
JIM DAVIS 1-13

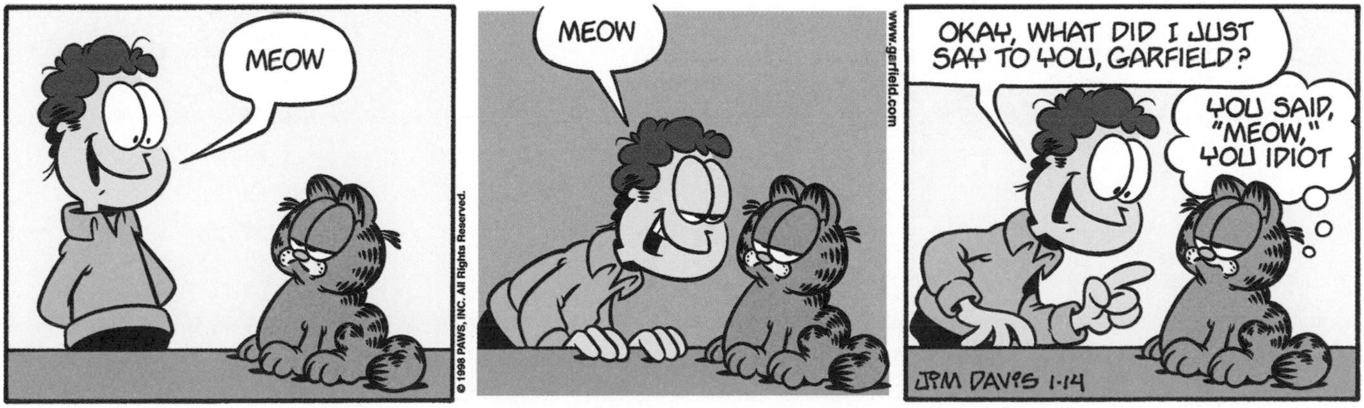
MEOW
© 1998 PAWS, INC. All Rights Reserved.
MEOW
www.garfield.com
OKAY, WHAT DID I JUST SAY TO YOU, GARFIELD?
YOU SAID, "MEOW," YOU IDIOT
JIM DAVIS 1-14

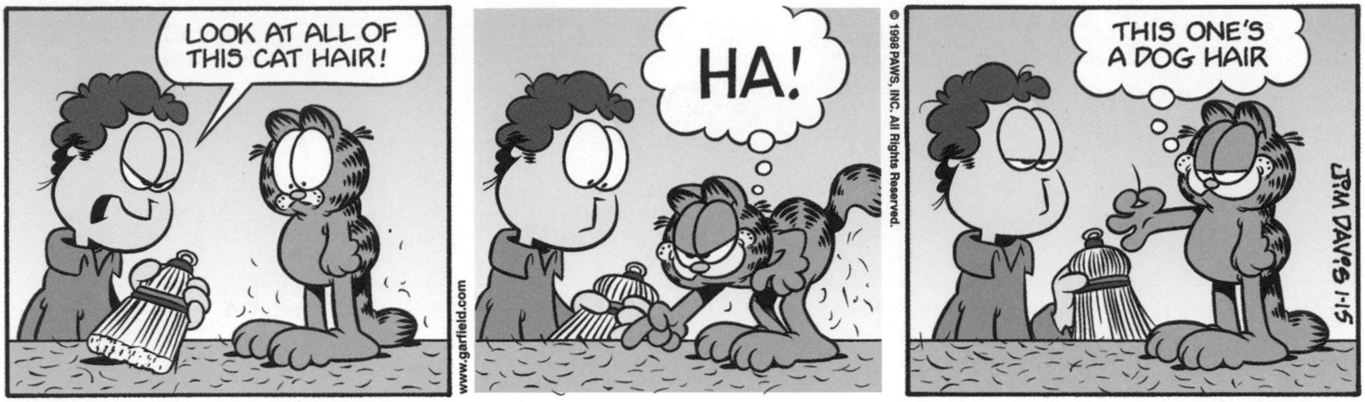
LOOK AT ALL OF THIS CAT HAIR!
HA!
THIS ONE'S A DOG HAIR
JIM DAVIS 1-15
© 1998 PAWS, INC. All Rights Reserved.
www.garfield.com

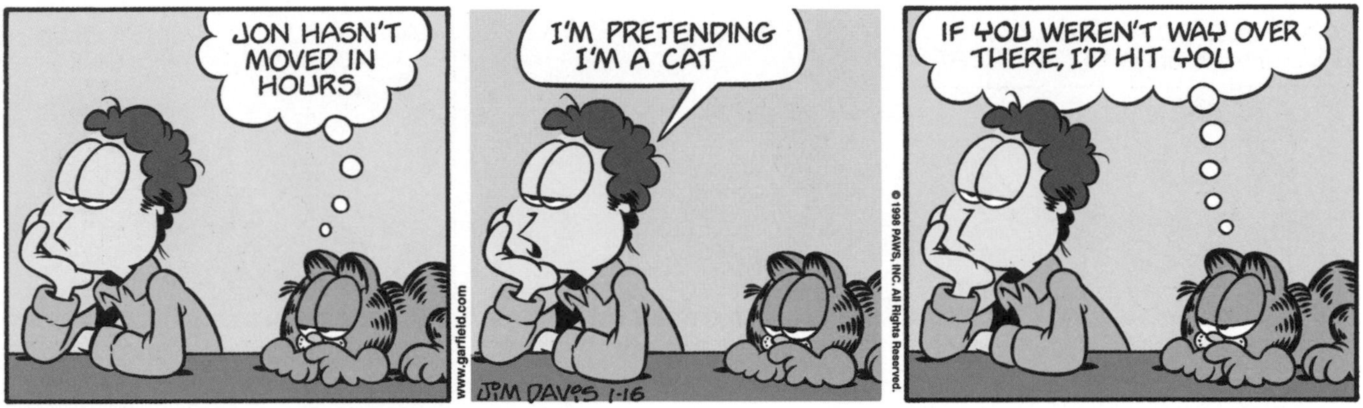
JON HASN'T MOVED IN HOURS
I'M PRETENDING I'M A CAT
IF YOU WEREN'T WAY OVER THERE, I'D HIT YOU
JIM DAVIS 1-16
© 1998 PAWS, INC. All Rights Reserved.
www.garfield.com

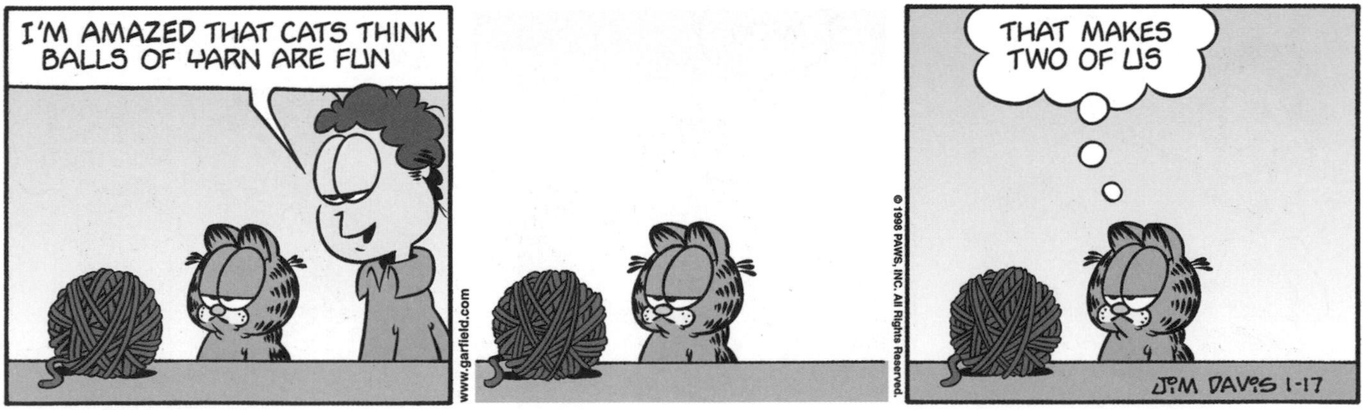
I'M AMAZED THAT CATS THINK BALLS OF YARN ARE FUN
THAT MAKES TWO OF US
JIM DAVIS 1-17
© 1998 PAWS, INC. All Rights Reserved.
www.garfield.com

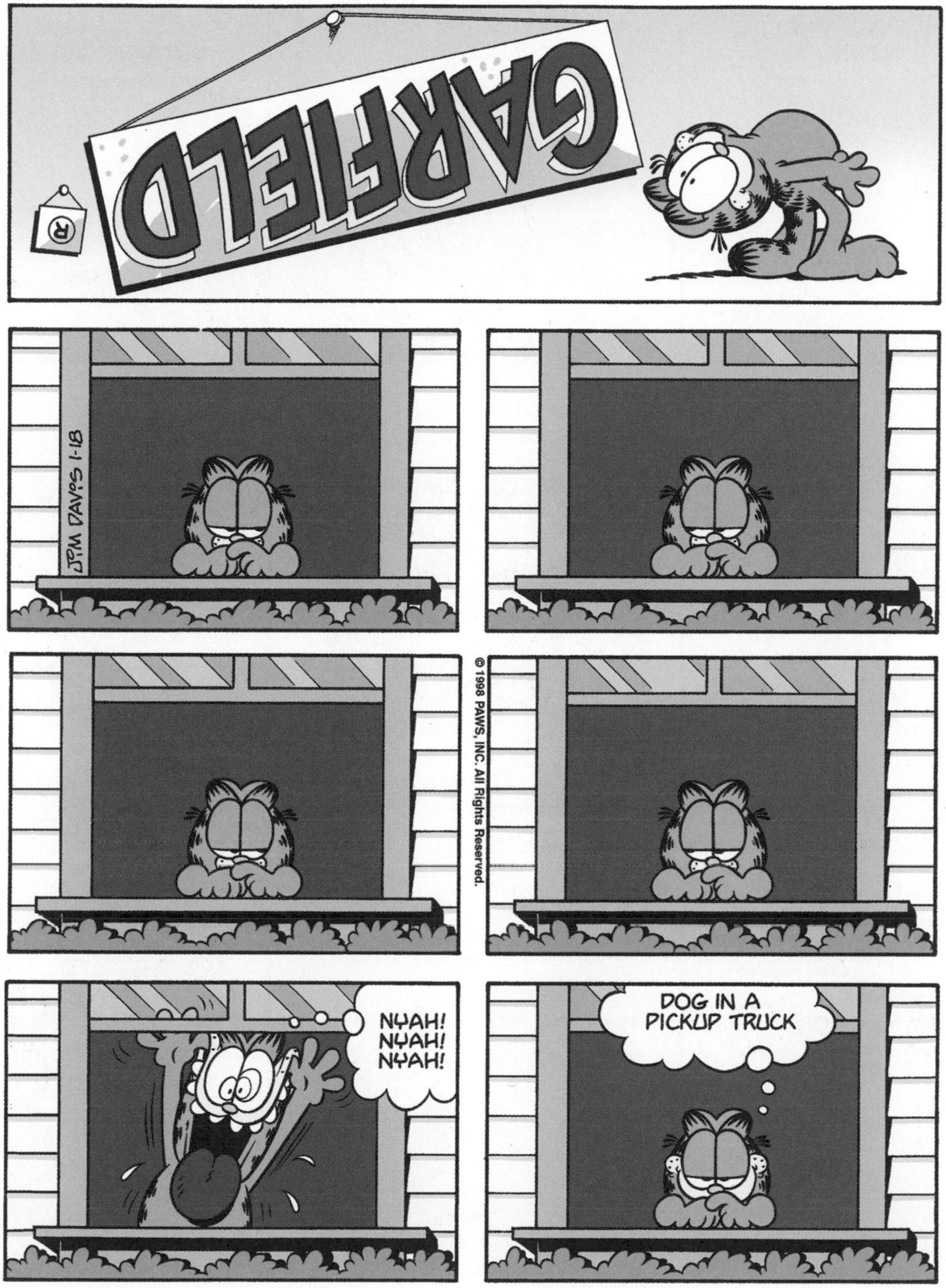
GARFIELD
JIM DAVIS 1-18
NYAH! NYAH! NYAH!
DOG IN A PICKUP TRUCK

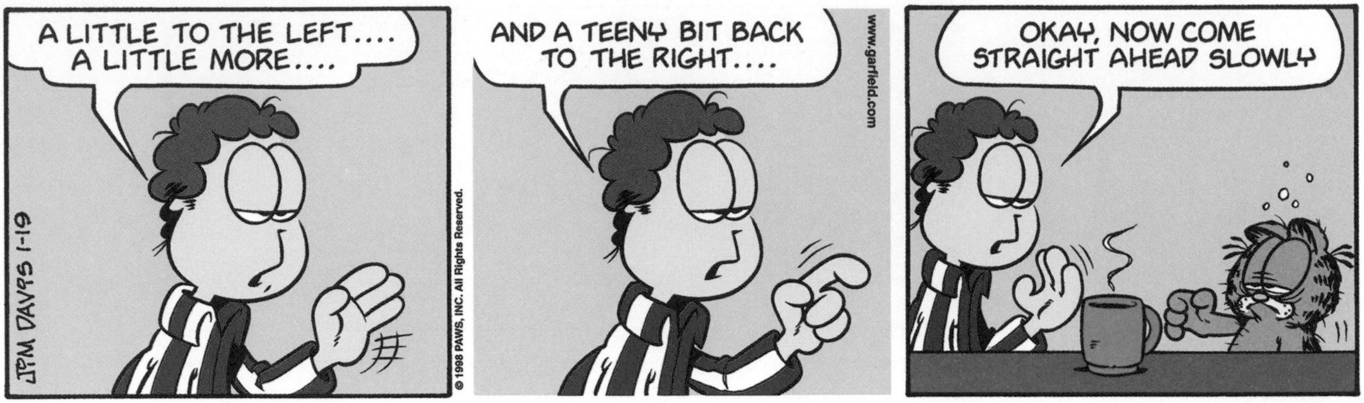
A LITTLE TO THE LEFT....
A LITTLE MORE....
JIM DAVIS 1-19
AND A TEENY BIT BACK TO THE RIGHT....
© 1998 PAWS, INC. All Rights Reserved.
www.garfield.com
OKAY, NOW COME STRAIGHT AHEAD SLOWLY

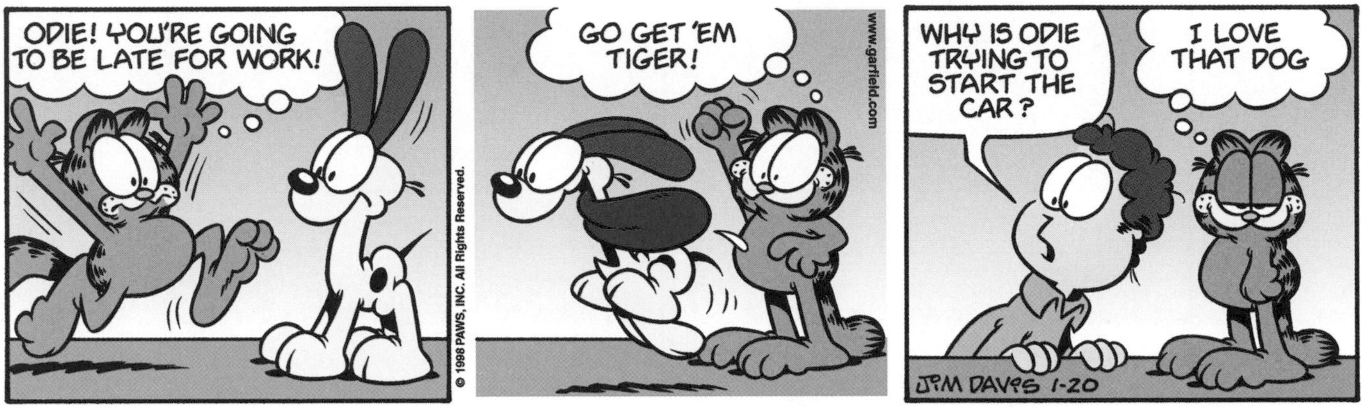
ODIE! YOU'RE GOING TO BE LATE FOR WORK!
GO GET 'EM TIGER!
© 1998 PAWS, INC. All Rights Reserved.
www.garfield.com
WHY IS ODIE TRYING TO START THE CAR?
I LOVE THAT DOG
JIM DAVIS 1-20

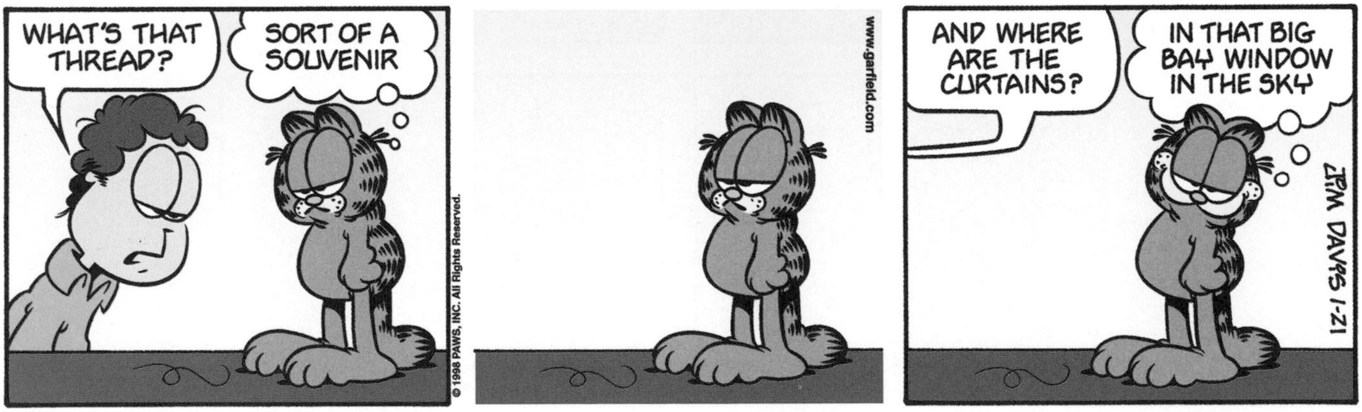
WHAT'S THAT THREAD?
SORT OF A SOUVENIR
© 1998 PAWS, INC. All Rights Reserved.
www.garfield.com
AND WHERE ARE THE CURTAINS?
IN THAT BIG BAY WINDOW IN THE SKY
JIM DAVIS 1-21

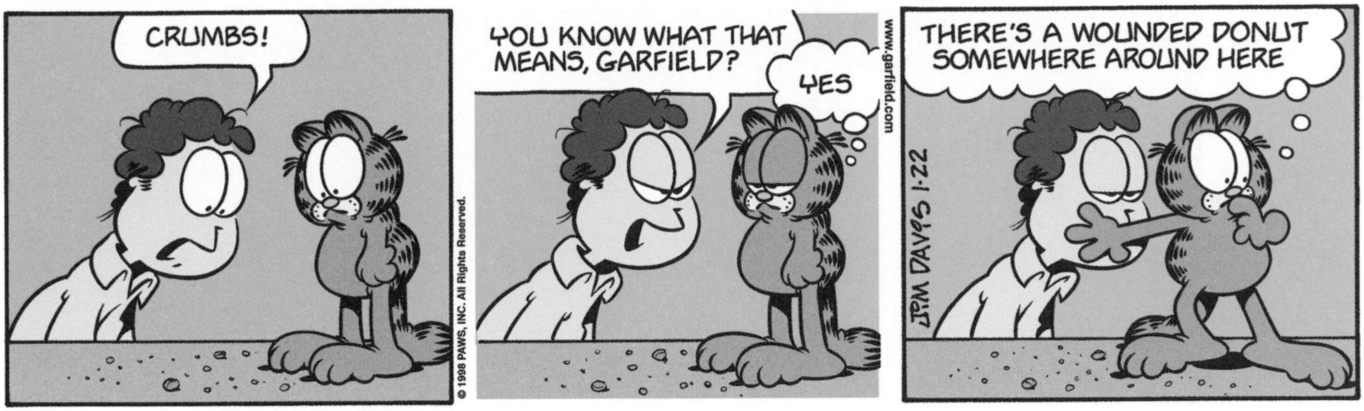
CRUMBS!
YOU KNOW WHAT THAT MEANS, GARFIELD?
YES
THERE'S A WOUNDED DONUT SOMEWHERE AROUND HERE
JIM DAVIS 1-22
© 1998 PAWS, INC. All Rights Reserved.
www.garfield.com

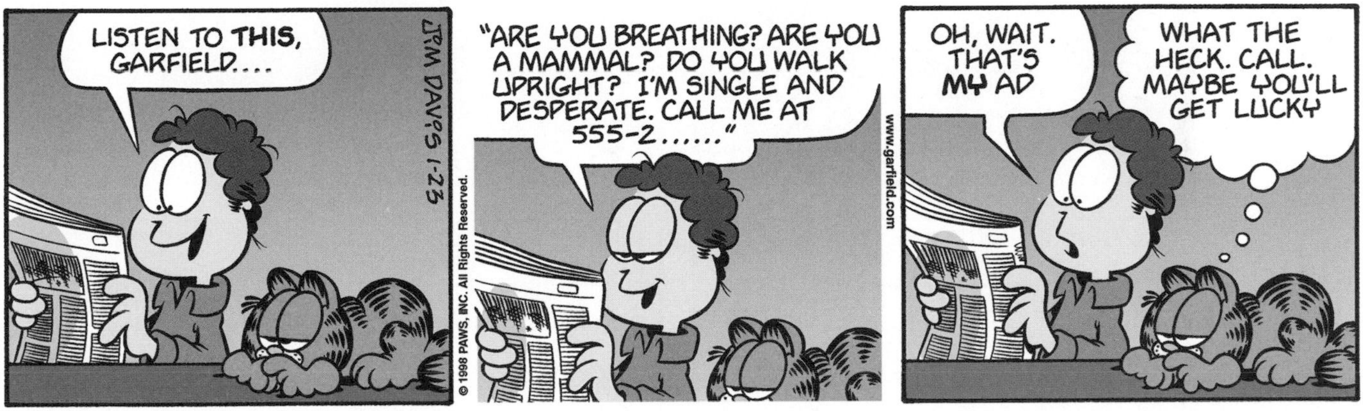
LISTEN TO **THIS**, GARFIELD....
"ARE YOU BREATHING? ARE YOU A MAMMAL? DO YOU WALK UPRIGHT? I'M SINGLE AND DESPERATE. CALL ME AT 555-2......"
OH, WAIT. THAT'S **MY** AD
WHAT THE HECK. CALL. MAYBE YOU'LL GET LUCKY
JIM DAVIS 1-23
© 1998 PAWS, INC. All Rights Reserved.
www.garfield.com

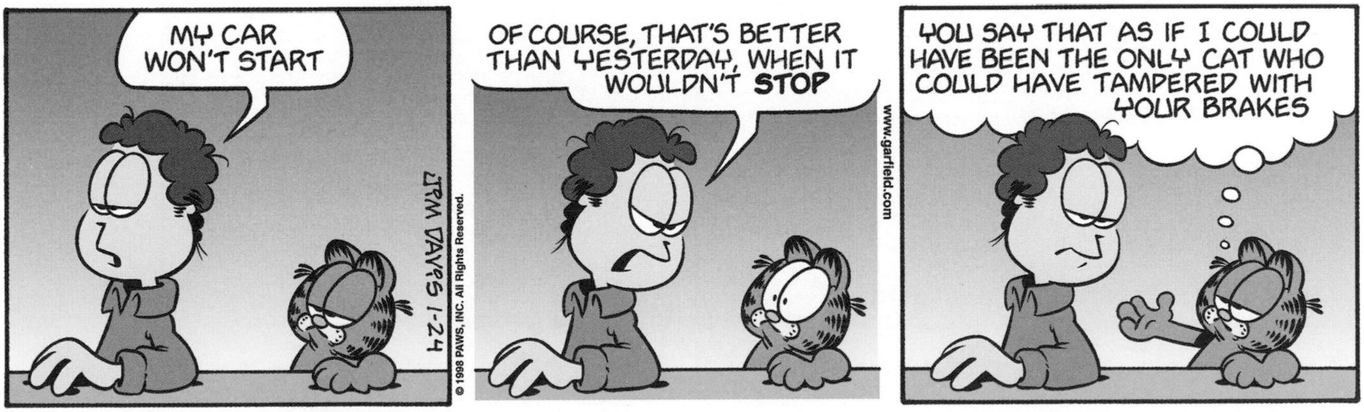
MY CAR WON'T START
OF COURSE, THAT'S BETTER THAN YESTERDAY, WHEN IT WOULDN'T **STOP**
YOU SAY THAT AS IF I COULD HAVE BEEN THE ONLY CAT WHO COULD HAVE TAMPERED WITH YOUR BRAKES
JIM DAVIS 1-24
© 1998 PAWS, INC. All Rights Reserved.
www.garfield.com

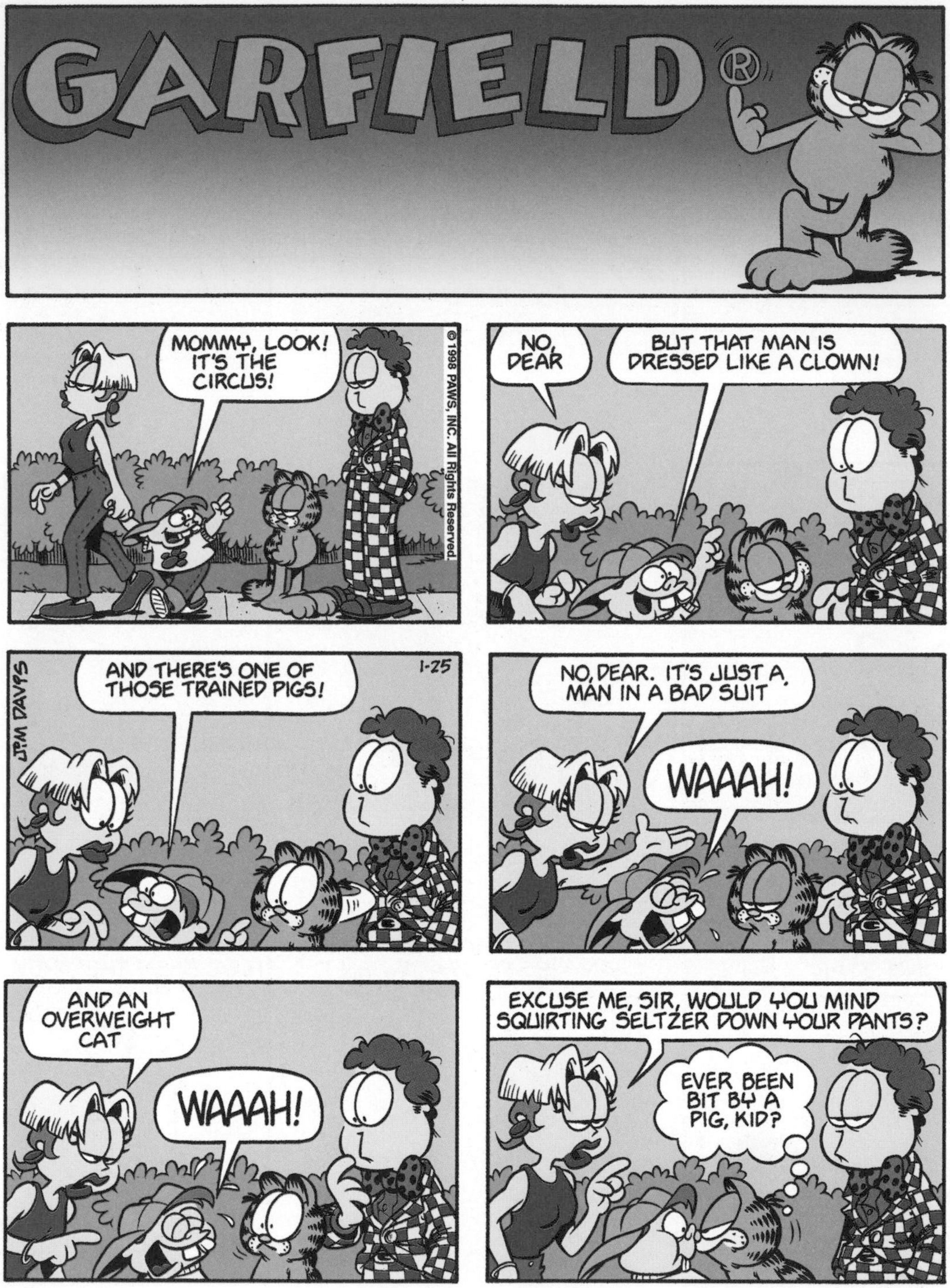
GARFIELD®
MOMMY, LOOK! IT'S THE CIRCUS!
© 1998 PAWS, INC. All Rights Reserved.
NO, DEAR
BUT THAT MAN IS DRESSED LIKE A CLOWN!
JIM DAVIS
1-25
AND THERE'S ONE OF THOSE TRAINED PIGS!
NO, DEAR. IT'S JUST A MAN IN A BAD SUIT
WAAAH!
AND AN OVERWEIGHT CAT
WAAAH!
EXCUSE ME, SIR, WOULD YOU MIND SQUIRTING SELTZER DOWN YOUR PANTS?
EVER BEEN BIT BY A PIG, KID?

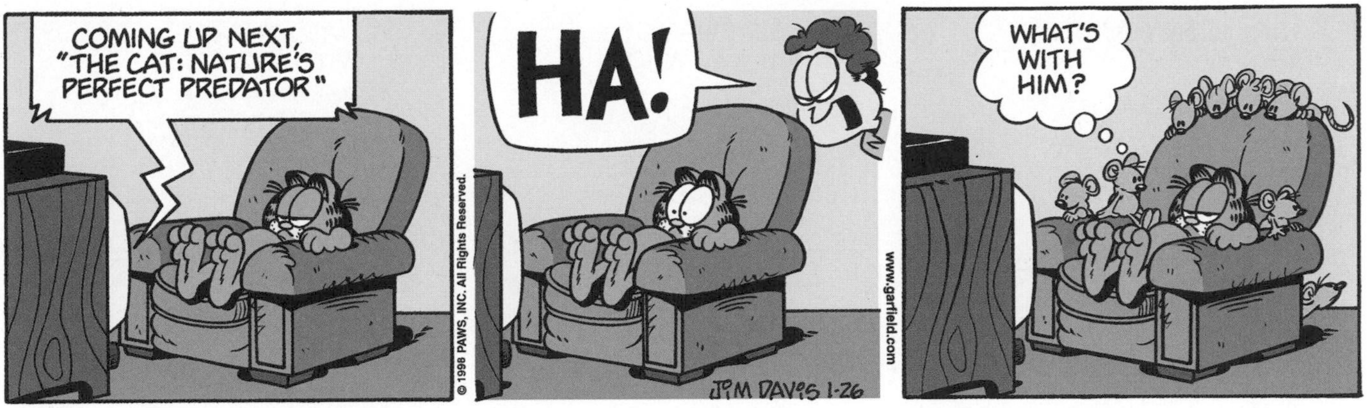
COMING UP NEXT, "THE CAT: NATURE'S PERFECT PREDATOR"
© 1998 PAWS, INC. All Rights Reserved.
HA!
JIM DAVIS 1-26
www.garfield.com
WHAT'S WITH HIM?

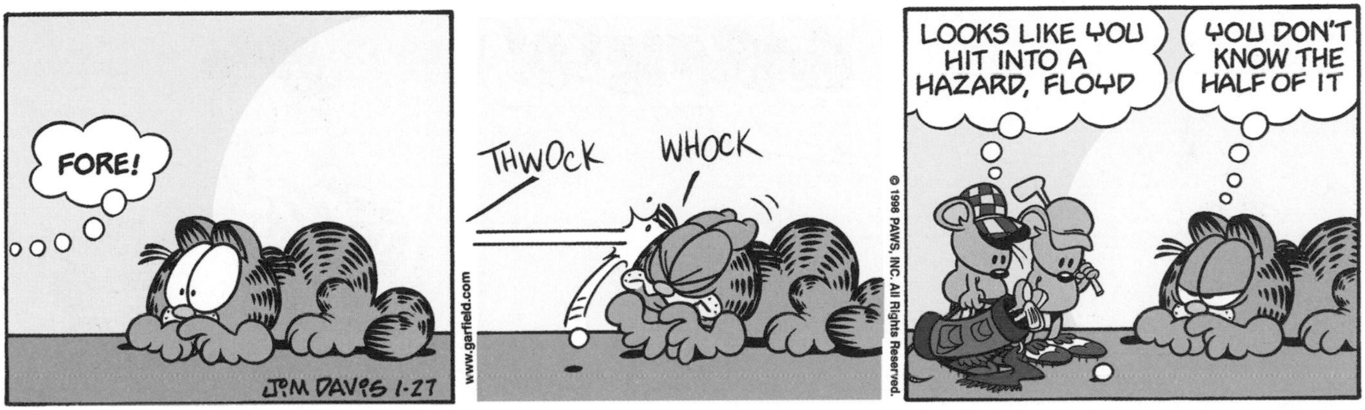
FORE!
JIM DAVIS 1-27
www.garfield.com
THWOCK
WHOCK
© 1998 PAWS, INC. All Rights Reserved.
LOOKS LIKE YOU HIT INTO A HAZARD, FLOYD
YOU DON'T KNOW THE HALF OF IT

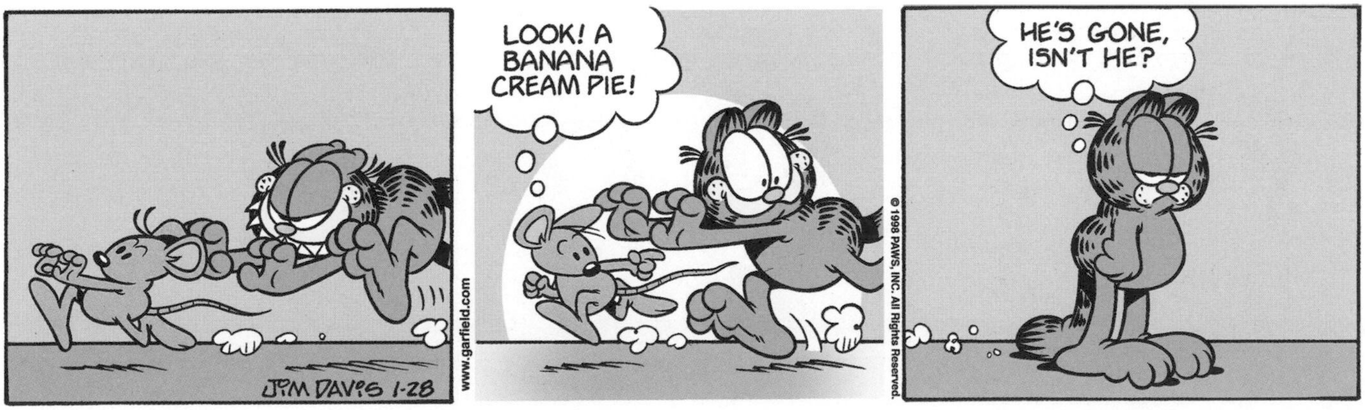
JIM DAVIS 1-28
www.garfield.com
LOOK! A BANANA CREAM PIE!
© 1998 PAWS, INC. All Rights Reserved.
HE'S GONE, ISN'T HE?

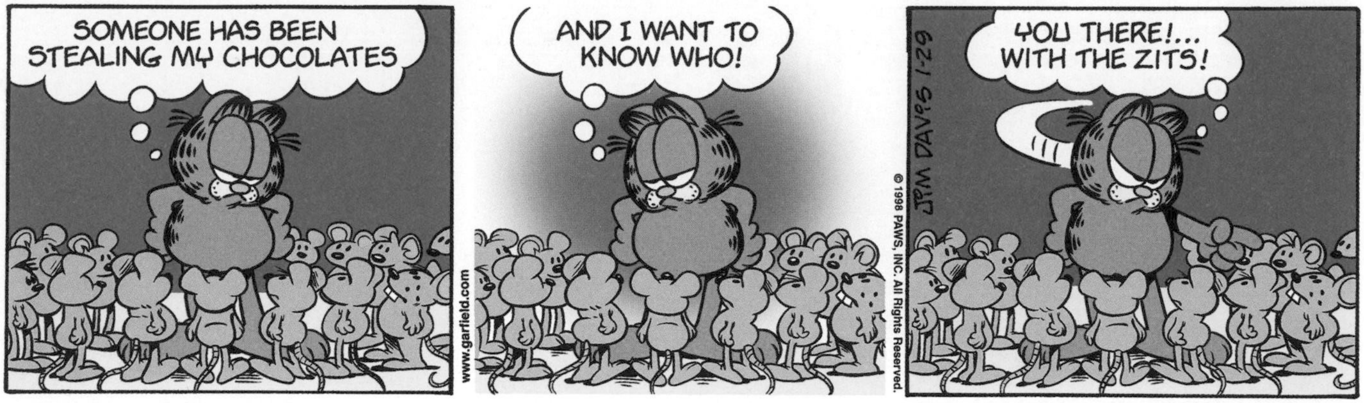
SOMEONE HAS BEEN STEALING MY CHOCOLATES
AND I WANT TO KNOW WHO!
YOU THERE!... WITH THE ZITS!
JIM DAVIS 1-29
www.garfield.com
© 1998 PAWS, INC. All Rights Reserved.

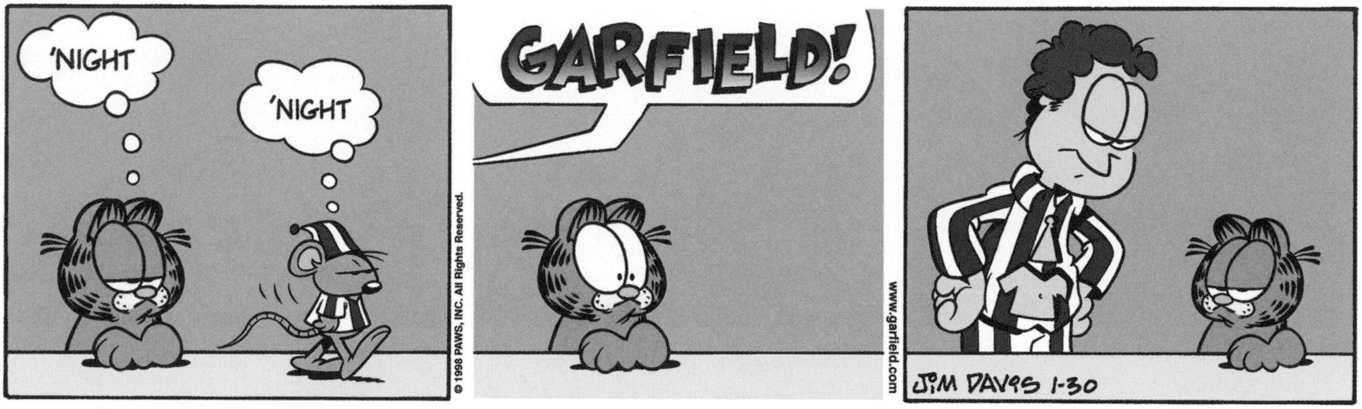
'NIGHT
'NIGHT
GARFIELD!
JIM DAVIS 1-30
© 1998 PAWS, INC. All Rights Reserved.
www.garfield.com

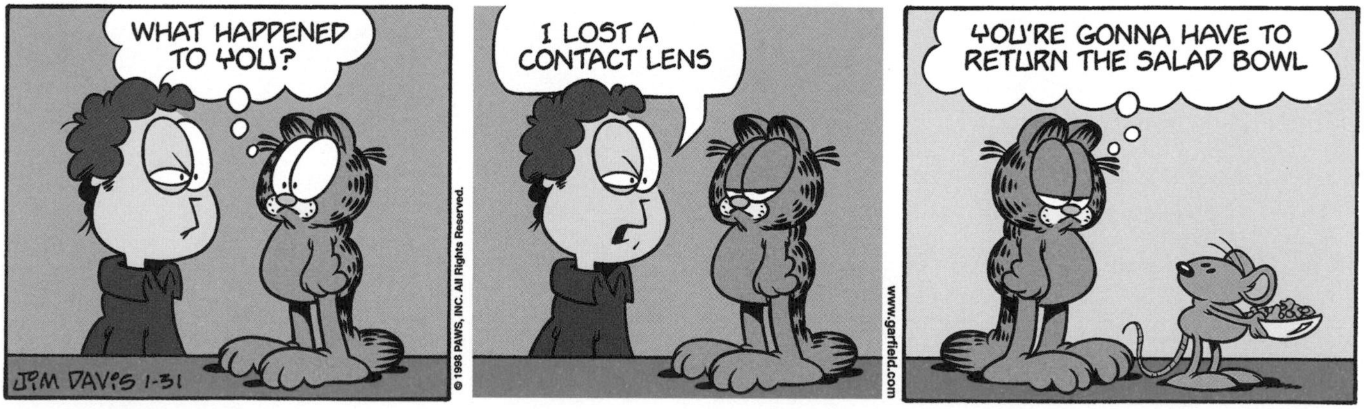
WHAT HAPPENED TO YOU?
I LOST A CONTACT LENS
YOU'RE GONNA HAVE TO RETURN THE SALAD BOWL
JIM DAVIS 1-31
© 1998 PAWS, INC. All Rights Reserved.
www.garfield.com

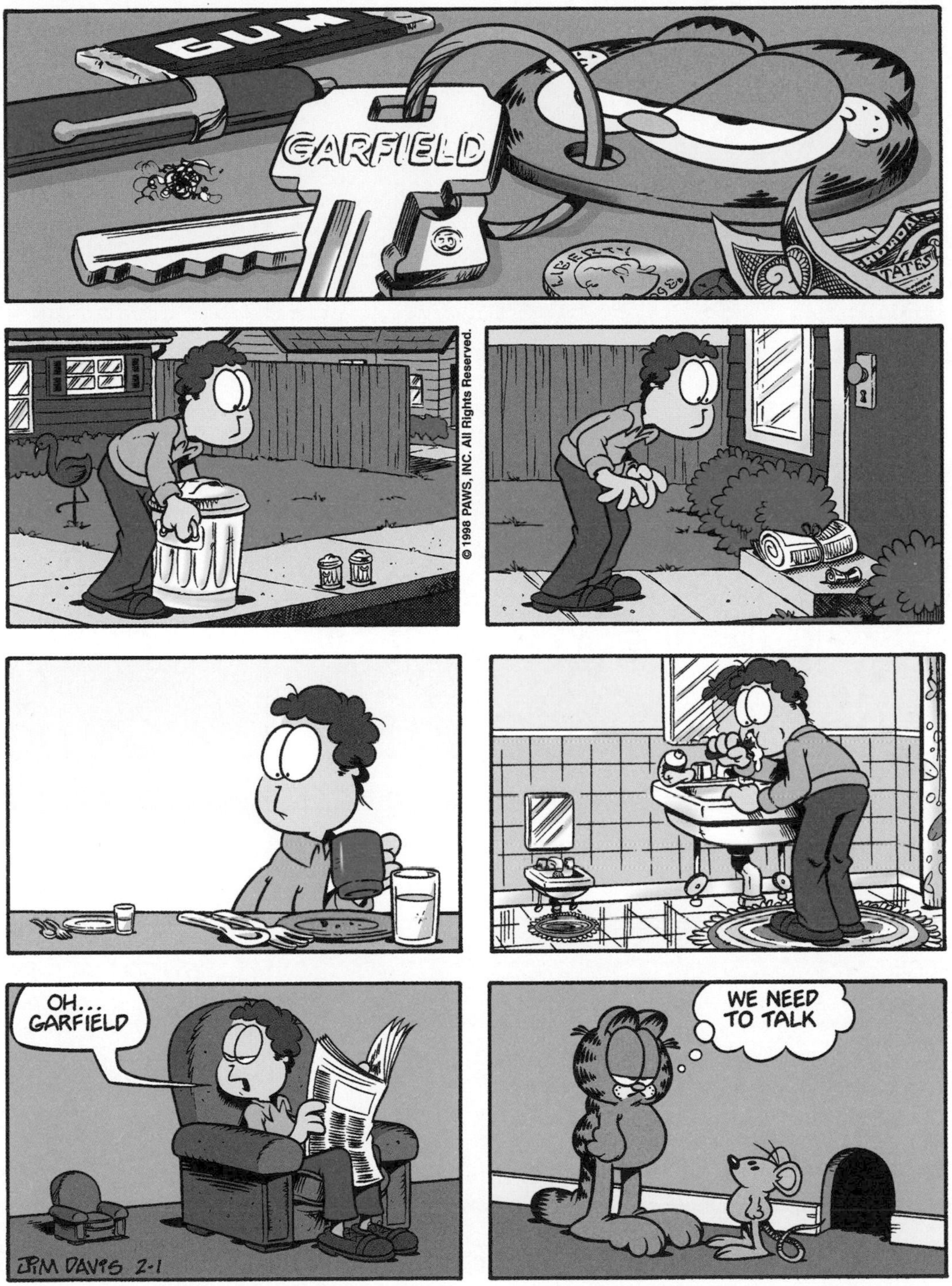
GUM
GARFIELD
OH... GARFIELD
WE NEED TO TALK
JIM DAVIS 2-1

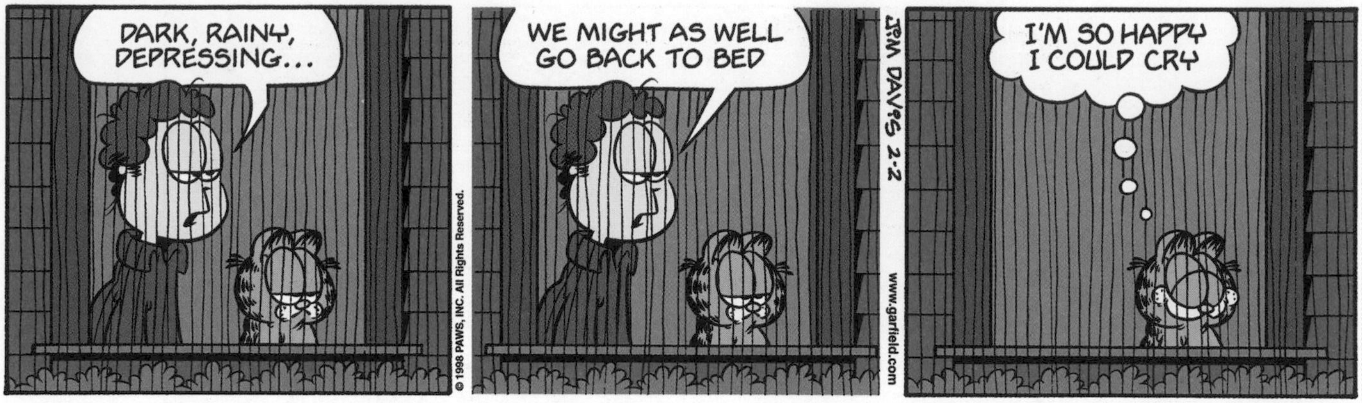
DARK, RAINY, DEPRESSING...
WE MIGHT AS WELL GO BACK TO BED
I'M SO HAPPY I COULD CRY
JIM DAVIS 2-2
© 1998 PAWS, INC. All Rights Reserved.
www.garfield.com

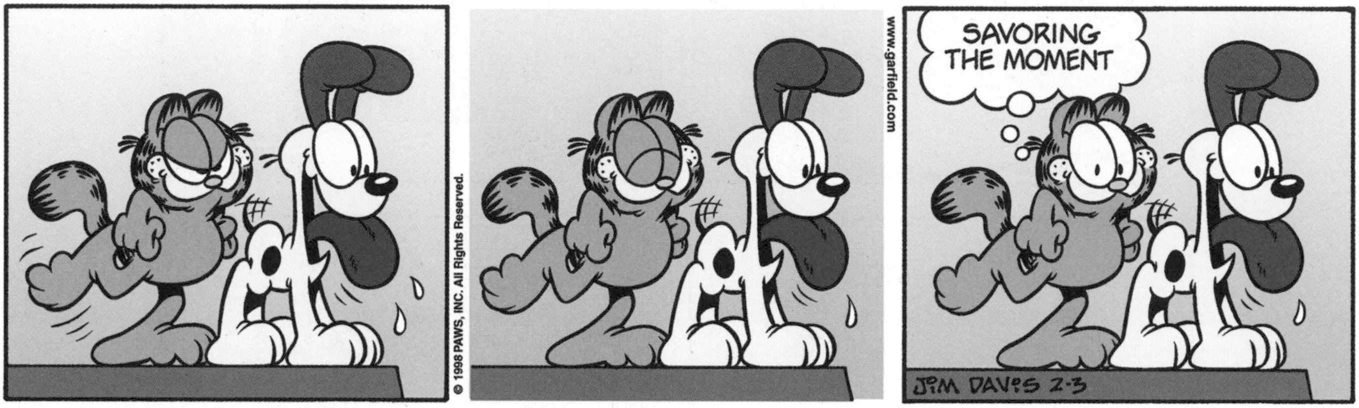
SAVORING THE MOMENT
JIM DAVIS 2-3
© 1998 PAWS, INC. All Rights Reserved.
www.garfield.com

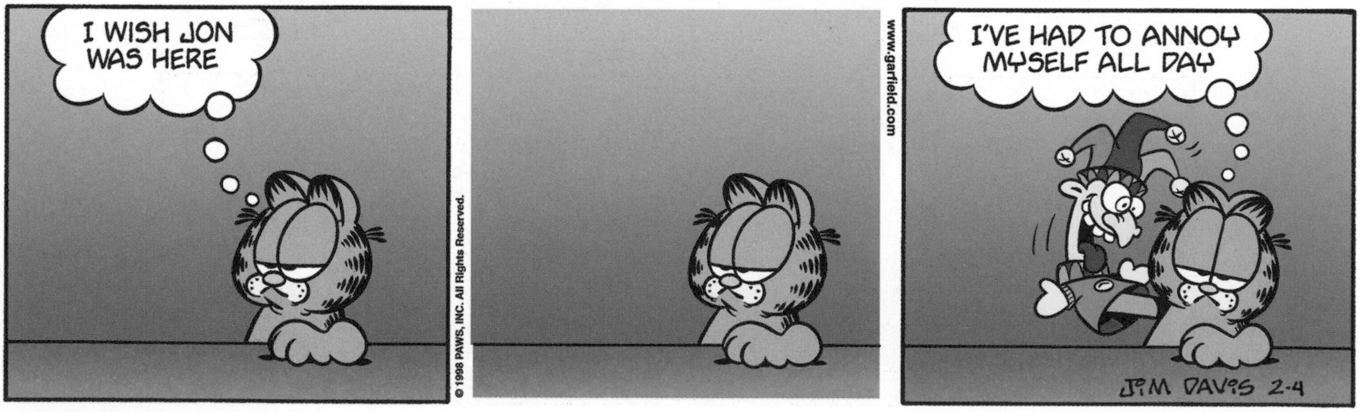
I WISH JON WAS HERE
I'VE HAD TO ANNOY MYSELF ALL DAY
JIM DAVIS 2-4
© 1998 PAWS, INC. All Rights Reserved.
www.garfield.com

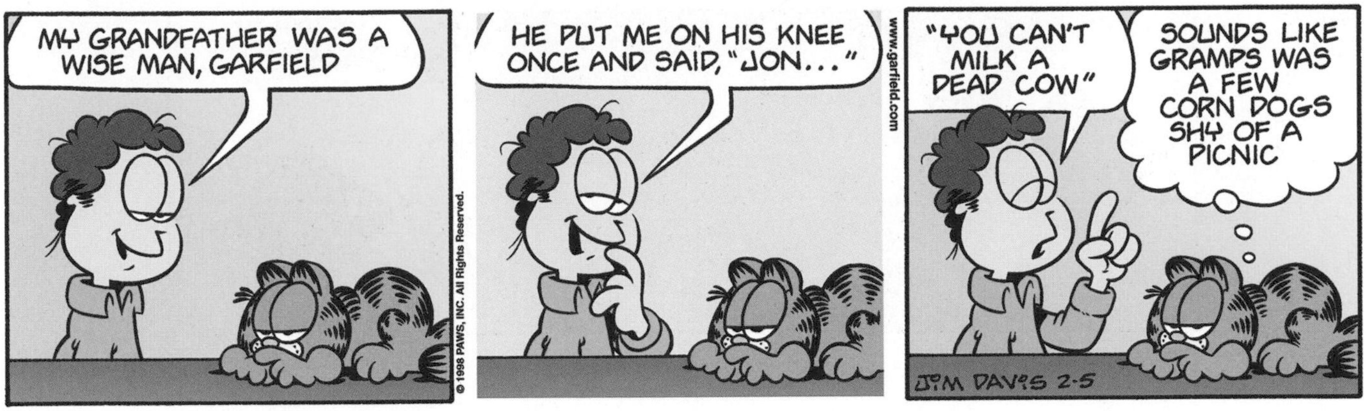
MY GRANDFATHER WAS A WISE MAN, GARFIELD
© 1998 PAWS, INC. All Rights Reserved.
HE PUT ME ON HIS KNEE ONCE AND SAID, "JON..."
www.garfield.com
"YOU CAN'T MILK A DEAD COW"
SOUNDS LIKE GRAMPS WAS A FEW CORN DOGS SHY OF A PICNIC
JIM DAVIS 2-5

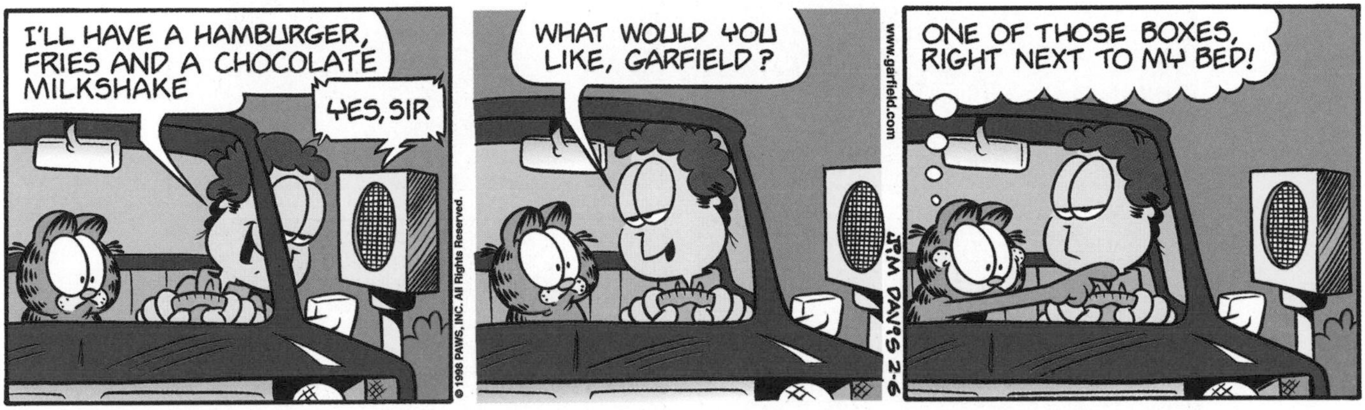
I'LL HAVE A HAMBURGER, FRIES AND A CHOCOLATE MILKSHAKE
YES, SIR
© 1998 PAWS, INC. All Rights Reserved.
WHAT WOULD YOU LIKE, GARFIELD?
JIM DAVIS 2-6
www.garfield.com
ONE OF THOSE BOXES, RIGHT NEXT TO MY BED!

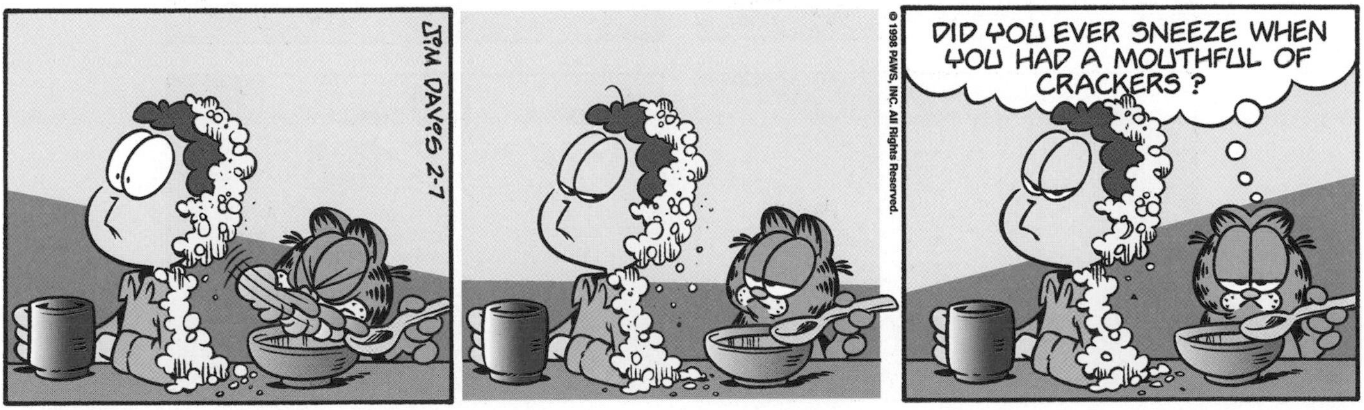
JIM DAVIS 2-7
© 1998 PAWS, INC. All Rights Reserved.
DID YOU EVER SNEEZE WHEN YOU HAD A MOUTHFUL OF CRACKERS?

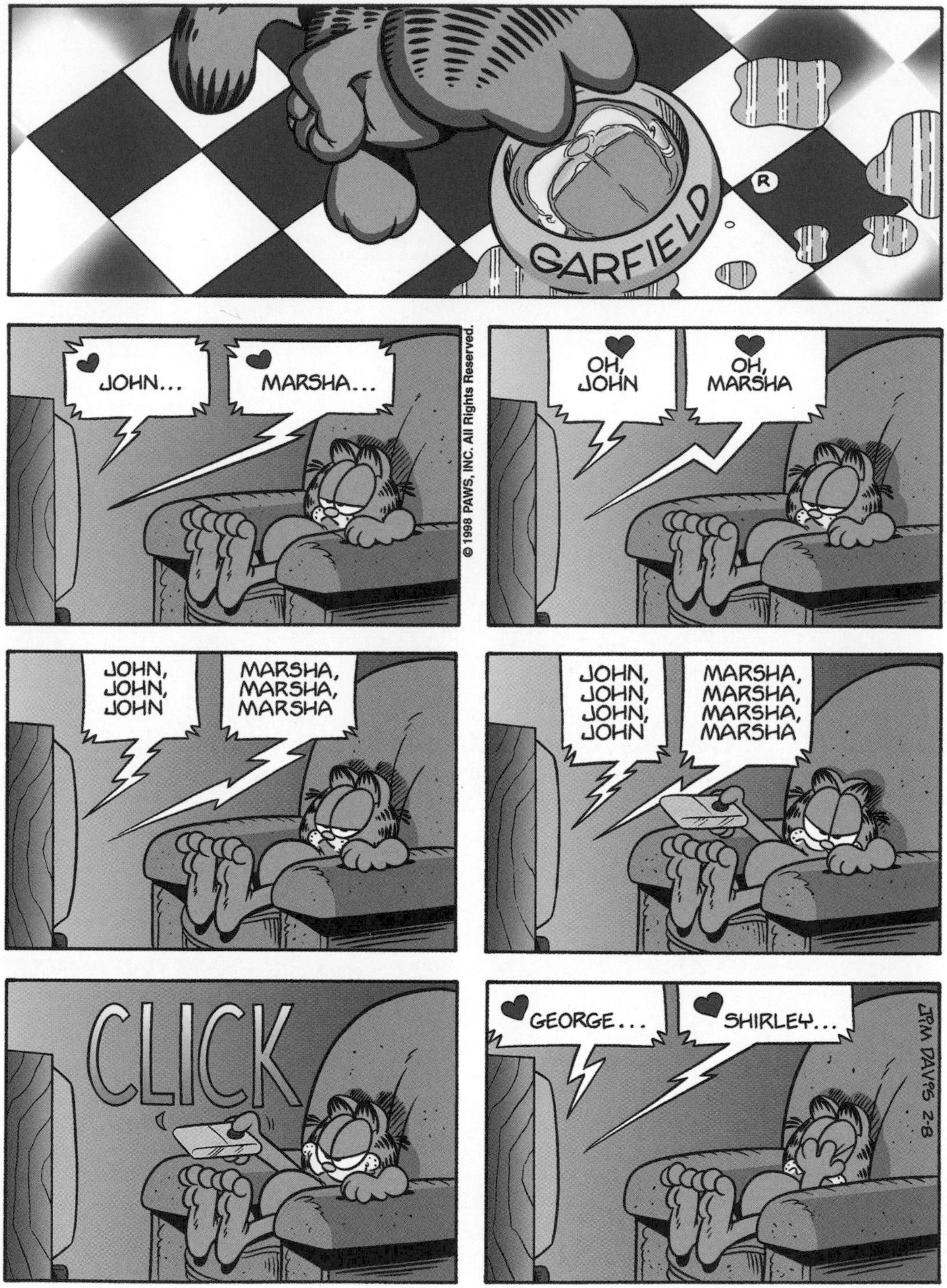
GARFIELD
JOHN...
MARSHA...
© 1998 PAWS, INC. All Rights Reserved.
OH, JOHN
OH, MARSHA
JOHN, JOHN, JOHN
MARSHA, MARSHA, MARSHA
JOHN, JOHN, JOHN, JOHN
MARSHA, MARSHA, MARSHA, MARSHA
CLICK
GEORGE...
SHIRLEY...
JIM DAVIS 2-8

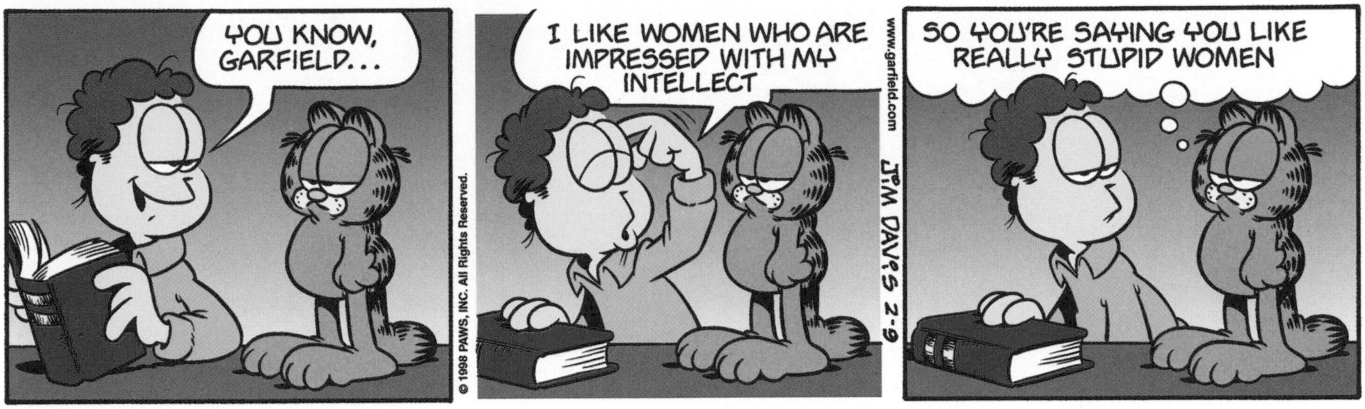
YOU KNOW, GARFIELD...
© 1998 PAWS, INC. All Rights Reserved.
I LIKE WOMEN WHO ARE IMPRESSED WITH MY INTELLECT
www.garfield.com
JIM DAVIS 2-9
SO YOU'RE SAYING YOU LIKE REALLY STUPID WOMEN

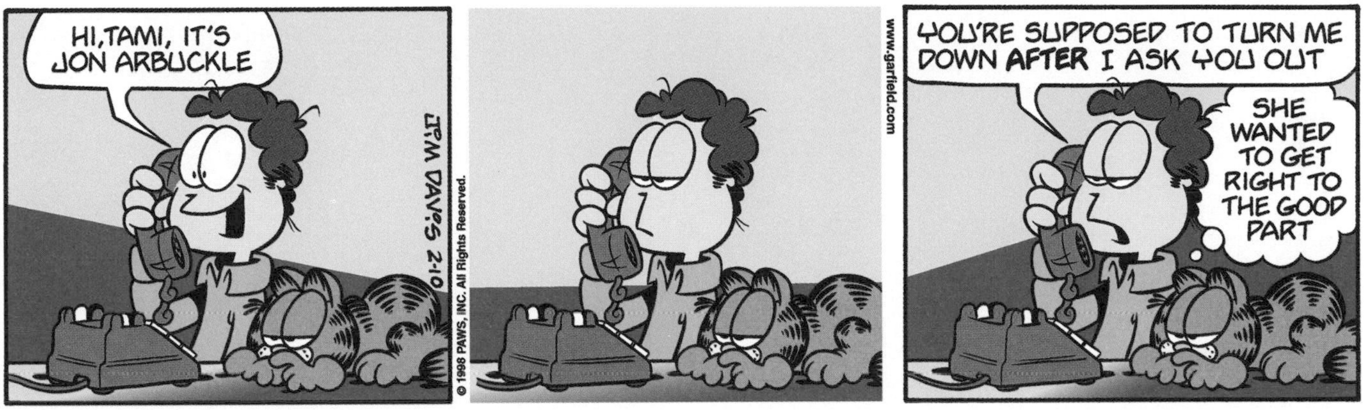
HI, TAMI, IT'S JON ARBUCKLE
JIM DAVIS 2-10
© 1998 PAWS, INC. All Rights Reserved.
www.garfield.com
YOU'RE SUPPOSED TO TURN ME DOWN **AFTER** I ASK YOU OUT
SHE WANTED TO GET RIGHT TO THE GOOD PART

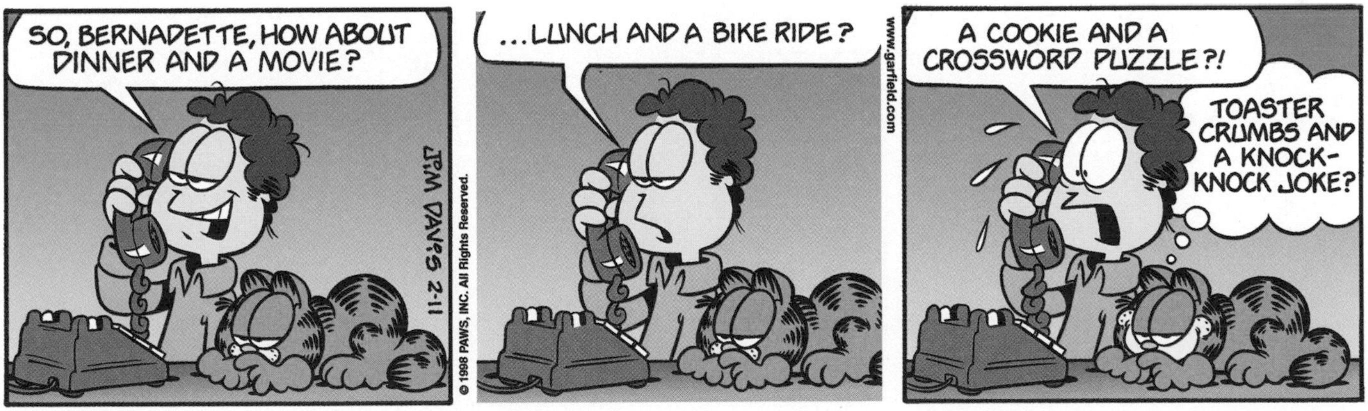
SO, BERNADETTE, HOW ABOUT DINNER AND A MOVIE?
JIM DAVIS 2-11
© 1998 PAWS, INC. All Rights Reserved.
...LUNCH AND A BIKE RIDE?
www.garfield.com
A COOKIE AND A CROSSWORD PUZZLE?!
TOASTER CRUMBS AND A KNOCK-KNOCK JOKE?

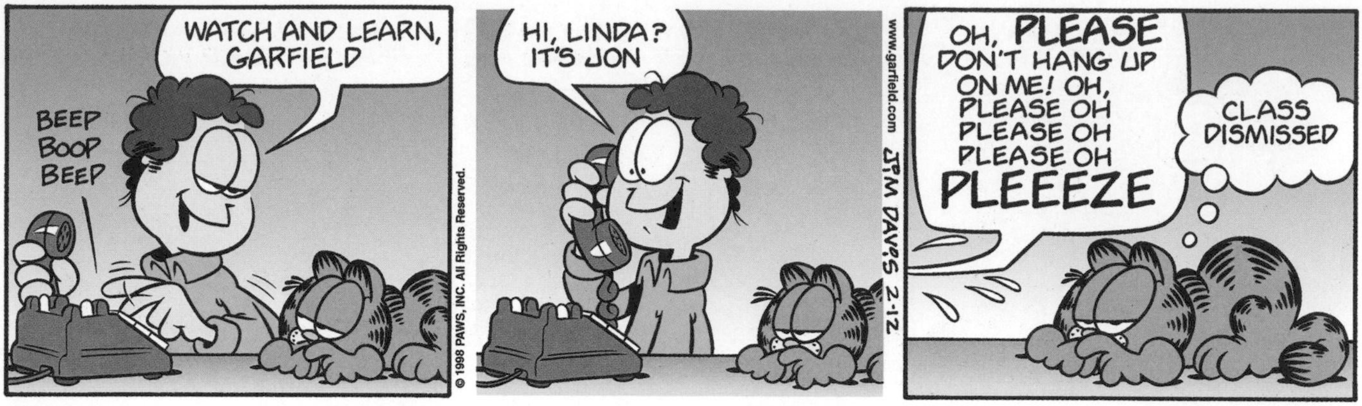
BEEP
BOOP
BEEP
WATCH AND LEARN, GARFIELD
© 1998 PAWS, INC. All Rights Reserved.
HI, LINDA? IT'S JON
www.garfield.com
JIM DAVIS 2-12
OH, PLEASE DON'T HANG UP ON ME! OH, PLEASE OH PLEASE OH PLEASE OH PLEEEZE
CLASS DISMISSED

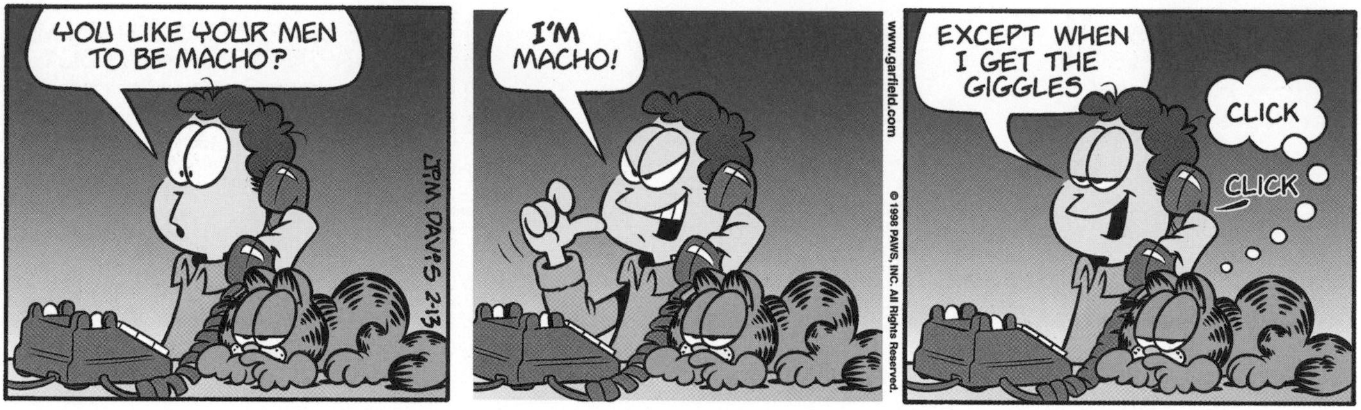
YOU LIKE YOUR MEN TO BE MACHO?
JIM DAVIS 2-13
I'M MACHO!
www.garfield.com
© 1998 PAWS, INC. All Rights Reserved.
EXCEPT WHEN I GET THE GIGGLES
CLICK
CLICK

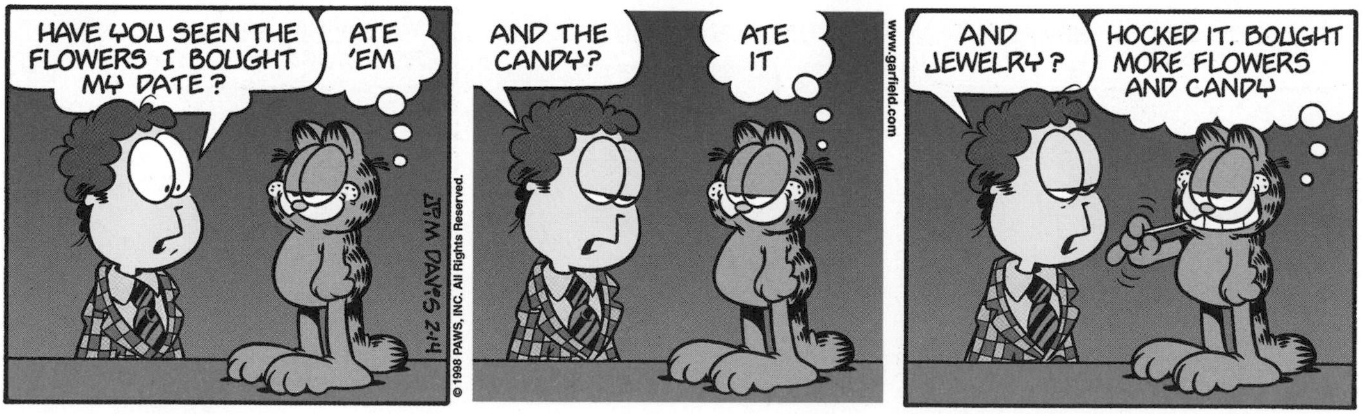
HAVE YOU SEEN THE FLOWERS I BOUGHT MY DATE?
ATE 'EM
JIM DAVIS 2-14
© 1998 PAWS, INC. All Rights Reserved.
AND THE CANDY?
ATE IT
www.garfield.com
AND JEWELRY?
HOCKED IT. BOUGHT MORE FLOWERS AND CANDY

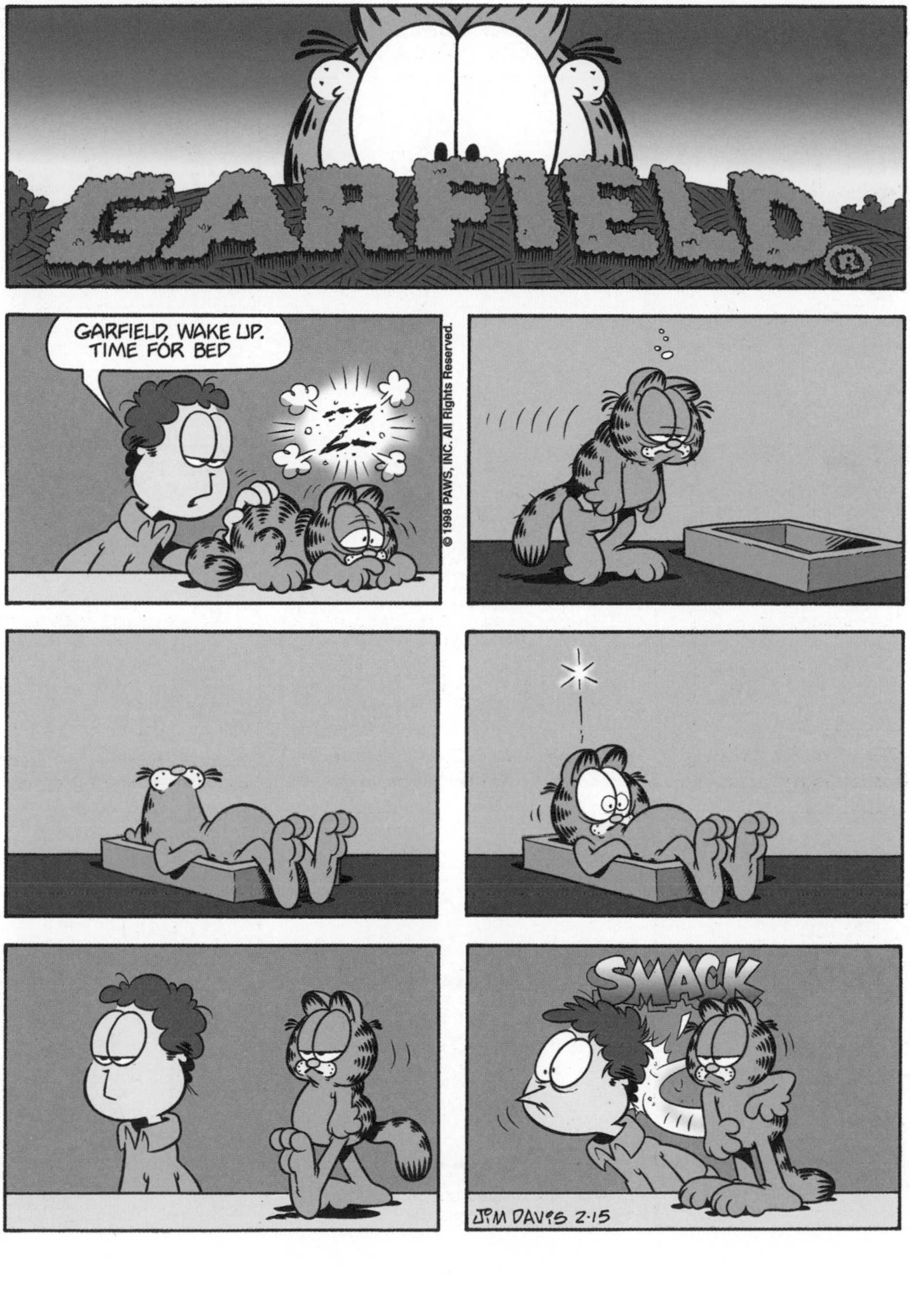
GARFIELD
GARFIELD, WAKE UP. TIME FOR BED
© 1998 PAWS, INC. All Rights Reserved.
Z
SMACK
JIM DAVIS 2·15

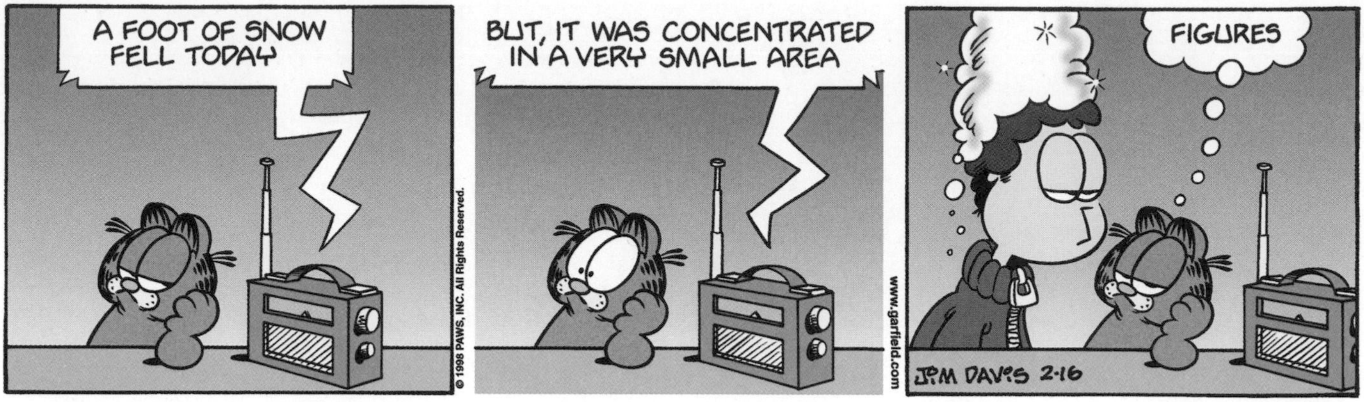
A FOOT OF SNOW FELL TODAY
BUT, IT WAS CONCENTRATED IN A VERY SMALL AREA
FIGURES
© 1998 PAWS, INC. All Rights Reserved.
www.garfield.com
JIM DAVIS 2-16

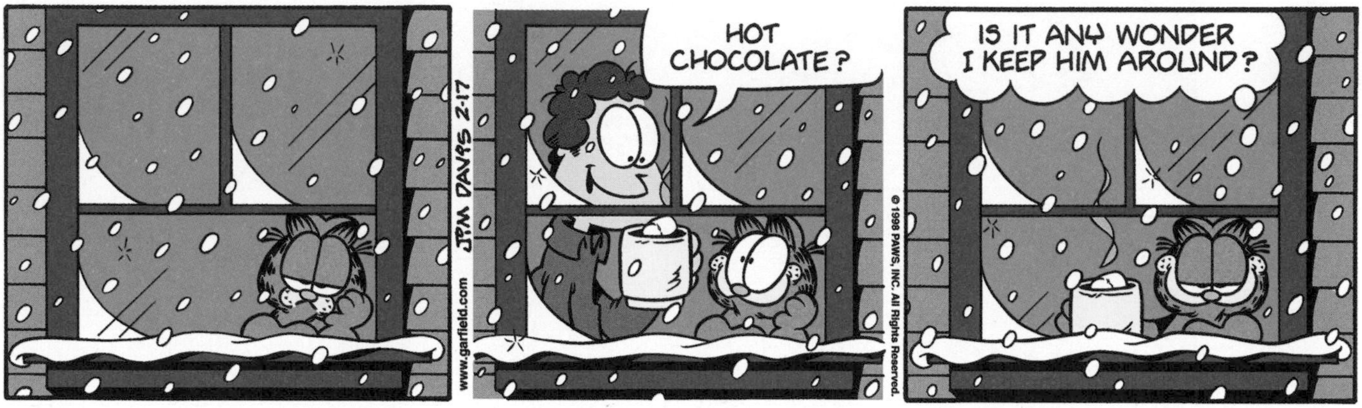
JIM DAVIS 2-17
www.garfield.com
HOT CHOCOLATE?
© 1998 PAWS, INC. All Rights Reserved.
IS IT ANY WONDER I KEEP HIM AROUND?

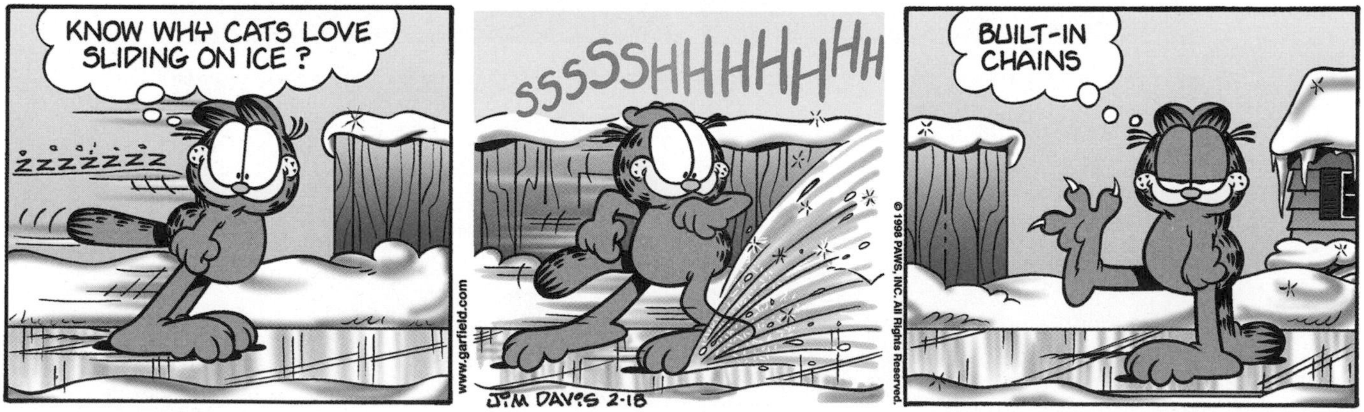
KNOW WHY CATS LOVE SLIDING ON ICE?
ZZZZZZZ
www.garfield.com
SSSSSHHHHHHHH
JIM DAVIS 2-18
© 1998 PAWS, INC. All Rights Reserved.
BUILT-IN CHAINS

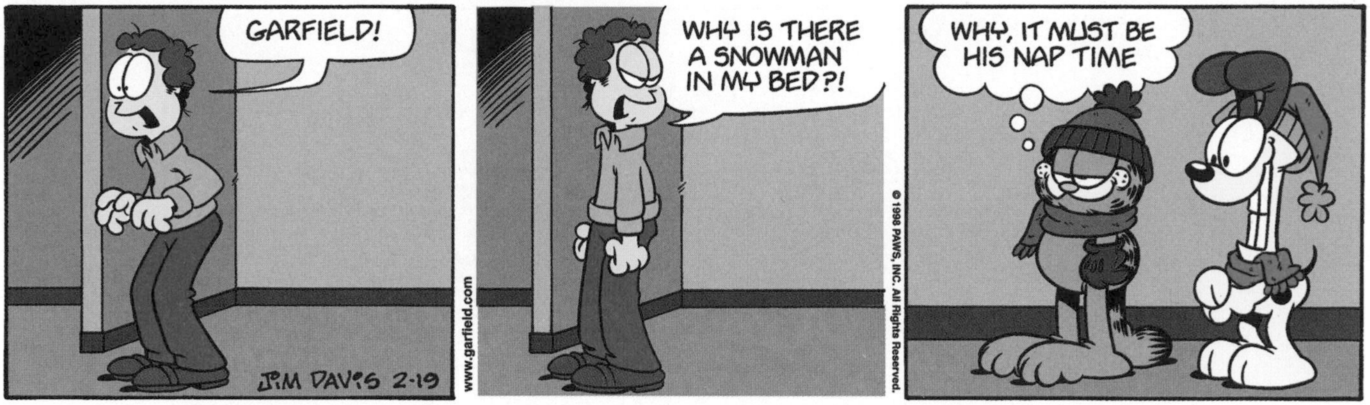
GARFIELD!
JIM DAVIS 2-19
www.garfield.com
WHY IS THERE A SNOWMAN IN MY BED?!
© 1998 PAWS, INC. All Rights Reserved.
WHY, IT MUST BE HIS NAP TIME

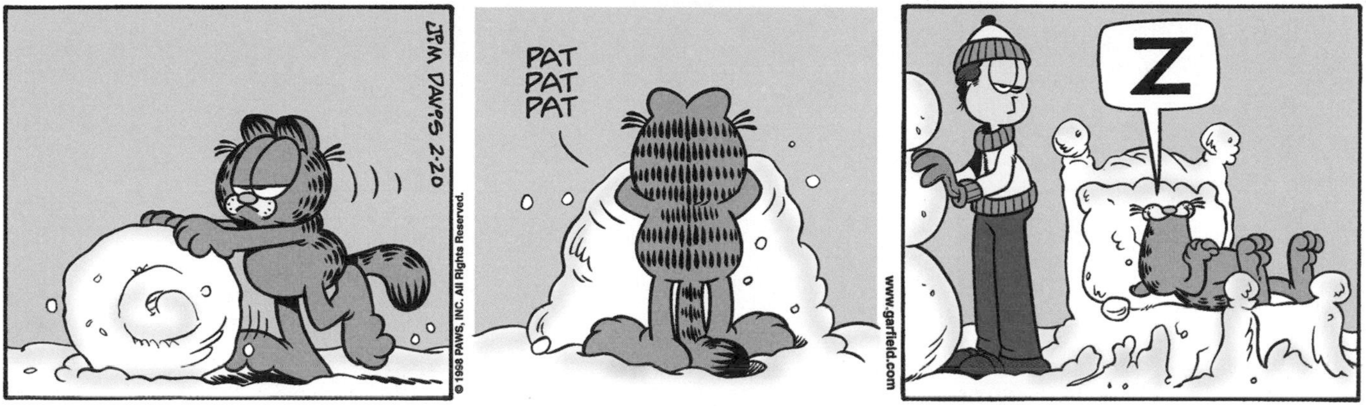
JIM DAVIS 2-20
© 1998 PAWS, INC. All Rights Reserved.
PAT PAT PAT
www.garfield.com
Z

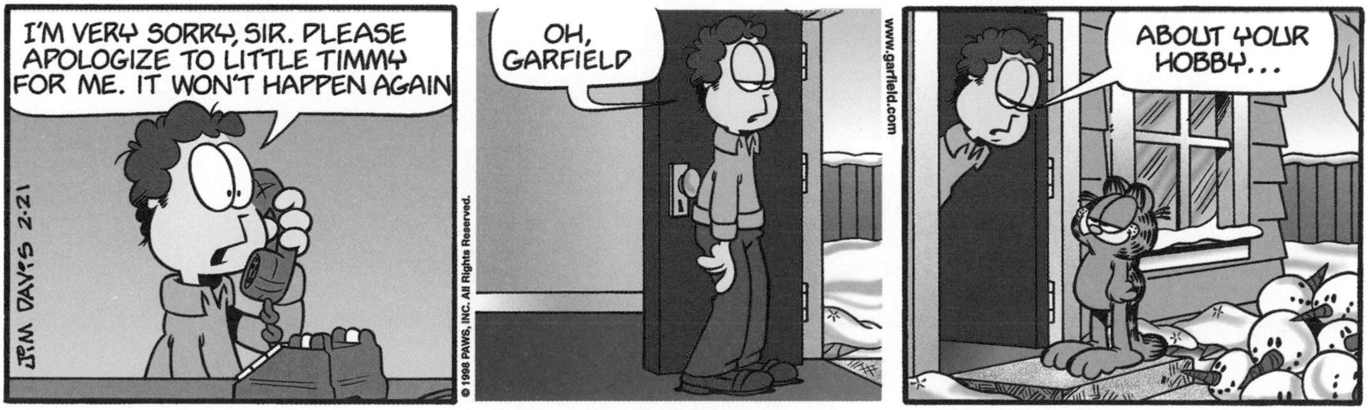
I'M VERY SORRY, SIR. PLEASE APOLOGIZE TO LITTLE TIMMY FOR ME. IT WON'T HAPPEN AGAIN
JIM DAVIS 2-21
© 1998 PAWS, INC. All Rights Reserved.
OH, GARFIELD
www.garfield.com
ABOUT YOUR HOBBY...

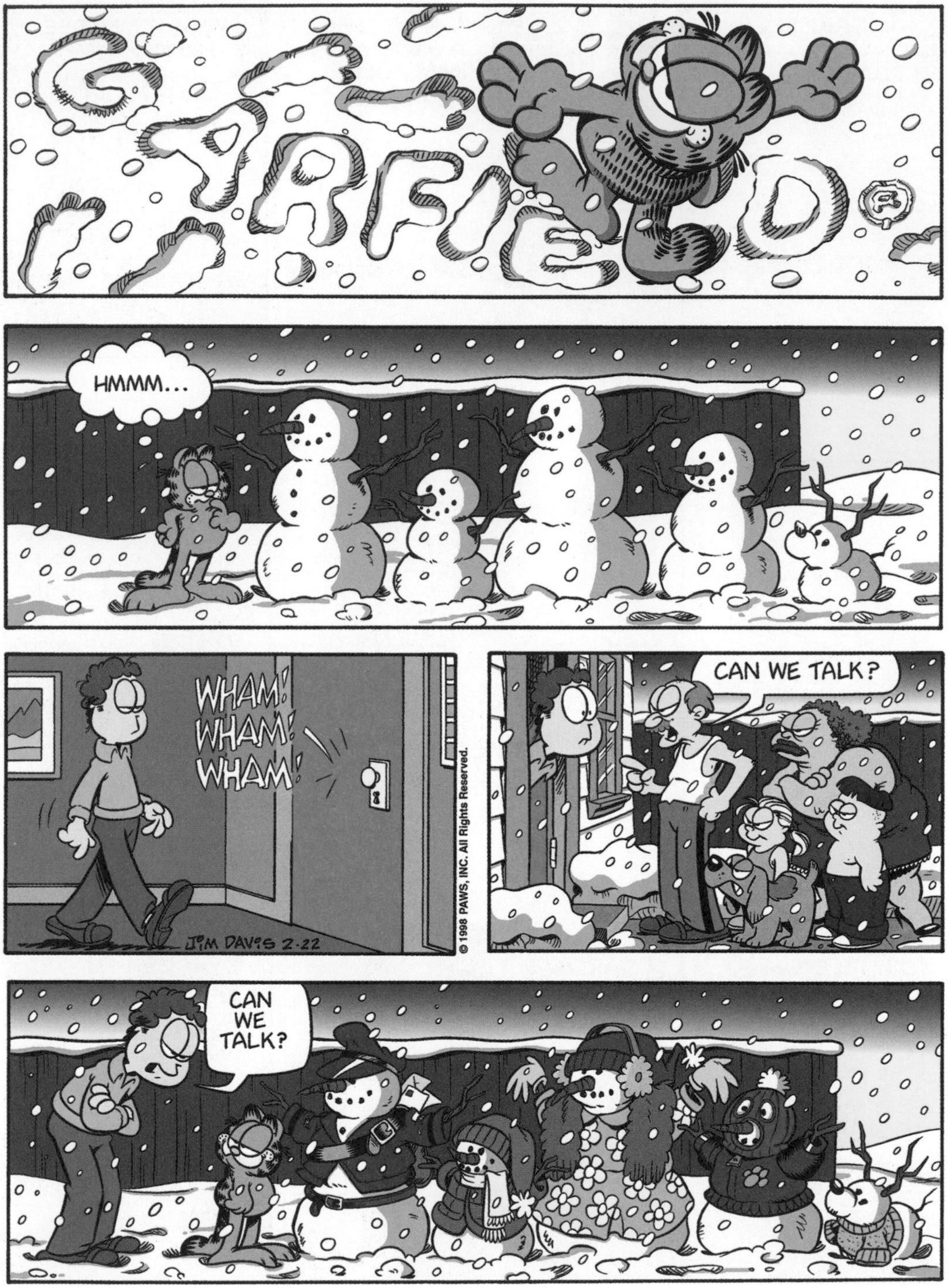
GARFIELD®
HMMM...
WHAM! WHAM! WHAM!
JIM DAVIS 2-22
© 1998 PAWS, INC. All Rights Reserved.
CAN WE TALK?
CAN WE TALK?

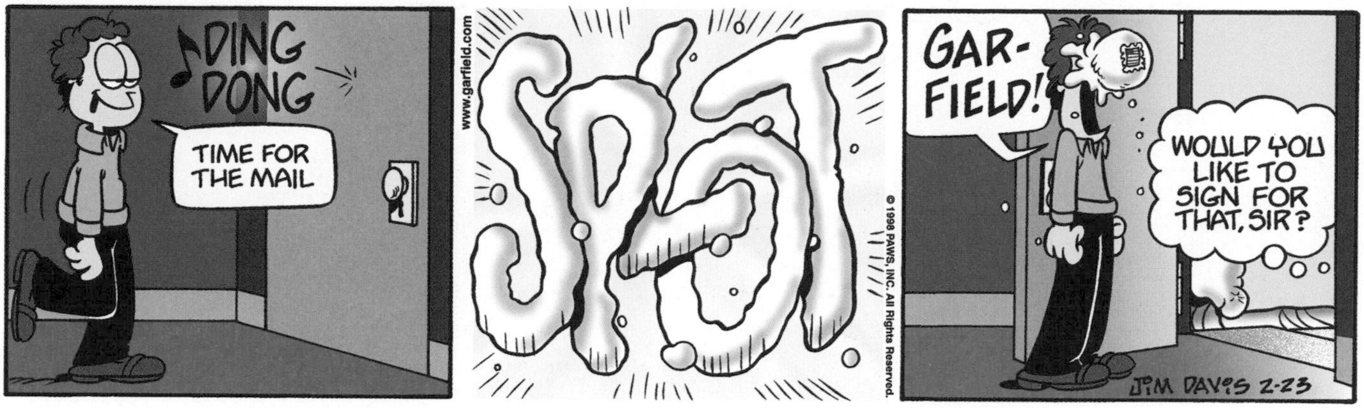
DING DONG
TIME FOR THE MAIL
www.garfield.com
SPLAT
© 1998 PAWS, INC. All Rights Reserved.
GAR-FIELD!
WOULD YOU LIKE TO SIGN FOR THAT, SIR?
JIM DAVIS 2-23

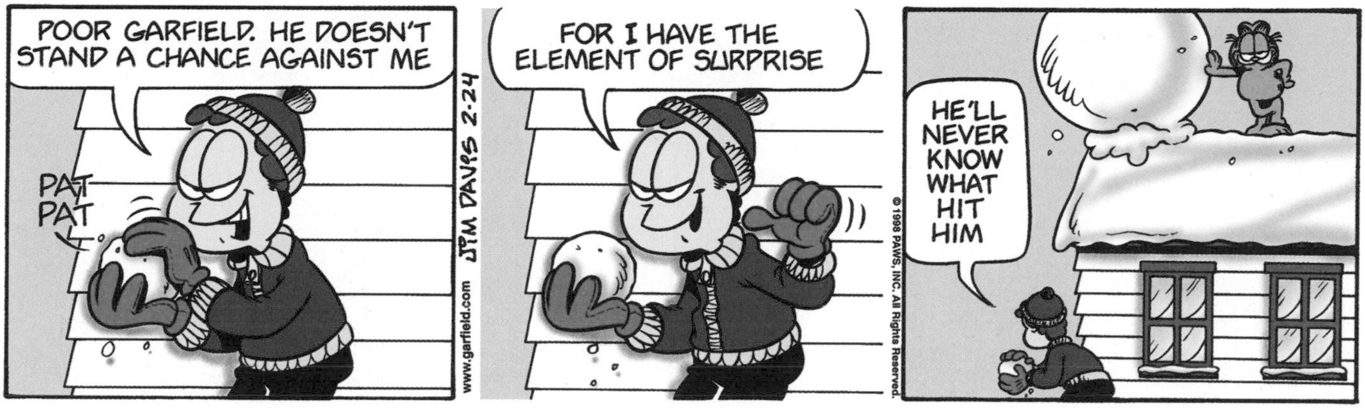
POOR GARFIELD. HE DOESN'T STAND A CHANCE AGAINST ME
PAT PAT
JIM DAVIS 2-24
www.garfield.com
FOR I HAVE THE ELEMENT OF SURPRISE
© 1998 PAWS, INC. All Rights Reserved.
HE'LL NEVER KNOW WHAT HIT HIM

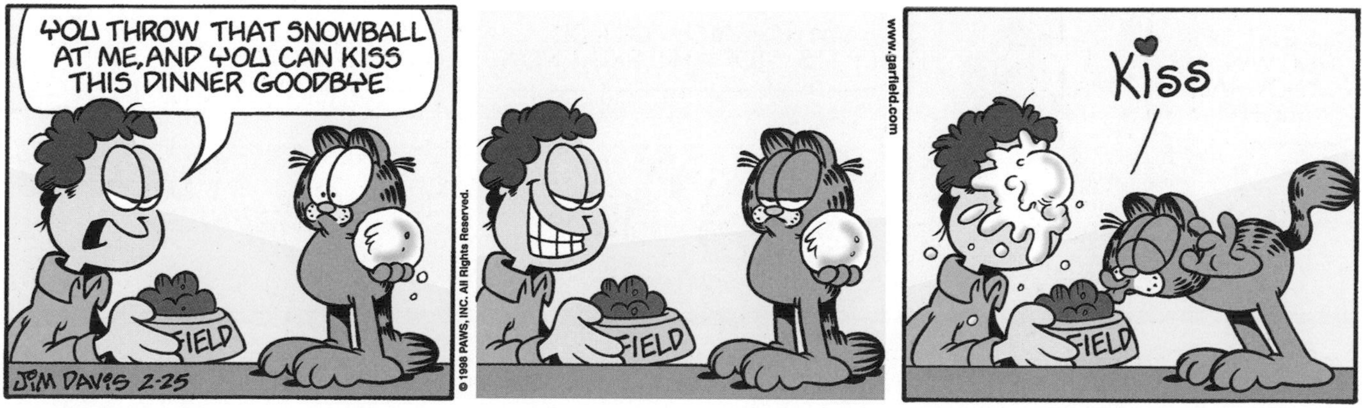
YOU THROW THAT SNOWBALL AT ME, AND YOU CAN KISS THIS DINNER GOODBYE
FIELD
JIM DAVIS 2-25
© 1998 PAWS, INC. All Rights Reserved.
FIELD
www.garfield.com
KISS
FIELD

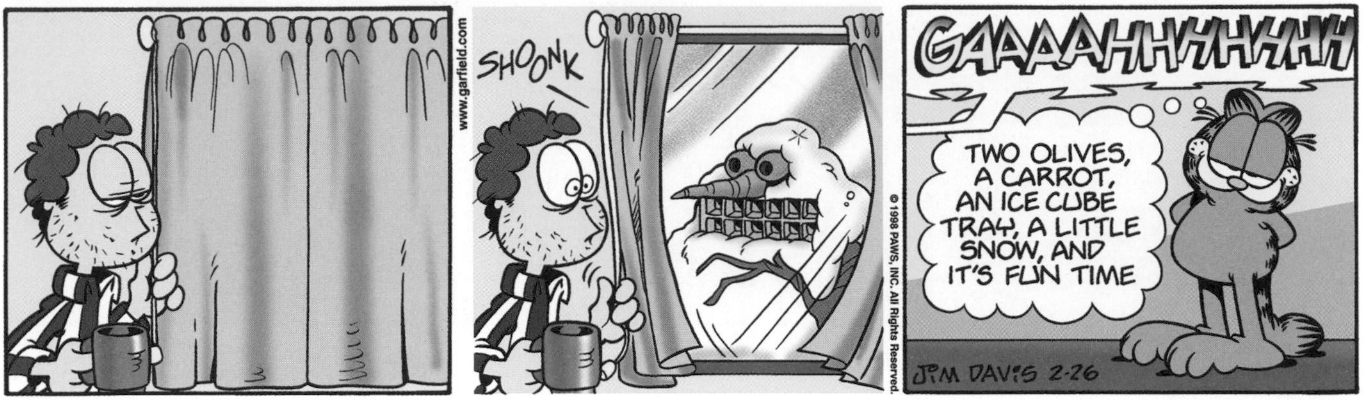
www.garfield.com
SHOONK
© 1998 PAWS, INC. All Rights Reserved.
GAAAAHHHHHHH
TWO OLIVES, A CARROT, AN ICE CUBE TRAY, A LITTLE SNOW, AND IT'S FUN TIME
JIM DAVIS 2-26

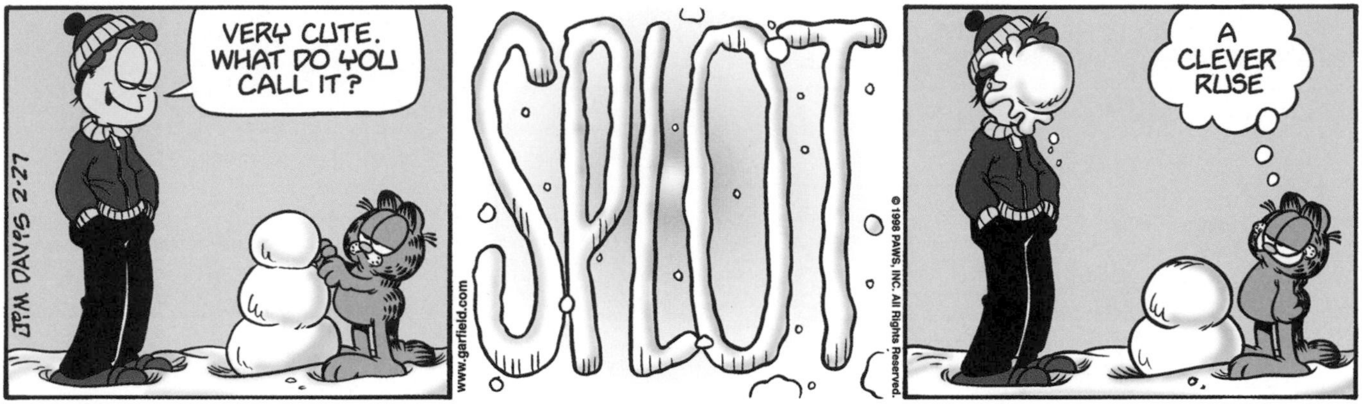
VERY CUTE. WHAT DO YOU CALL IT?
JIM DAVIS 2-27
www.garfield.com
SPLOT
© 1998 PAWS, INC. All Rights Reserved.
A CLEVER RUSE

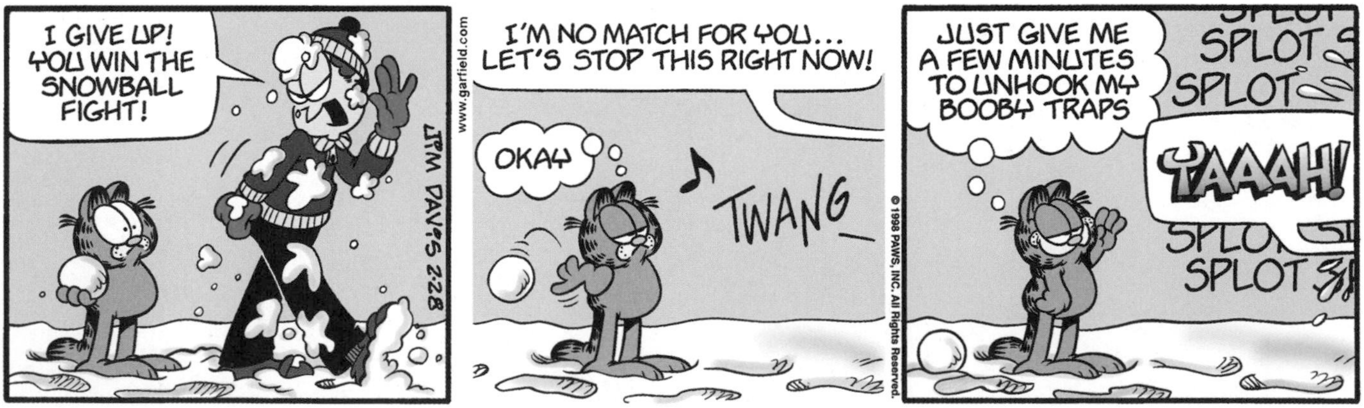
I GIVE UP! YOU WIN THE SNOWBALL FIGHT!
JIM DAVIS 2-28
www.garfield.com
I'M NO MATCH FOR YOU... LET'S STOP THIS RIGHT NOW!
OKAY
TWANG
© 1998 PAWS, INC. All Rights Reserved.
JUST GIVE ME A FEW MINUTES TO UNHOOK MY BOOBY TRAPS
SPLOT
SPLOT
YAAAH!
SPLOT

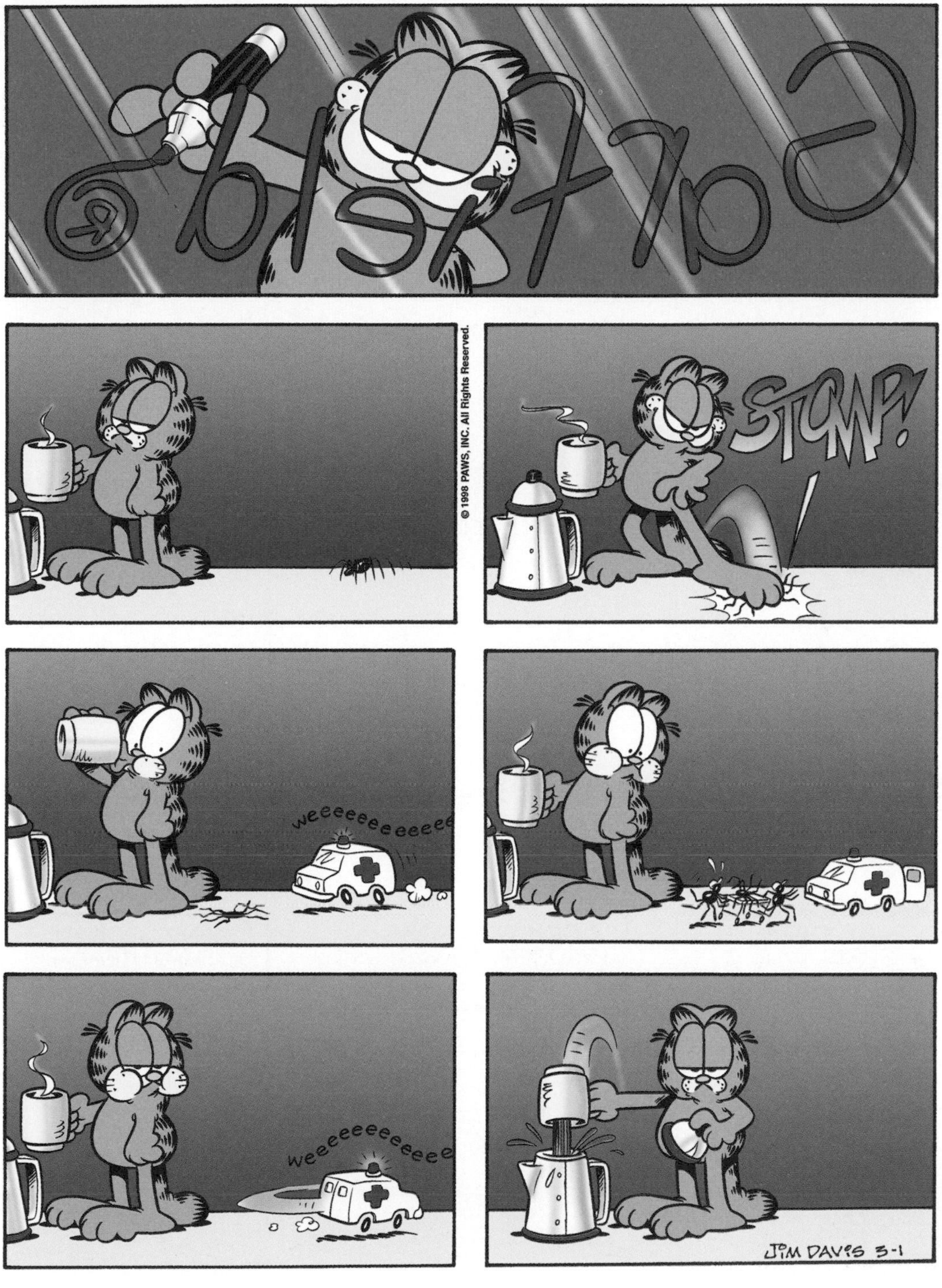
© 1998 PAWS, INC. All Rights Reserved.
STOMP!
weeeeeeeeeeeee
weeeeeeeeeeee
JIM DAVIS 3-1

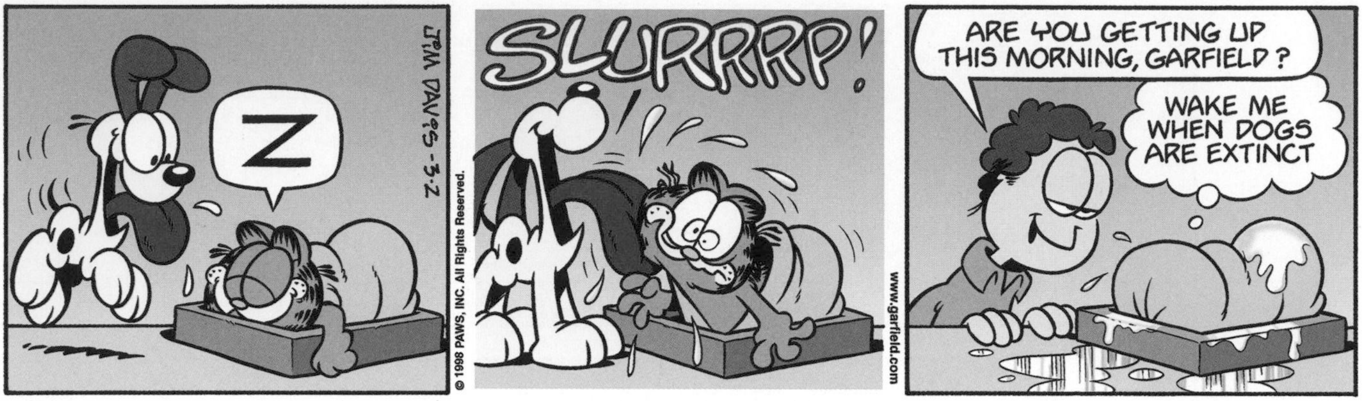
JIM DAVIS 3-2
Z
SLURRRP!
© 1998 PAWS, INC. All Rights Reserved.
www.garfield.com
ARE YOU GETTING UP THIS MORNING, GARFIELD ?
WAKE ME WHEN DOGS ARE EXTINCT

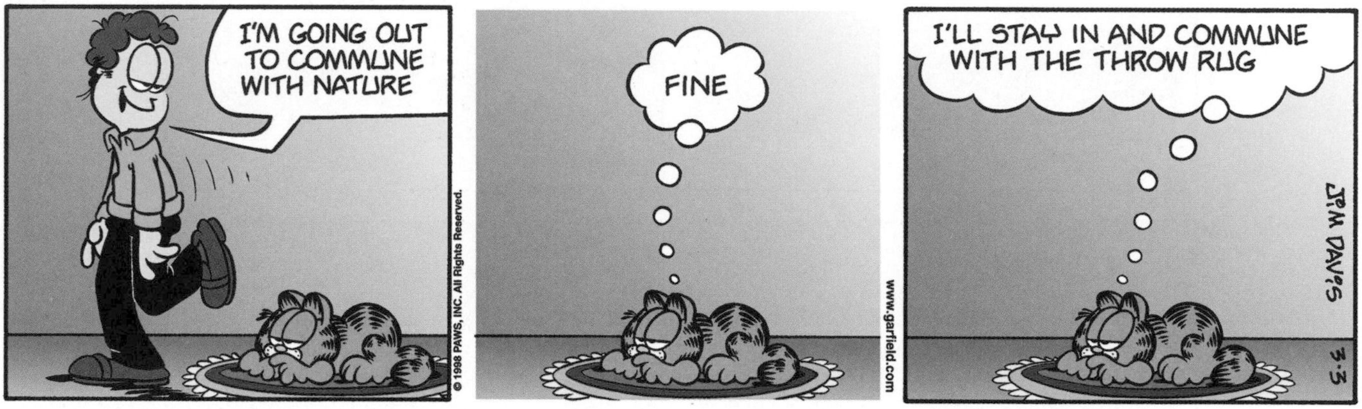
I'M GOING OUT TO COMMUNE WITH NATURE
© 1998 PAWS, INC. All Rights Reserved.
FINE
www.garfield.com
I'LL STAY IN AND COMMUNE WITH THE THROW RUG
JIM DAVIS 3-3

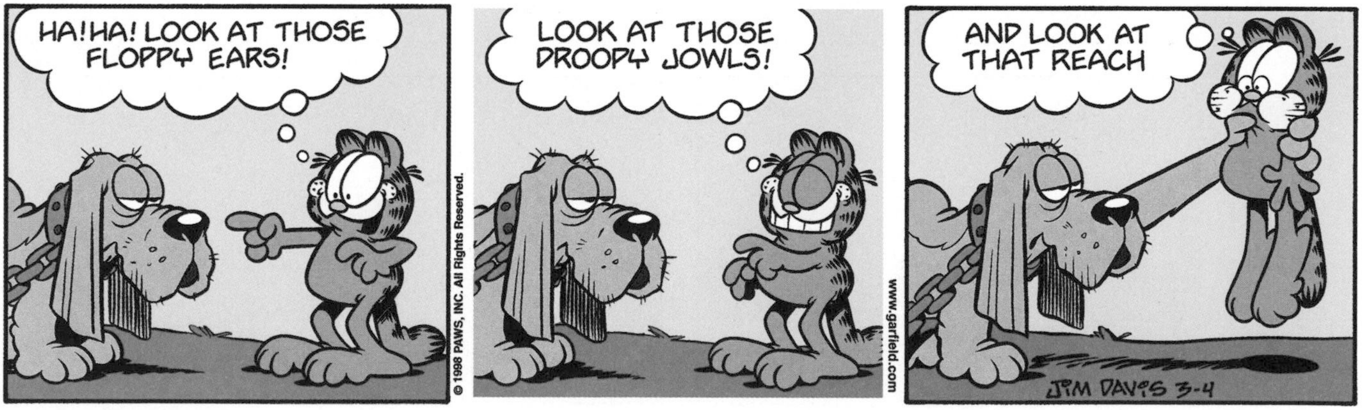
HA! HA! LOOK AT THOSE FLOPPY EARS!
© 1998 PAWS, INC. All Rights Reserved.
LOOK AT THOSE DROOPY JOWLS!
www.garfield.com
AND LOOK AT THAT REACH
JIM DAVIS 3-4

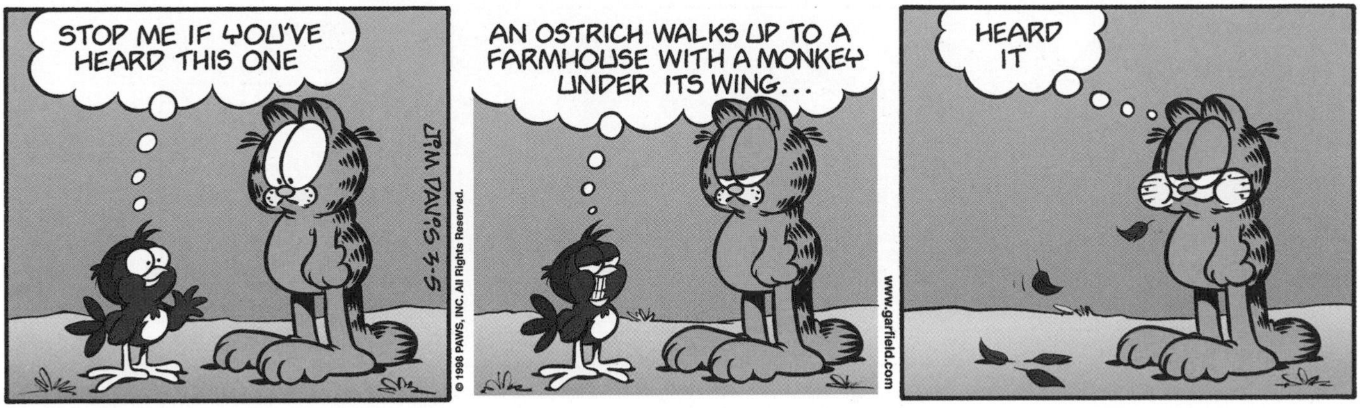
STOP ME IF YOU'VE HEARD THIS ONE
JIM DAVIS 3-5
© 1998 PAWS, INC. All Rights Reserved.
AN OSTRICH WALKS UP TO A FARMHOUSE WITH A MONKEY UNDER ITS WING...
www.garfield.com
HEARD IT

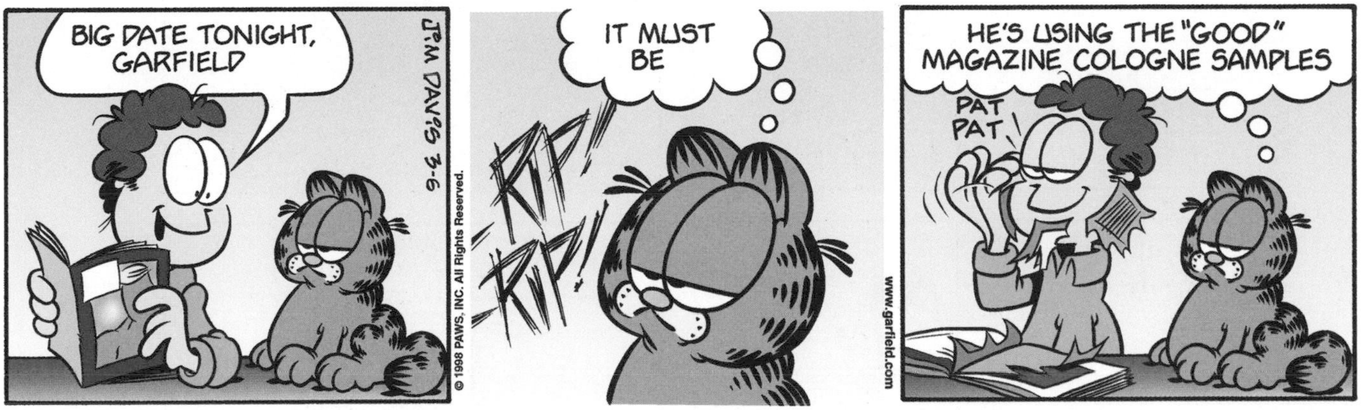
BIG DATE TONIGHT, GARFIELD
JIM DAVIS 3-6
© 1998 PAWS, INC. All Rights Reserved.
IT MUST BE
RIP! RIP!
www.garfield.com
HE'S USING THE "GOOD" MAGAZINE COLOGNE SAMPLES
PAT PAT

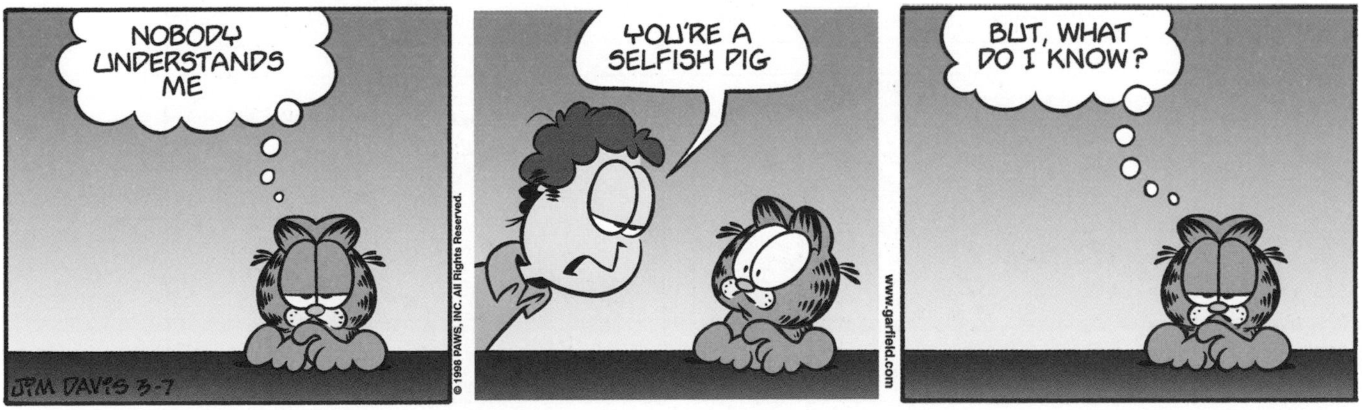
NOBODY UNDERSTANDS ME
JIM DAVIS 3-7
© 1998 PAWS, INC. All Rights Reserved.
YOU'RE A SELFISH PIG
www.garfield.com
BUT, WHAT DO I KNOW?

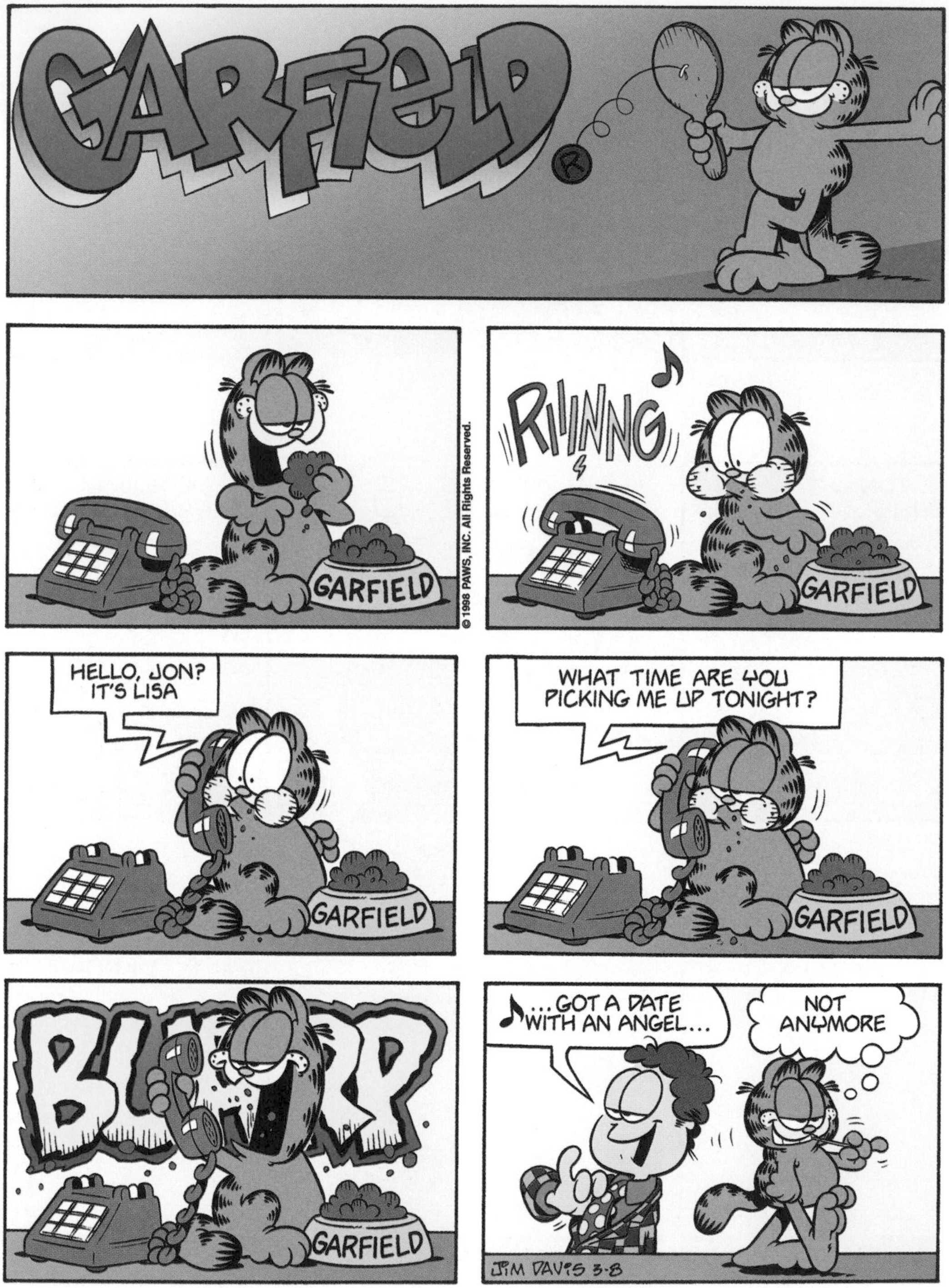
GARFIELD ®
GARFIELD
© 1998 PAWS, INC. All Rights Reserved.
RIIINNG
GARFIELD
HELLO, JON? IT'S LISA
GARFIELD
WHAT TIME ARE YOU PICKING ME UP TONIGHT?
GARFIELD
GARFIELD
...GOT A DATE WITH AN ANGEL...
NOT ANYMORE
JIM DAVIS 3-8

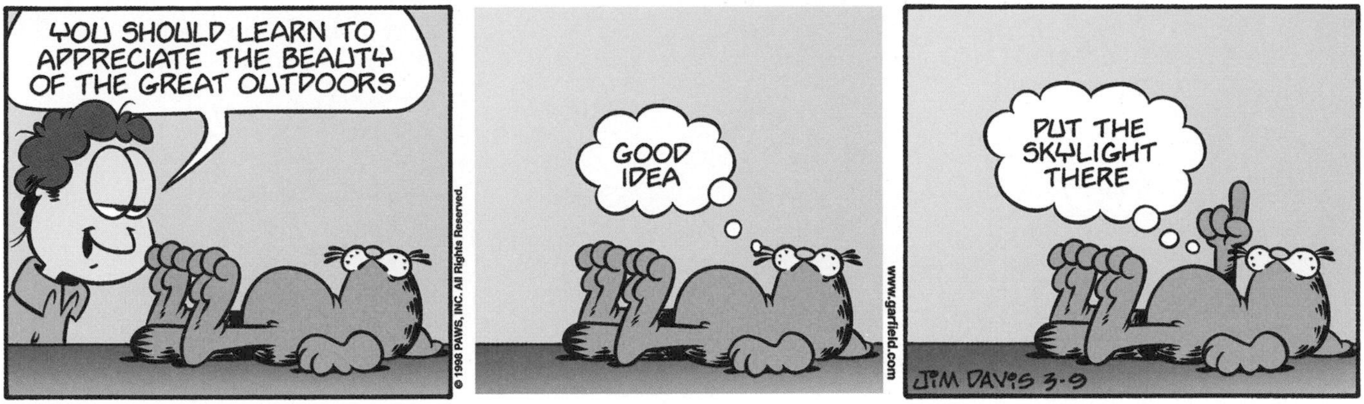
YOU SHOULD LEARN TO APPRECIATE THE BEAUTY OF THE GREAT OUTDOORS
GOOD IDEA
PUT THE SKYLIGHT THERE
JIM DAVIS 3-9
© 1998 PAWS, INC. All Rights Reserved.
www.garfield.com

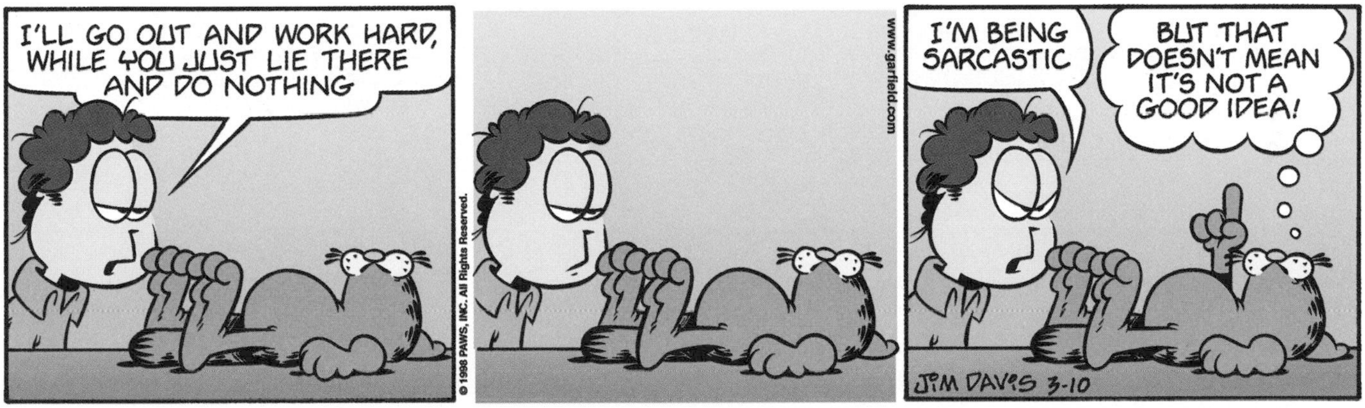
I'LL GO OUT AND WORK HARD, WHILE YOU JUST LIE THERE AND DO NOTHING
I'M BEING SARCASTIC
BUT THAT DOESN'T MEAN IT'S NOT A GOOD IDEA!
JIM DAVIS 3-10
© 1998 PAWS, INC. All Rights Reserved.
www.garfield.com

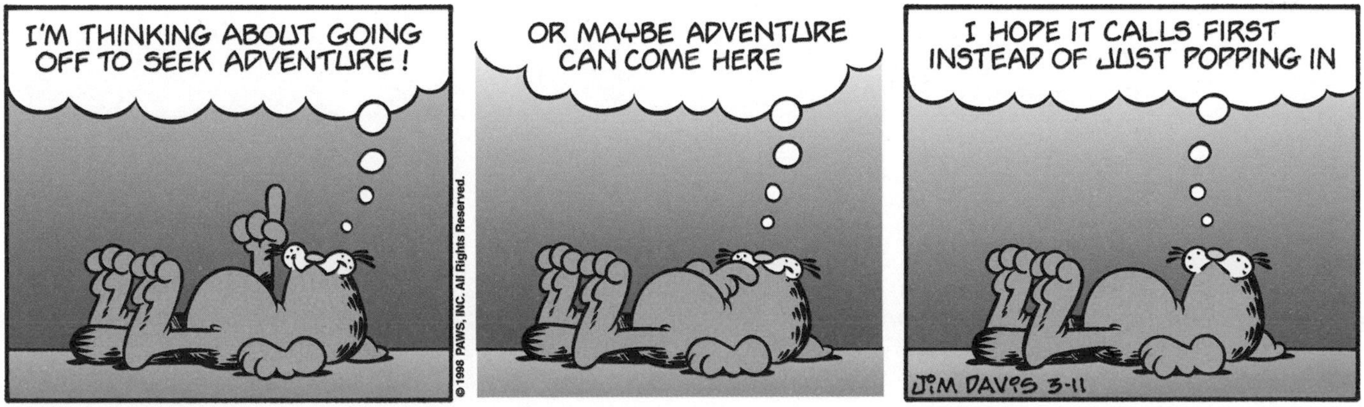
I'M THINKING ABOUT GOING OFF TO SEEK ADVENTURE!
OR MAYBE ADVENTURE CAN COME HERE
I HOPE IT CALLS FIRST INSTEAD OF JUST POPPING IN
JIM DAVIS 3-11
© 1998 PAWS, INC. All Rights Reserved.

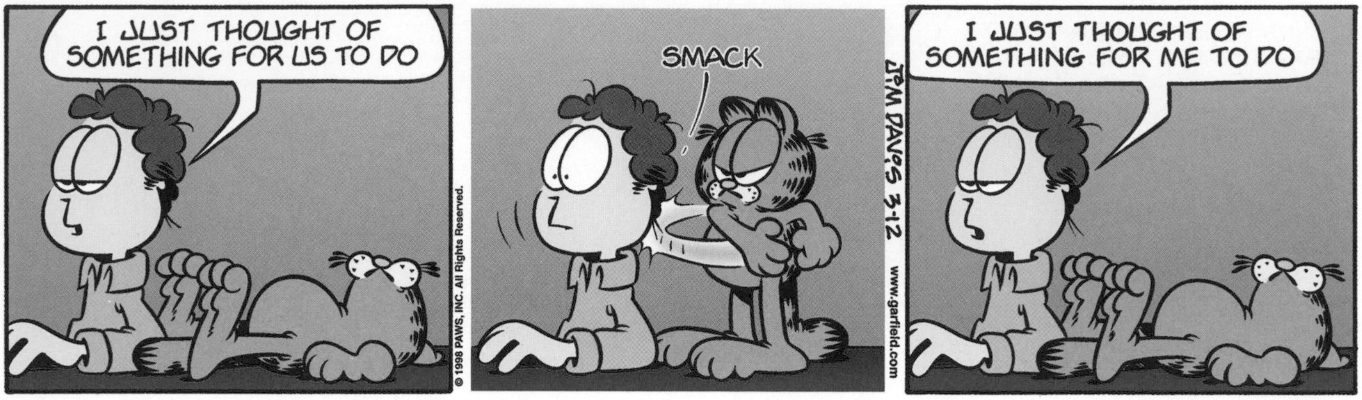
I JUST THOUGHT OF SOMETHING FOR US TO DO
SMACK
I JUST THOUGHT OF SOMETHING FOR ME TO DO
JIM DAVIS 3-12
© 1998 PAWS, INC. All Rights Reserved.
www.garfield.com

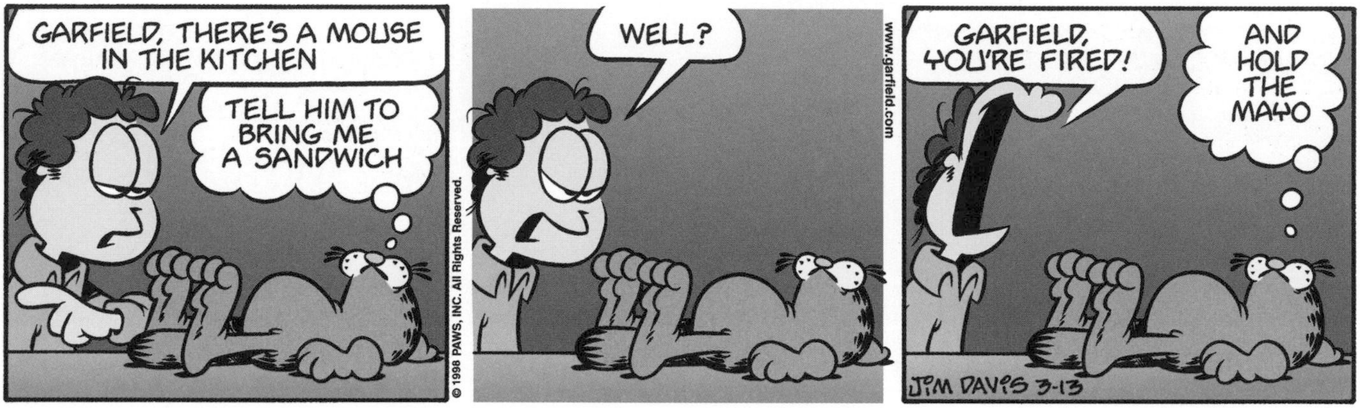
GARFIELD, THERE'S A MOUSE IN THE KITCHEN
TELL HIM TO BRING ME A SANDWICH
WELL?
GARFIELD, YOU'RE FIRED!
AND HOLD THE MAYO
JIM DAVIS 3-13
© 1998 PAWS, INC. All Rights Reserved.
www.garfield.com

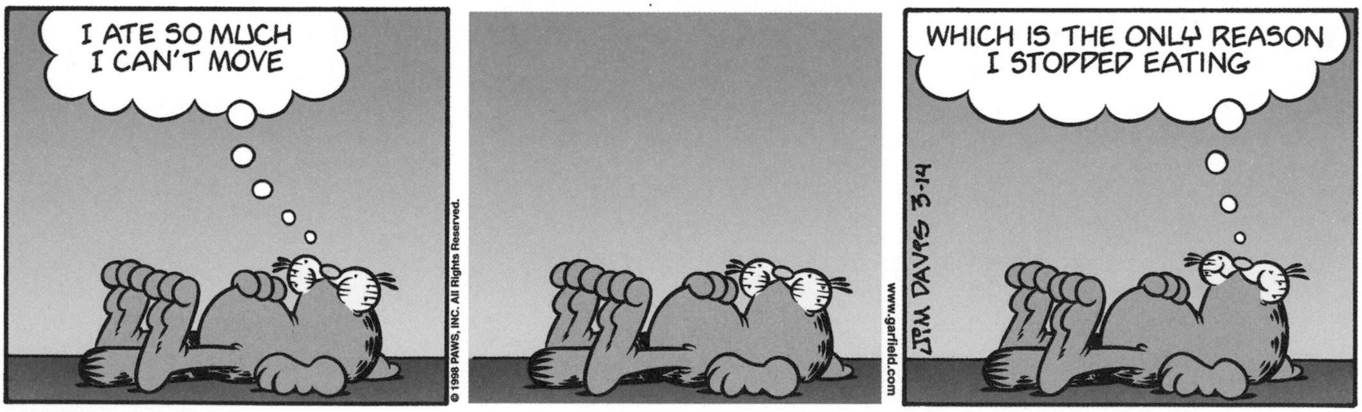
I ATE SO MUCH I CAN'T MOVE
WHICH IS THE ONLY REASON I STOPPED EATING
JIM DAVIS 3-14
© 1998 PAWS, INC. All Rights Reserved.
www.garfield.com

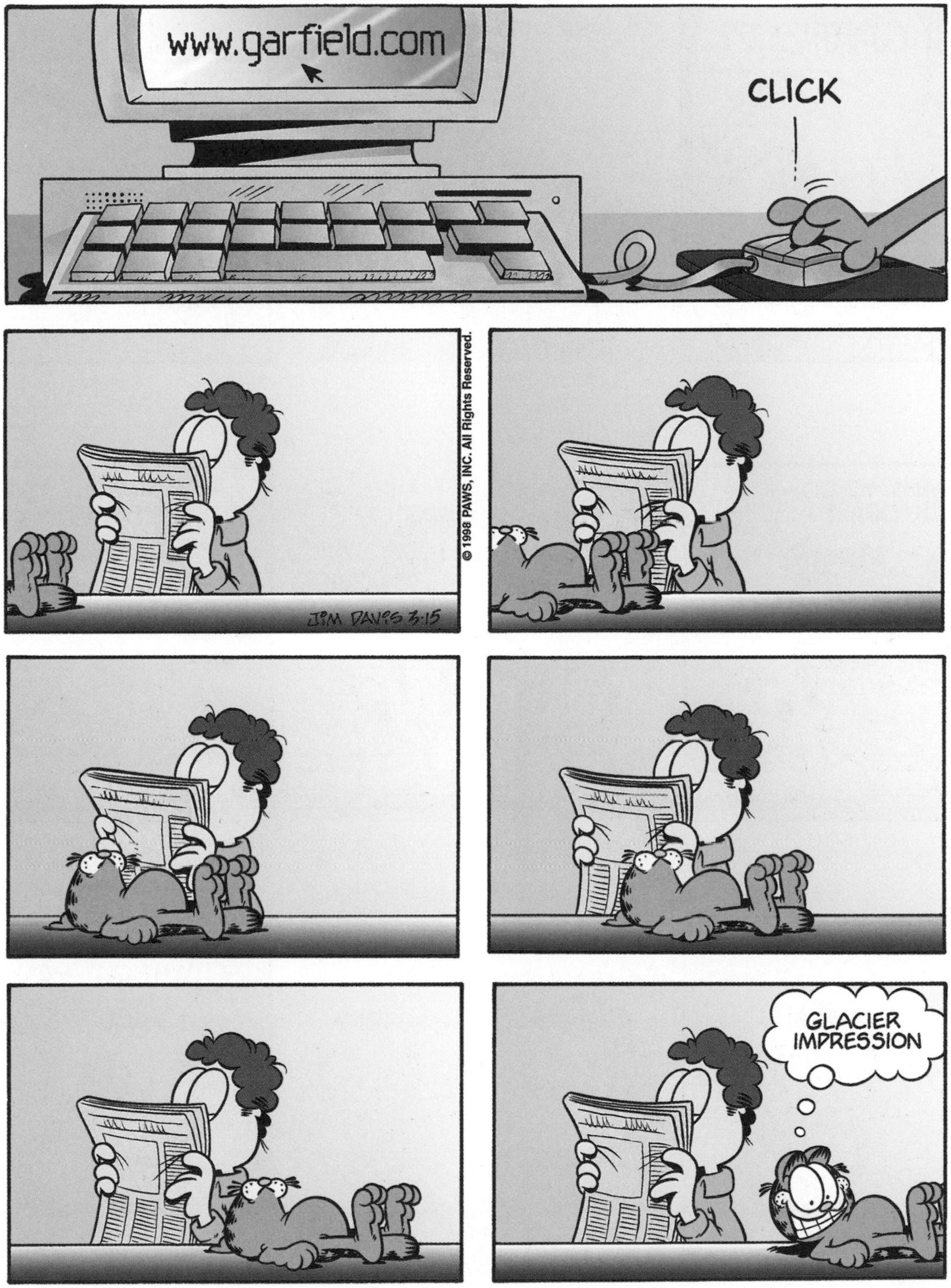
www.garfield.com
CLICK
© 1998 PAWS, INC. All Rights Reserved.
JIM DAVIS 3-15
GLACIER IMPRESSION

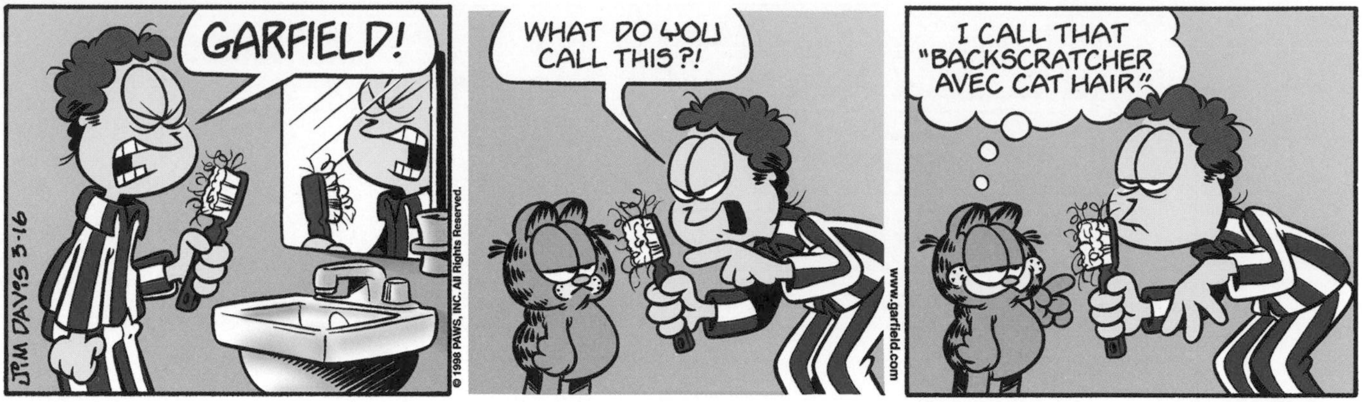
GARFIELD!
JIM DAVIS 3-16
© 1998 PAWS, INC. All Rights Reserved.
WHAT DO YOU CALL THIS?!
www.garfield.com
I CALL THAT "BACKSCRATCHER AVEC CAT HAIR"

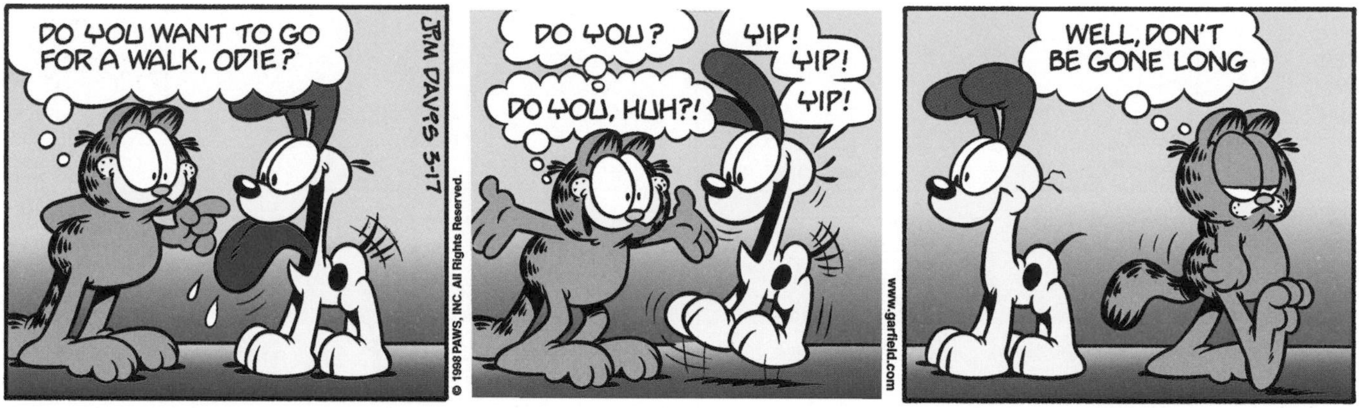
DO YOU WANT TO GO FOR A WALK, ODIE?
JIM DAVIS 3-17
© 1998 PAWS, INC. All Rights Reserved.
DO YOU?
DO YOU, HUH?!
YIP!
YIP!
YIP!
www.garfield.com
WELL, DON'T BE GONE LONG

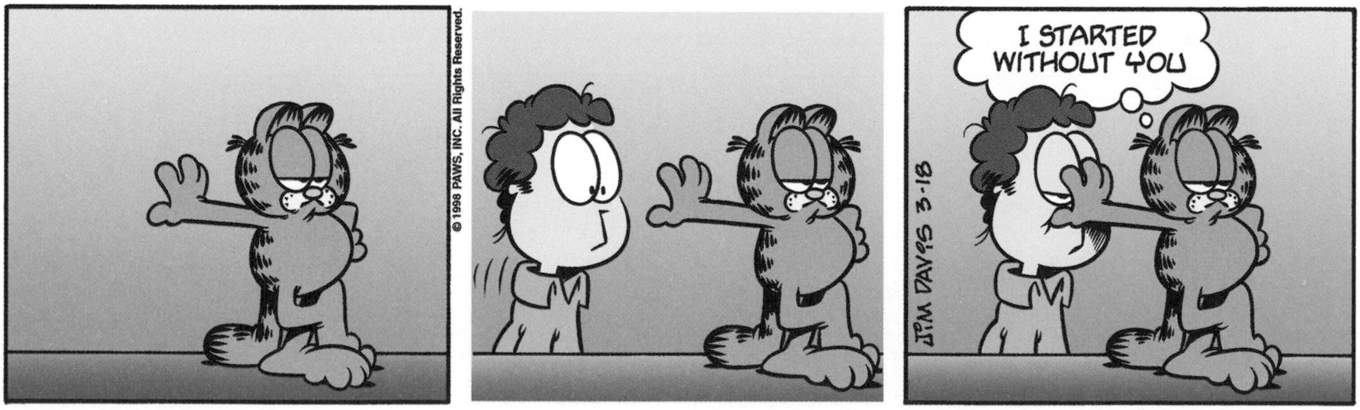
© 1998 PAWS, INC. All Rights Reserved.
JIM DAVIS 3-18
I STARTED WITHOUT YOU

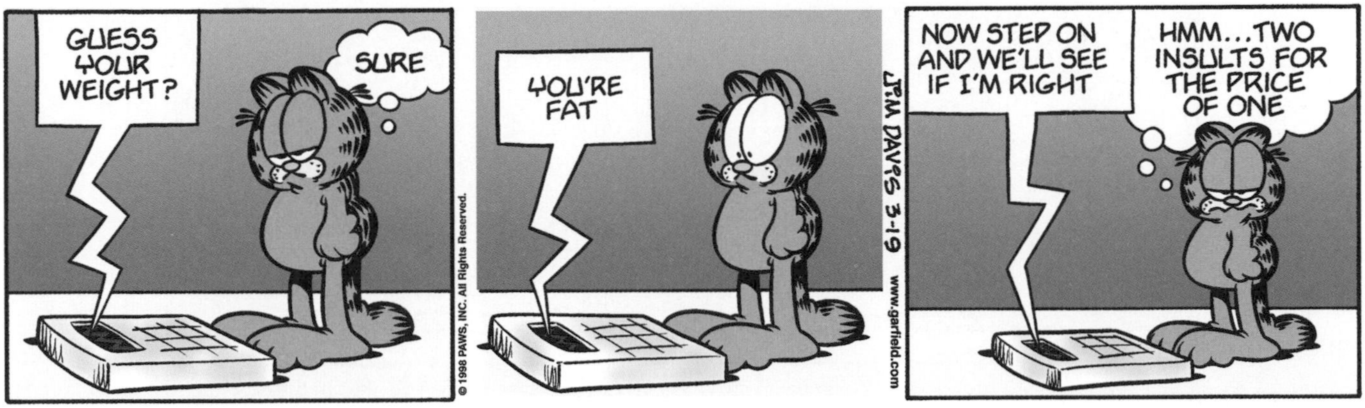
GUESS YOUR WEIGHT?
SURE
YOU'RE FAT
NOW STEP ON AND WE'LL SEE IF I'M RIGHT
HMM...TWO INSULTS FOR THE PRICE OF ONE
JIM DAVIS 3-19
© 1998 PAWS, INC. All Rights Reserved.
www.garfield.com

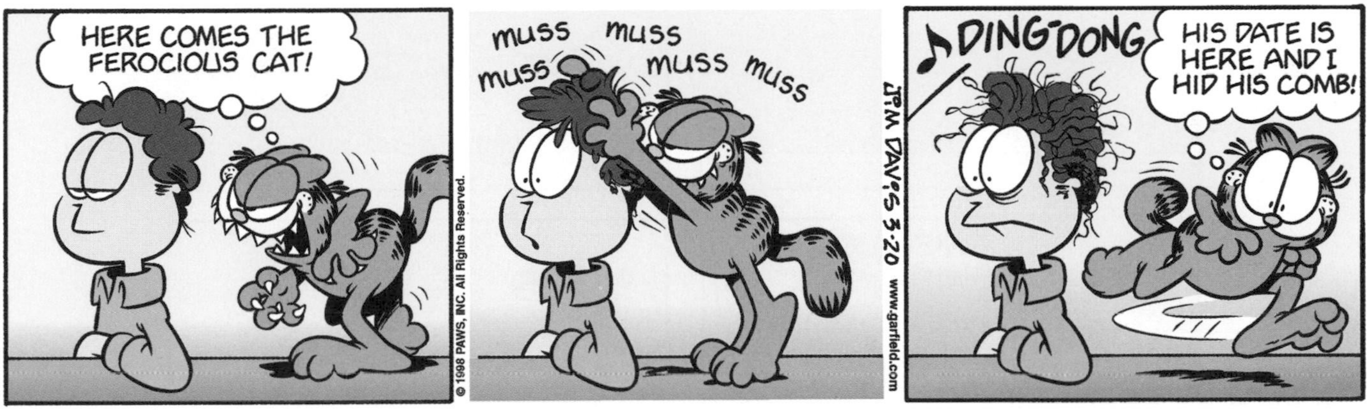
HERE COMES THE FEROCIOUS CAT!
muss muss muss muss muss
DING-DONG
HIS DATE IS HERE AND I HID HIS COMB!
JIM DAVIS 3-20
© 1998 PAWS, INC. All Rights Reserved.
www.garfield.com

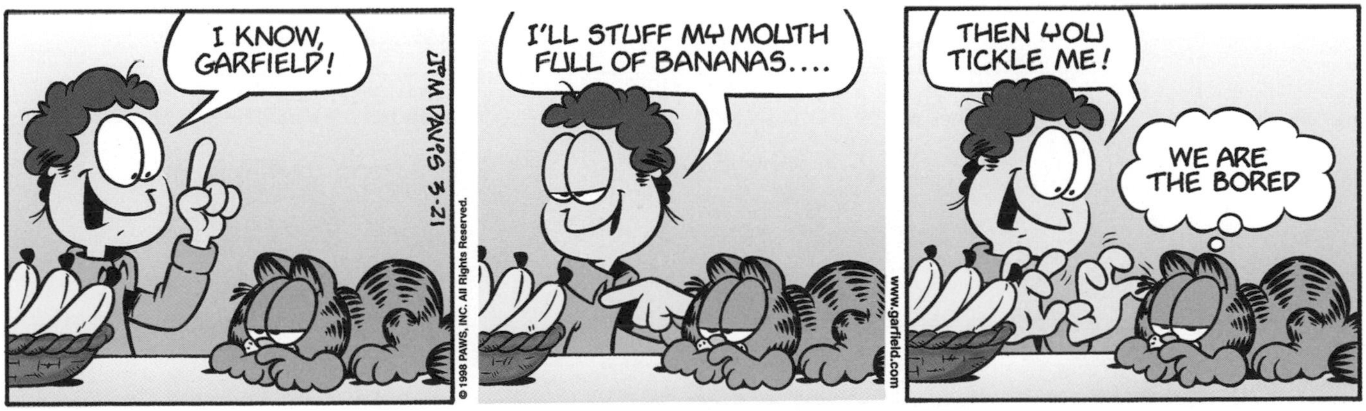
I KNOW, GARFIELD!
I'LL STUFF MY MOUTH FULL OF BANANAS....
THEN YOU TICKLE ME!
WE ARE THE BORED
JIM DAVIS 3-21
© 1998 PAWS, INC. All Rights Reserved.
www.garfield.com

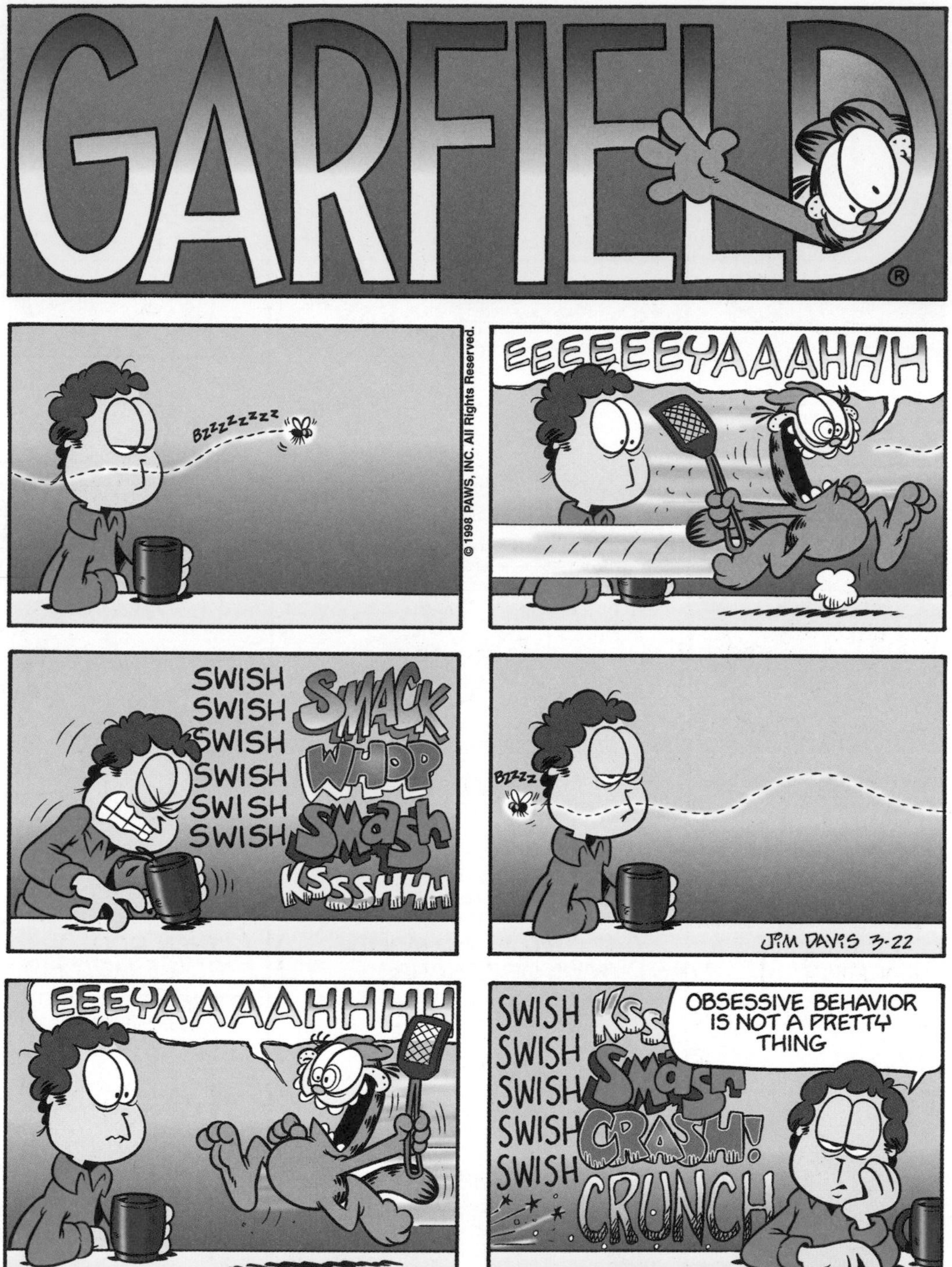
GARFIELD®
© 1998 PAWS, INC. All Rights Reserved.
BZZZZZZZZ
EEEEEEEYAAAHHH
SWISH
SWISH
SWISH
SWISH
SWISH
SWISH
SMACK
WHOP
SMASH
KSSSHHH
BZZZZ
JIM DAVIS 3-22
EEEYAAAAHHHH
SWISH
SWISH
SWISH
SWISH
SWISH
SMASH
CRASH!
CRUNCH
OBSESSIVE BEHAVIOR IS NOT A PRETTY THING

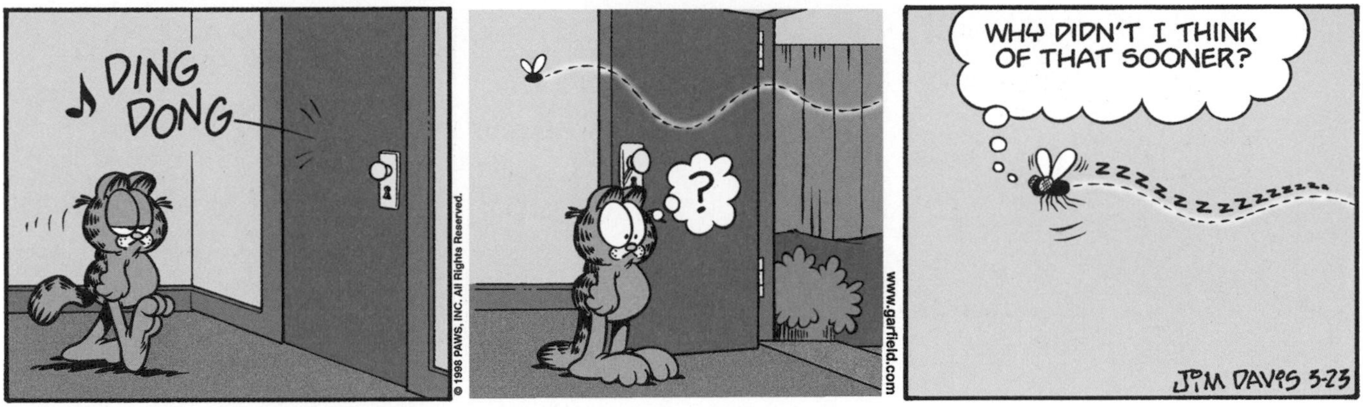
DING
DONG
?
WHY DIDN'T I THINK OF THAT SOONER?
JIM DAVIS 3-23
© 1998 PAWS, INC. All Rights Reserved.
www.garfield.com

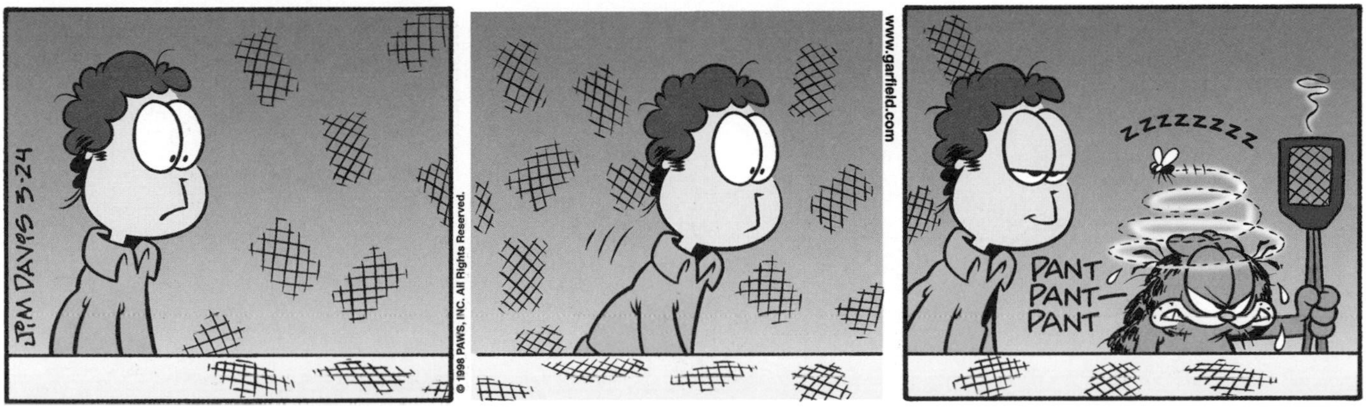
JIM DAVIS 3-24
© 1998 PAWS, INC. All Rights Reserved.
www.garfield.com
ZZZZZZZZ
PANT
PANT—
PANT

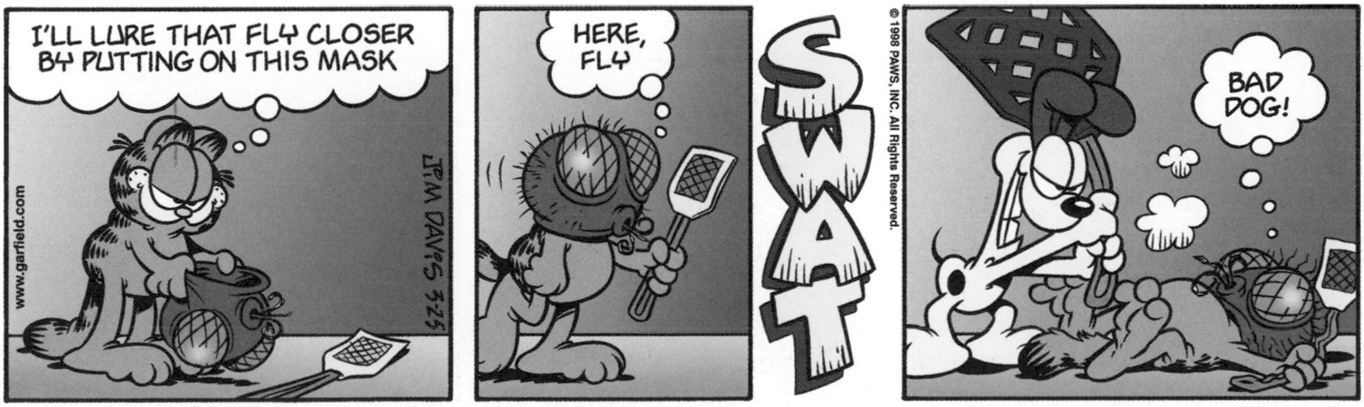
I'LL LURE THAT FLY CLOSER BY PUTTING ON THIS MASK
JIM DAVIS 3-25
www.garfield.com
HERE, FLY
SWAT
© 1998 PAWS, INC. All Rights Reserved.
BAD DOG!

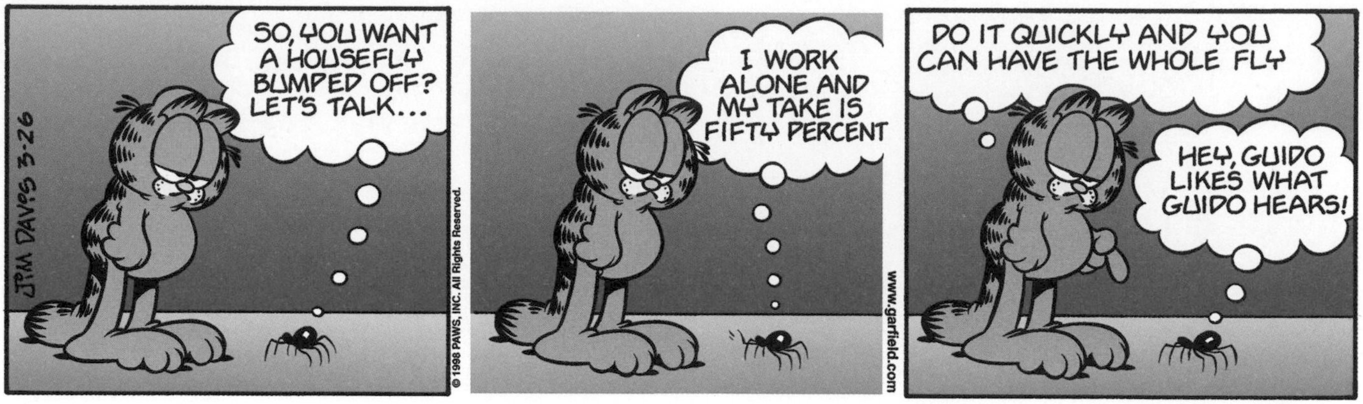
JIM DAVIS 3-26
SO, YOU WANT A HOUSEFLY BUMPED OFF? LET'S TALK...
© 1998 PAWS, INC. All Rights Reserved.
I WORK ALONE AND MY TAKE IS FIFTY PERCENT
www.garfield.com
DO IT QUICKLY AND YOU CAN HAVE THE WHOLE FLY
HEY, GUIDO LIKES WHAT GUIDO HEARS!

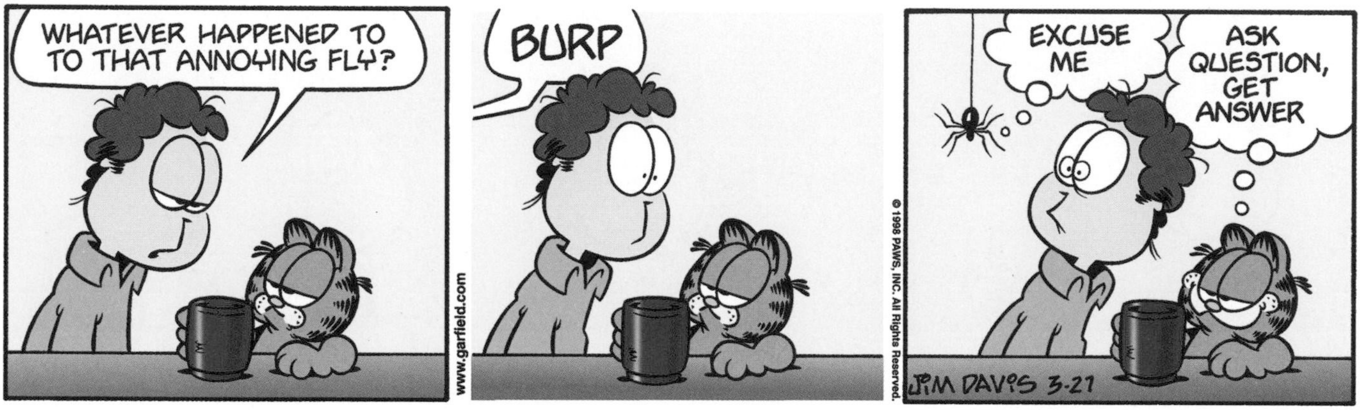
WHATEVER HAPPENED TO TO THAT ANNOYING FLY?
www.garfield.com
BURP
© 1998 PAWS, INC. All Rights Reserved.
EXCUSE ME
ASK QUESTION, GET ANSWER
JIM DAVIS 3-27

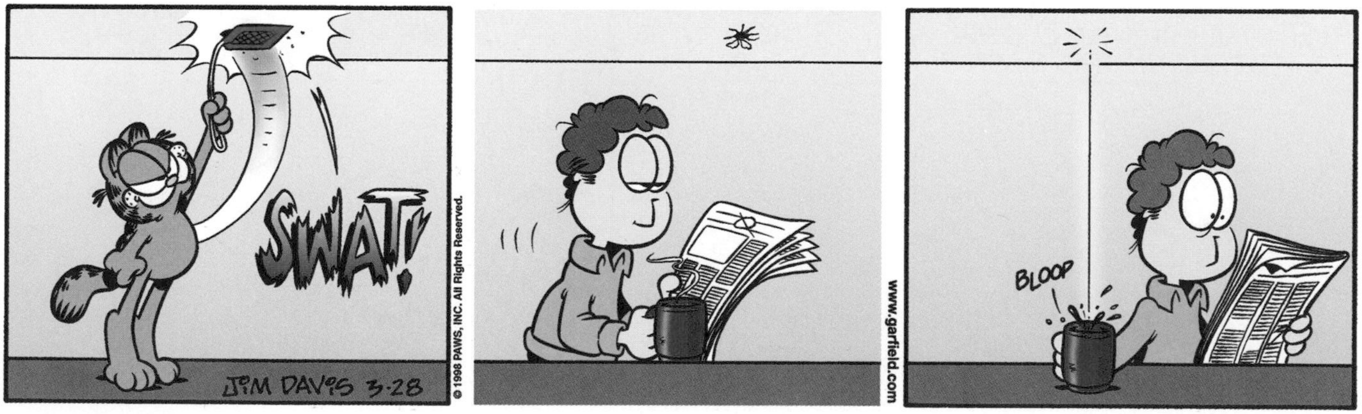
SWAT!
JIM DAVIS 3-28
© 1998 PAWS, INC. All Rights Reserved.
www.garfield.com
BLOOP

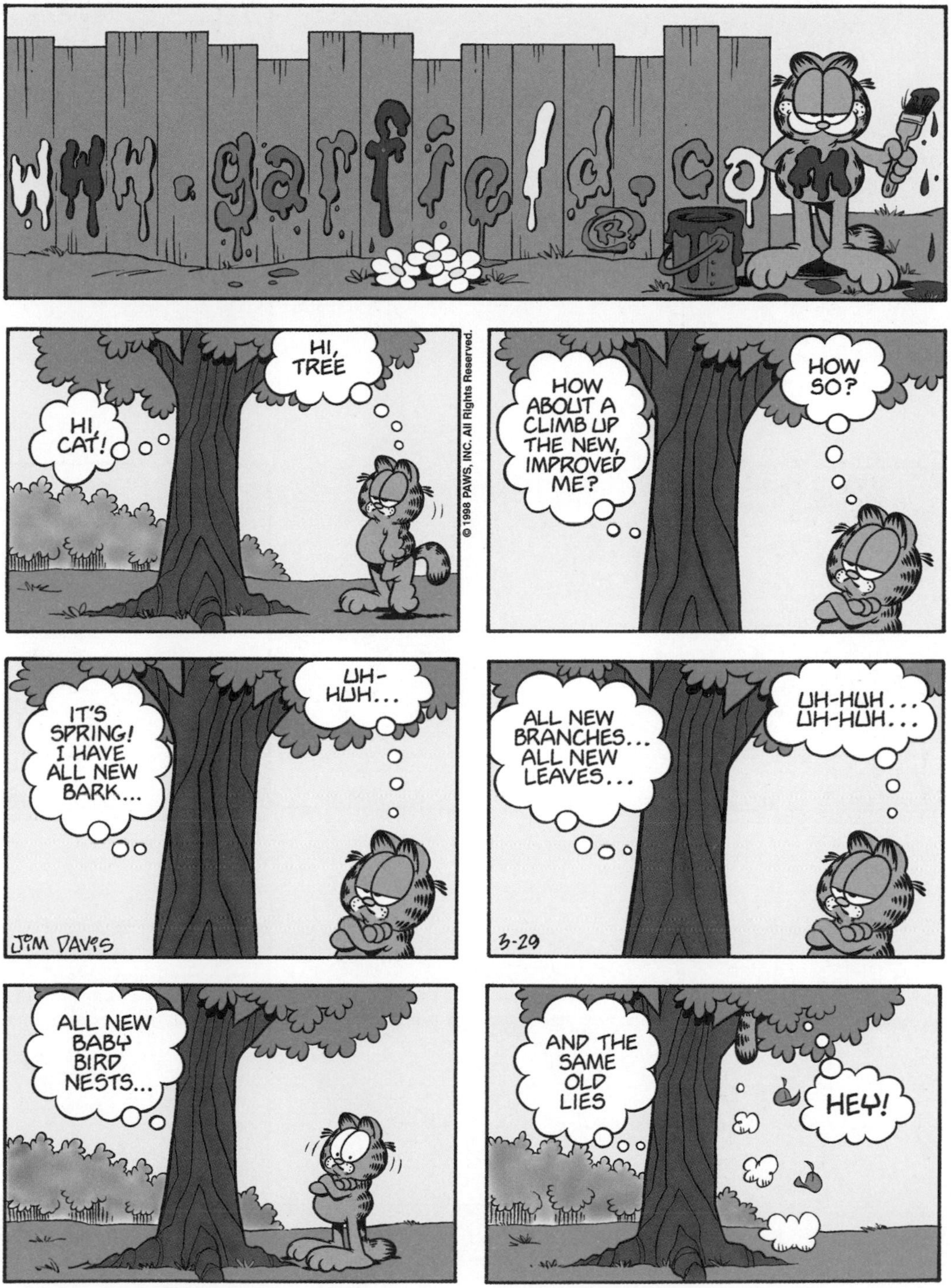
www.garfield.com
®
HI, TREE
HI, CAT!
© 1998 PAWS, INC. All Rights Reserved.
HOW ABOUT A CLIMB UP THE NEW, IMPROVED ME?
HOW SO?
IT'S SPRING! I HAVE ALL NEW BARK...
UH-HUH...
JIM DAVIS
ALL NEW BRANCHES... ALL NEW LEAVES...
UH-HUH... UH-HUH...
3-29
ALL NEW BABY BIRD NESTS...
AND THE SAME OLD LIES
HEY!

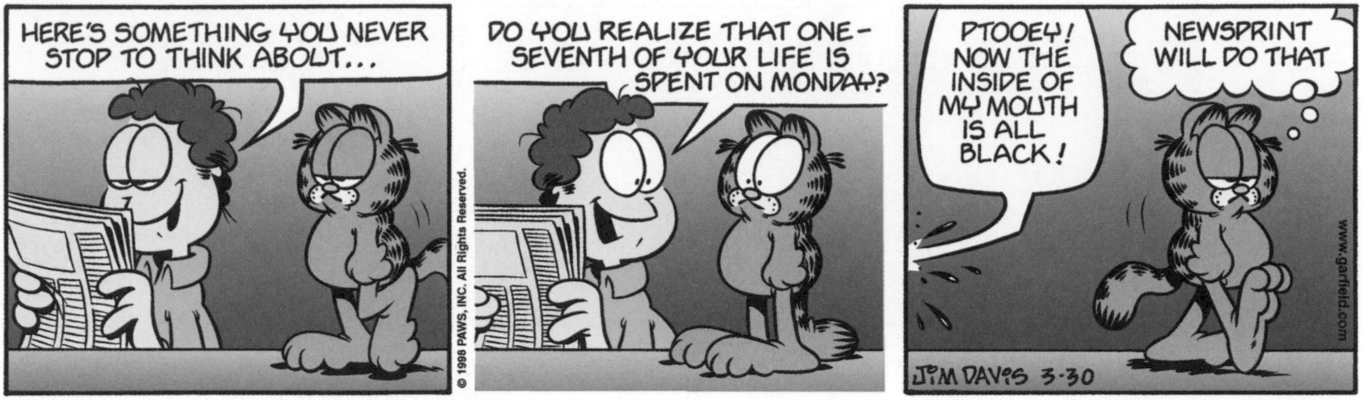
HERE'S SOMETHING YOU NEVER STOP TO THINK ABOUT...
© 1998 PAWS, INC. All Rights Reserved.
DO YOU REALIZE THAT ONE-SEVENTH OF YOUR LIFE IS SPENT ON MONDAY?
PTOOEY! NOW THE INSIDE OF MY MOUTH IS ALL BLACK!
NEWSPRINT WILL DO THAT
www.garfield.com
JIM DAVIS 3-30

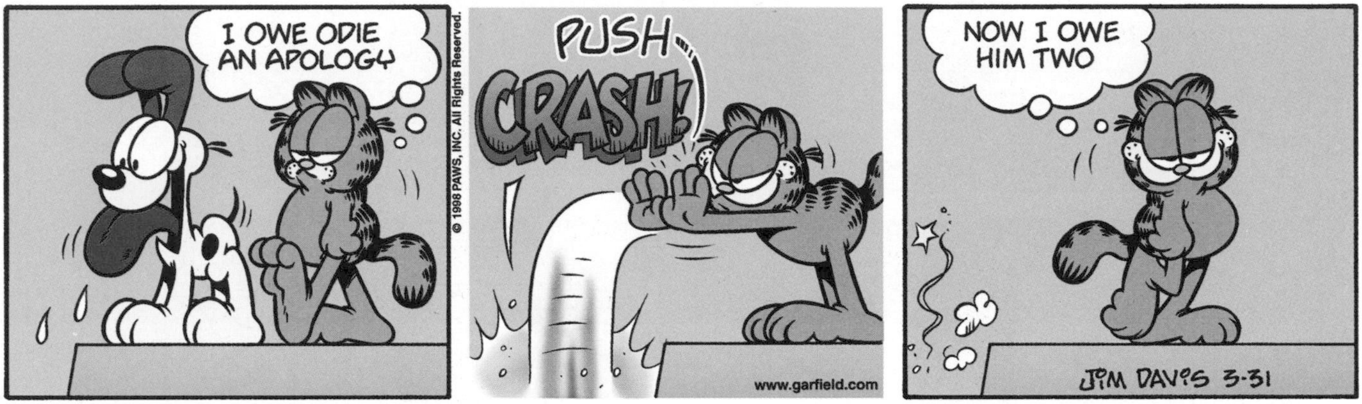
I OWE ODIE AN APOLOGY
© 1998 PAWS, INC. All Rights Reserved.
PUSH
CRASH!
www.garfield.com
NOW I OWE HIM TWO
JIM DAVIS 3-31

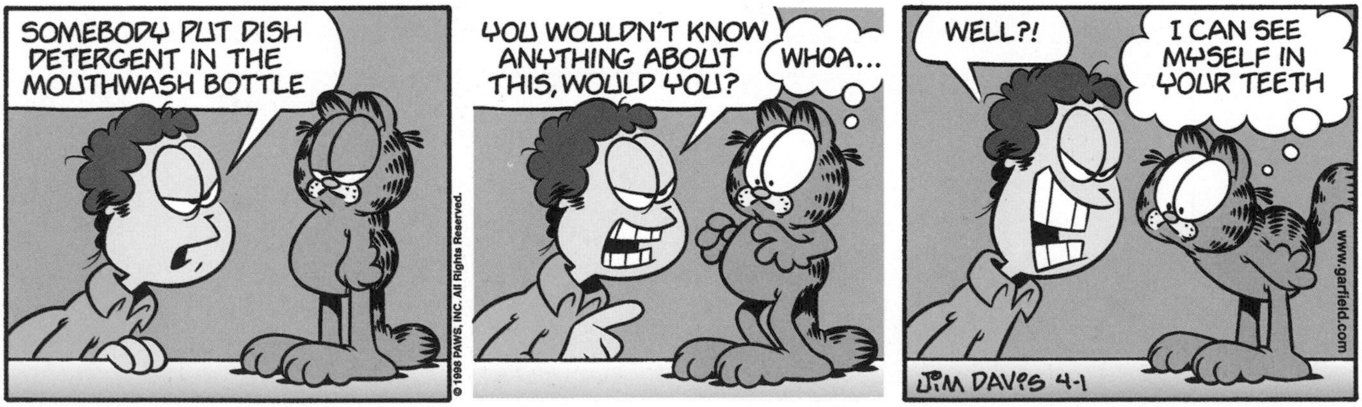
SOMEBODY PUT DISH DETERGENT IN THE MOUTHWASH BOTTLE
© 1998 PAWS, INC. All Rights Reserved.
YOU WOULDN'T KNOW ANYTHING ABOUT THIS, WOULD YOU?
WHOA...
WELL?!
I CAN SEE MYSELF IN YOUR TEETH
www.garfield.com
JIM DAVIS 4-1

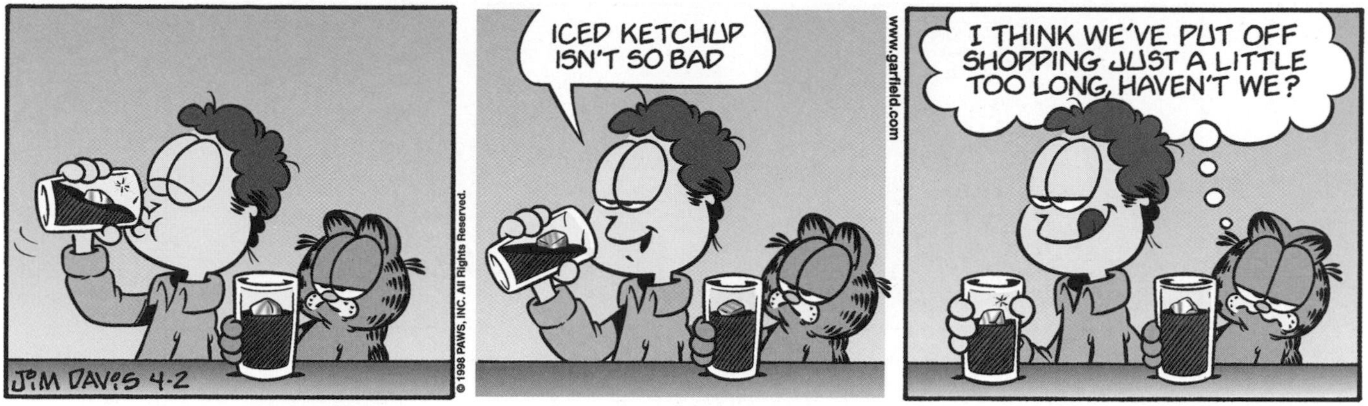
JIM DAVIS 4-2
© 1998 PAWS, INC. All Rights Reserved.
ICED KETCHUP ISN'T SO BAD
www.garfield.com
I THINK WE'VE PUT OFF SHOPPING JUST A LITTLE TOO LONG, HAVEN'T WE?

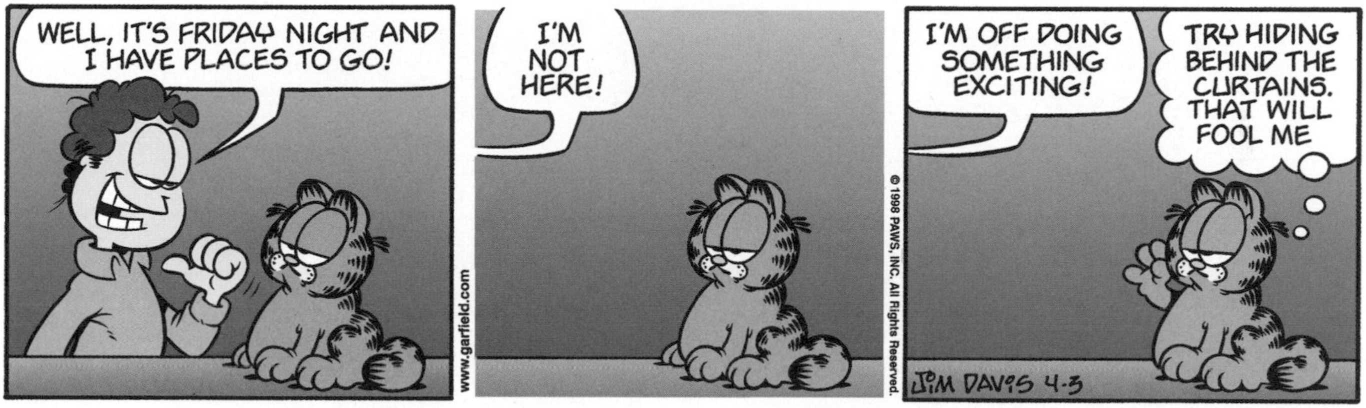
WELL, IT'S FRIDAY NIGHT AND I HAVE PLACES TO GO!
www.garfield.com
I'M NOT HERE!
© 1998 PAWS, INC. All Rights Reserved.
I'M OFF DOING SOMETHING EXCITING!
TRY HIDING BEHIND THE CURTAINS. THAT WILL FOOL ME
JIM DAVIS 4-3

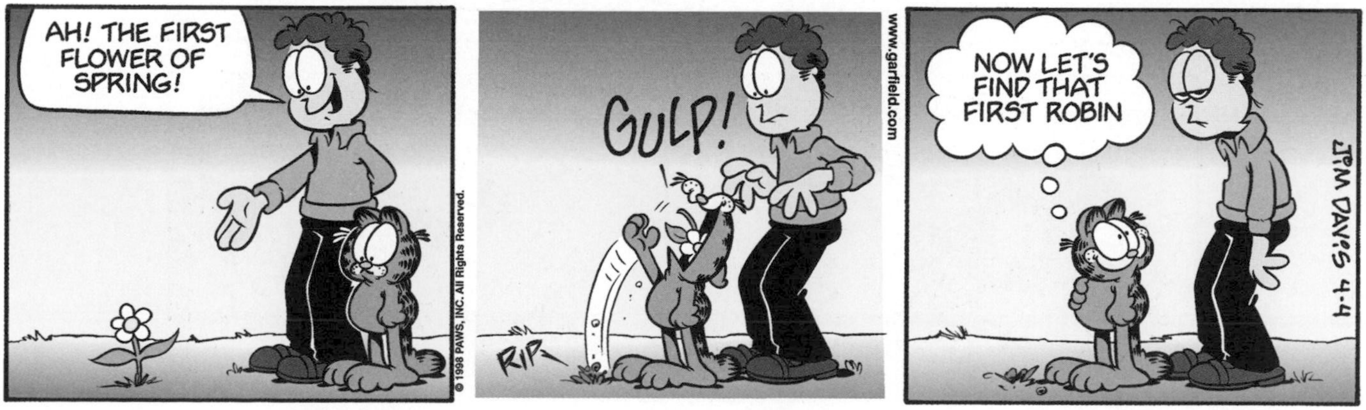
AH! THE FIRST FLOWER OF SPRING!
© 1998 PAWS, INC. All Rights Reserved.
GULP!
RIP
www.garfield.com
NOW LET'S FIND THAT FIRST ROBIN
JIM DAVIS 4-4

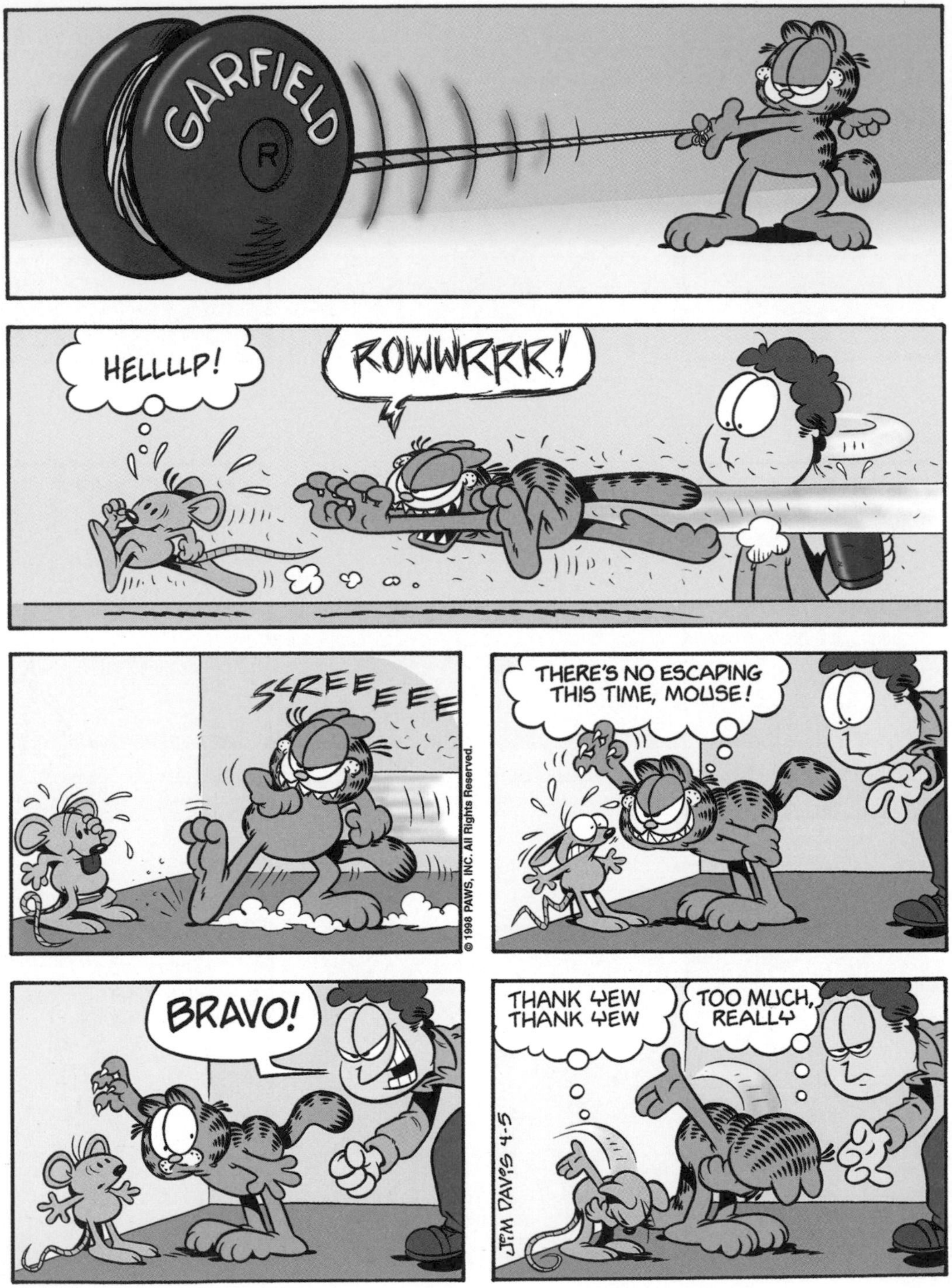
GARFIELD
R
HELLLLP!
ROWWRRR!
SCREEEEEEE
© 1998 PAWS, INC. All Rights Reserved.
THERE'S NO ESCAPING THIS TIME, MOUSE!
BRAVO!
JIM DAVIS 4-5
THANK YEW THANK YEW
TOO MUCH, REALLY

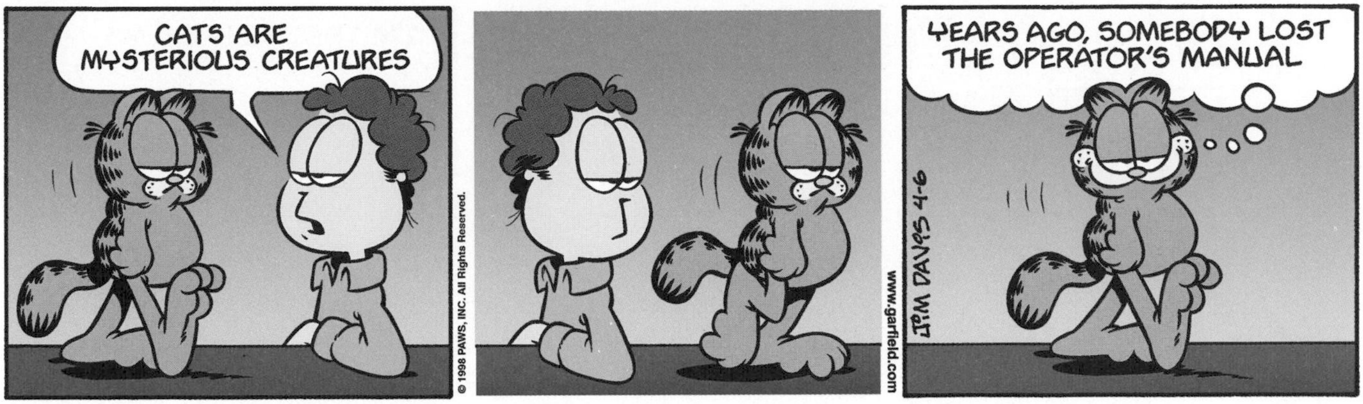
CATS ARE MYSTERIOUS CREATURES
YEARS AGO, SOMEBODY LOST THE OPERATOR'S MANUAL
© 1998 PAWS, INC. All Rights Reserved.
www.garfield.com

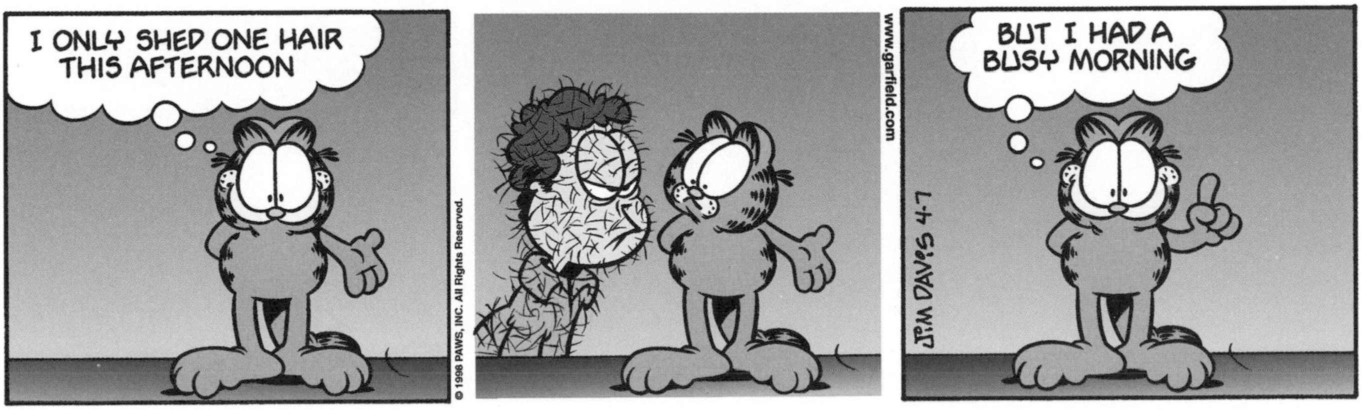
I ONLY SHED ONE HAIR THIS AFTERNOON
BUT I HAD A BUSY MORNING
© 1998 PAWS, INC. All Rights Reserved.
www.garfield.com

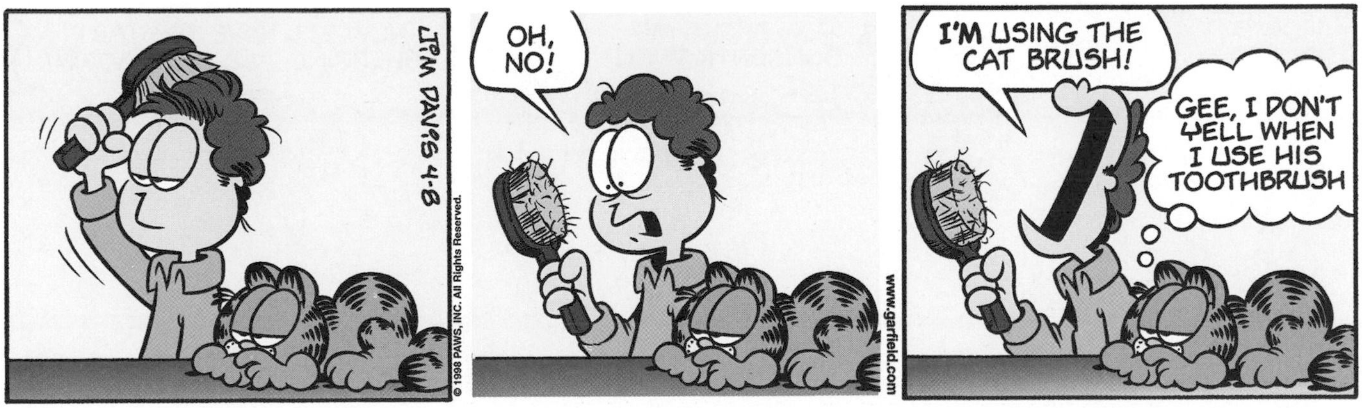
OH, NO!
I'M USING THE CAT BRUSH!
GEE, I DON'T YELL WHEN I USE HIS TOOTHBRUSH
© 1998 PAWS, INC. All Rights Reserved.
www.garfield.com

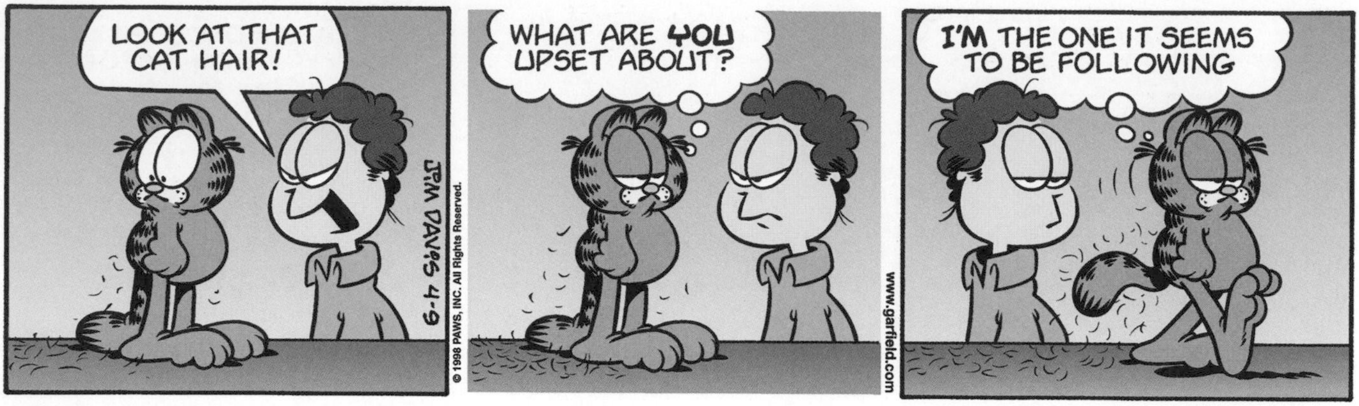
LOOK AT THAT CAT HAIR!
JIM DAVIS 4-9
© 1998 PAWS, INC. All Rights Reserved.
WHAT ARE YOU UPSET ABOUT?
www.garfield.com
I'M THE ONE IT SEEMS TO BE FOLLOWING

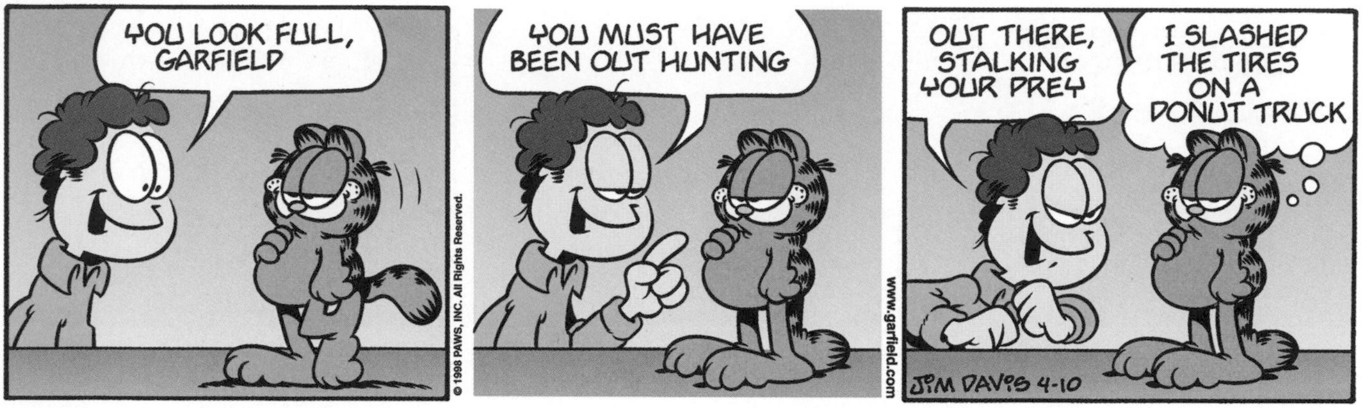
YOU LOOK FULL, GARFIELD
© 1998 PAWS, INC. All Rights Reserved.
YOU MUST HAVE BEEN OUT HUNTING
www.garfield.com
OUT THERE, STALKING YOUR PREY
I SLASHED THE TIRES ON A DONUT TRUCK
JIM DAVIS 4-10

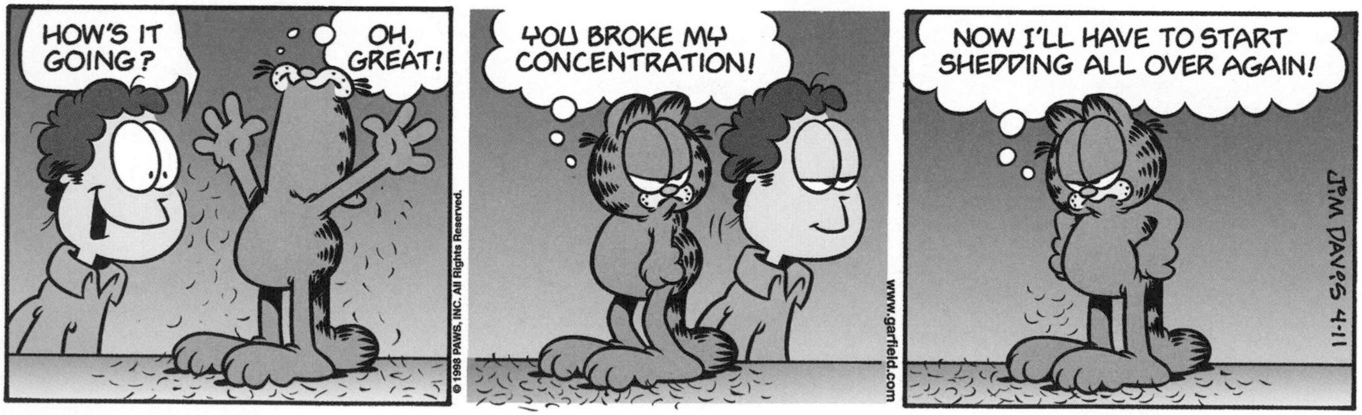
HOW'S IT GOING?
OH, GREAT!
© 1998 PAWS, INC. All Rights Reserved.
YOU BROKE MY CONCENTRATION!
www.garfield.com
NOW I'LL HAVE TO START SHEDDING ALL OVER AGAIN!
JIM DAVIS 4-11

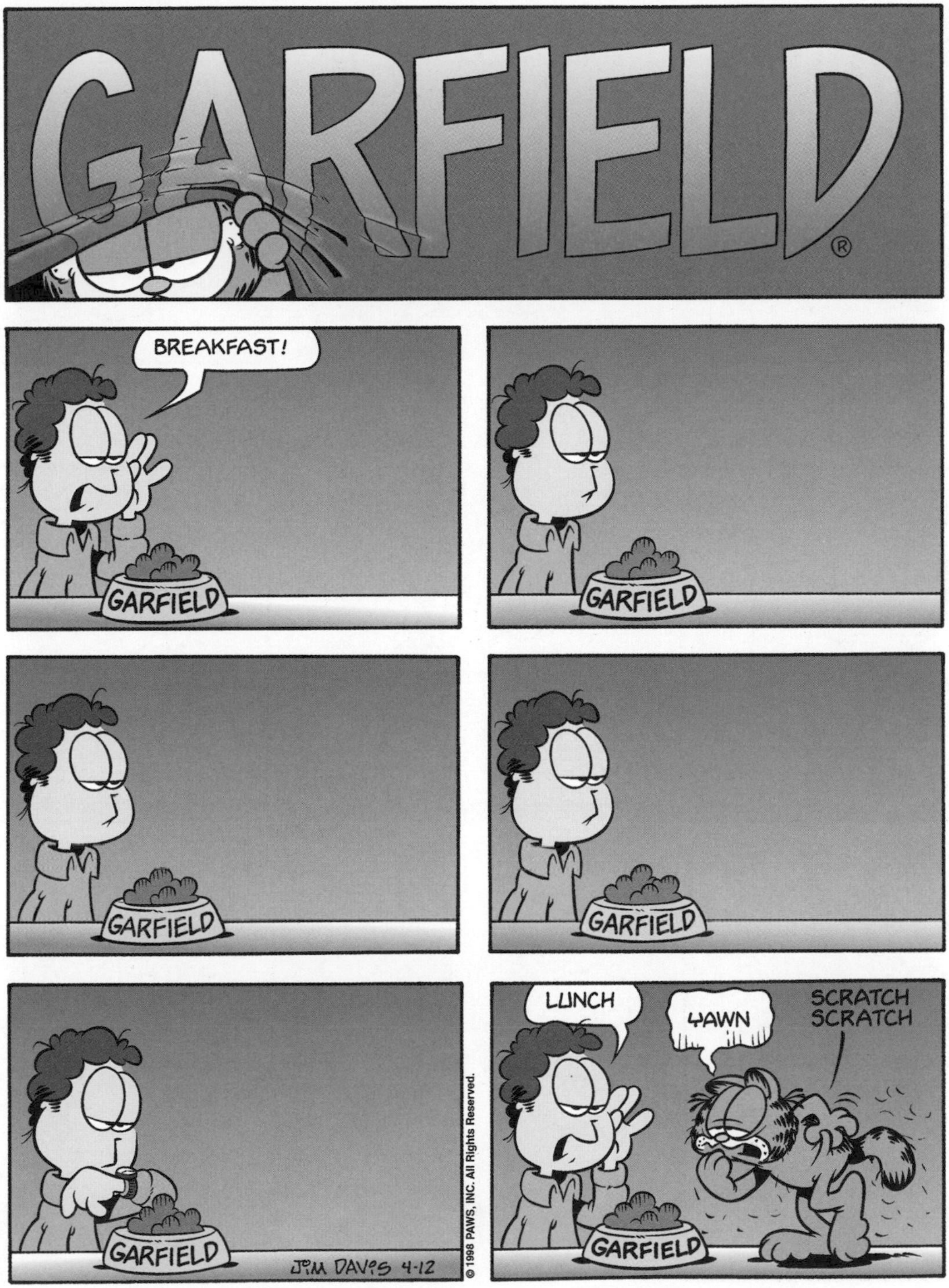
GARFIELD®
BREAKFAST!
GARFIELD
GARFIELD
GARFIELD
GARFIELD
GARFIELD
JIM DAVIS 4-12
LUNCH
YAWN
SCRATCH SCRATCH
GARFIELD

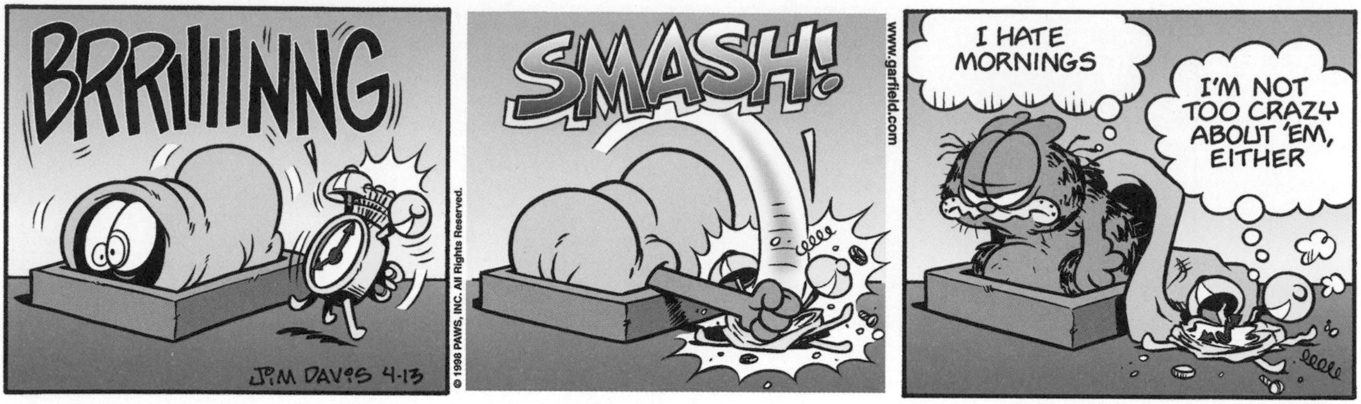
BRRIIIINNG
JIM DAVIS 4-13
© 1998 PAWS, INC. All Rights Reserved.
SMASH!
www.garfield.com
I HATE MORNINGS
I'M NOT TOO CRAZY ABOUT 'EM, EITHER

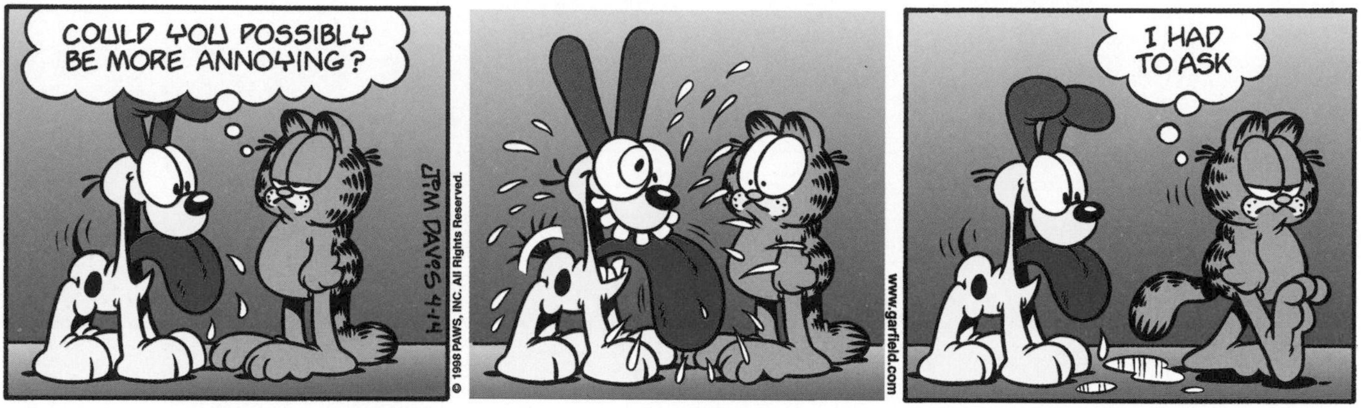
COULD YOU POSSIBLY BE MORE ANNOYING?
JIM DAVIS 4-14
© 1998 PAWS, INC. All Rights Reserved.
www.garfield.com
I HAD TO ASK

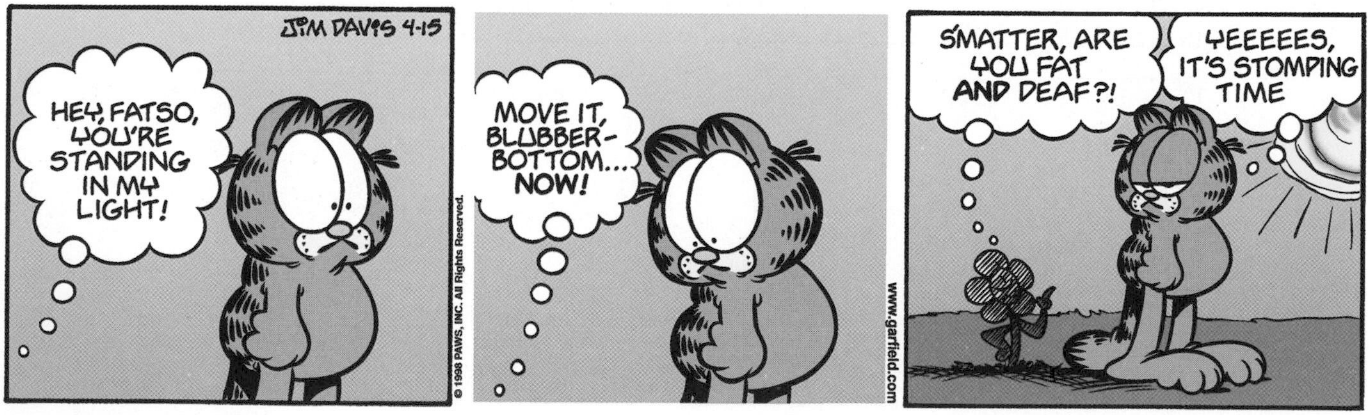
JIM DAVIS 4-15
HEY, FATSO, YOU'RE STANDING IN MY LIGHT!
© 1998 PAWS, INC. All Rights Reserved.
MOVE IT, BLUBBER-BOTTOM... NOW!
www.garfield.com
S'MATTER, ARE YOU FAT AND DEAF?!
YEEEEES, IT'S STOMPING TIME

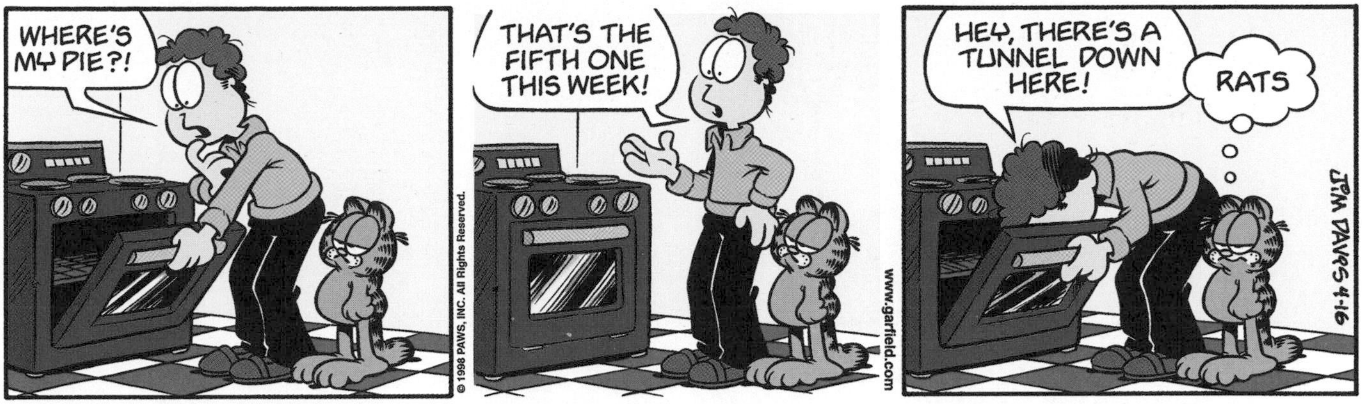
WHERE'S MY PIE?!
THAT'S THE FIFTH ONE THIS WEEK!
HEY, THERE'S A TUNNEL DOWN HERE!
RATS
JIM DAVIS 4-16
© 1998 PAWS, INC. All Rights Reserved.
www.garfield.com

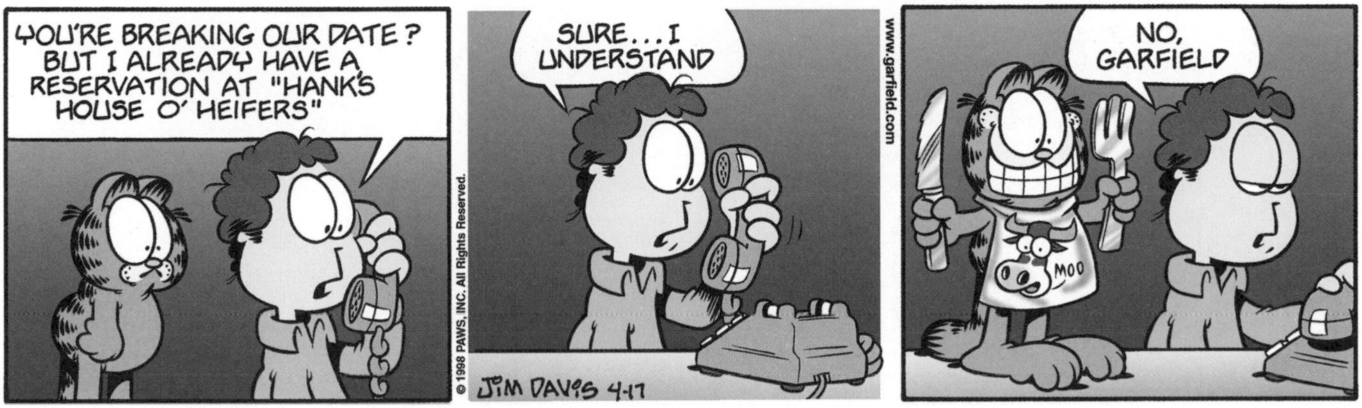
YOU'RE BREAKING OUR DATE? BUT I ALREADY HAVE A RESERVATION AT "HANK'S HOUSE O' HEIFERS"
SURE... I UNDERSTAND
NO, GARFIELD
MOO
JIM DAVIS 4-17
© 1998 PAWS, INC. All Rights Reserved.
www.garfield.com

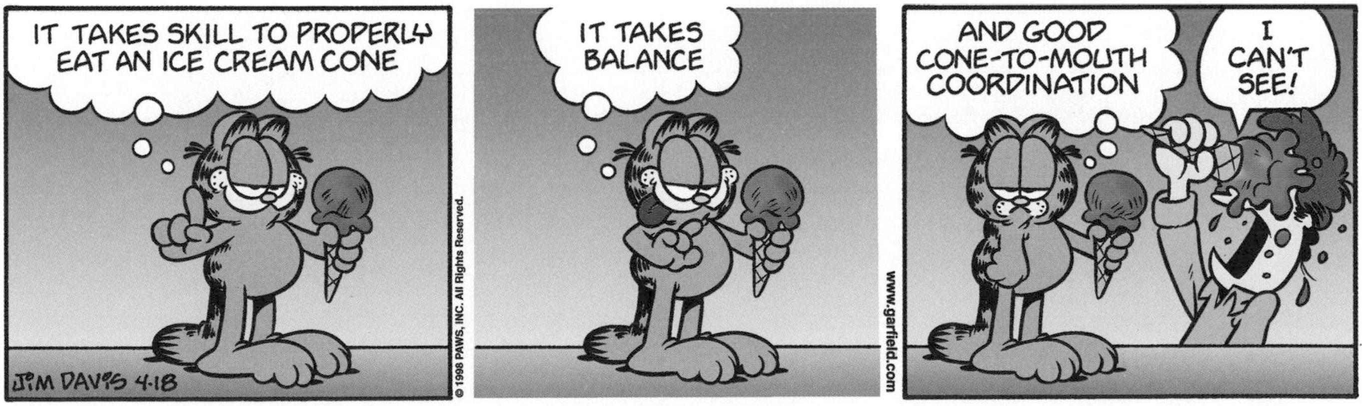
IT TAKES SKILL TO PROPERLY EAT AN ICE CREAM CONE
IT TAKES BALANCE
AND GOOD CONE-TO-MOUTH COORDINATION
I CAN'T SEE!
JIM DAVIS 4-18
© 1998 PAWS, INC. All Rights Reserved.
www.garfield.com

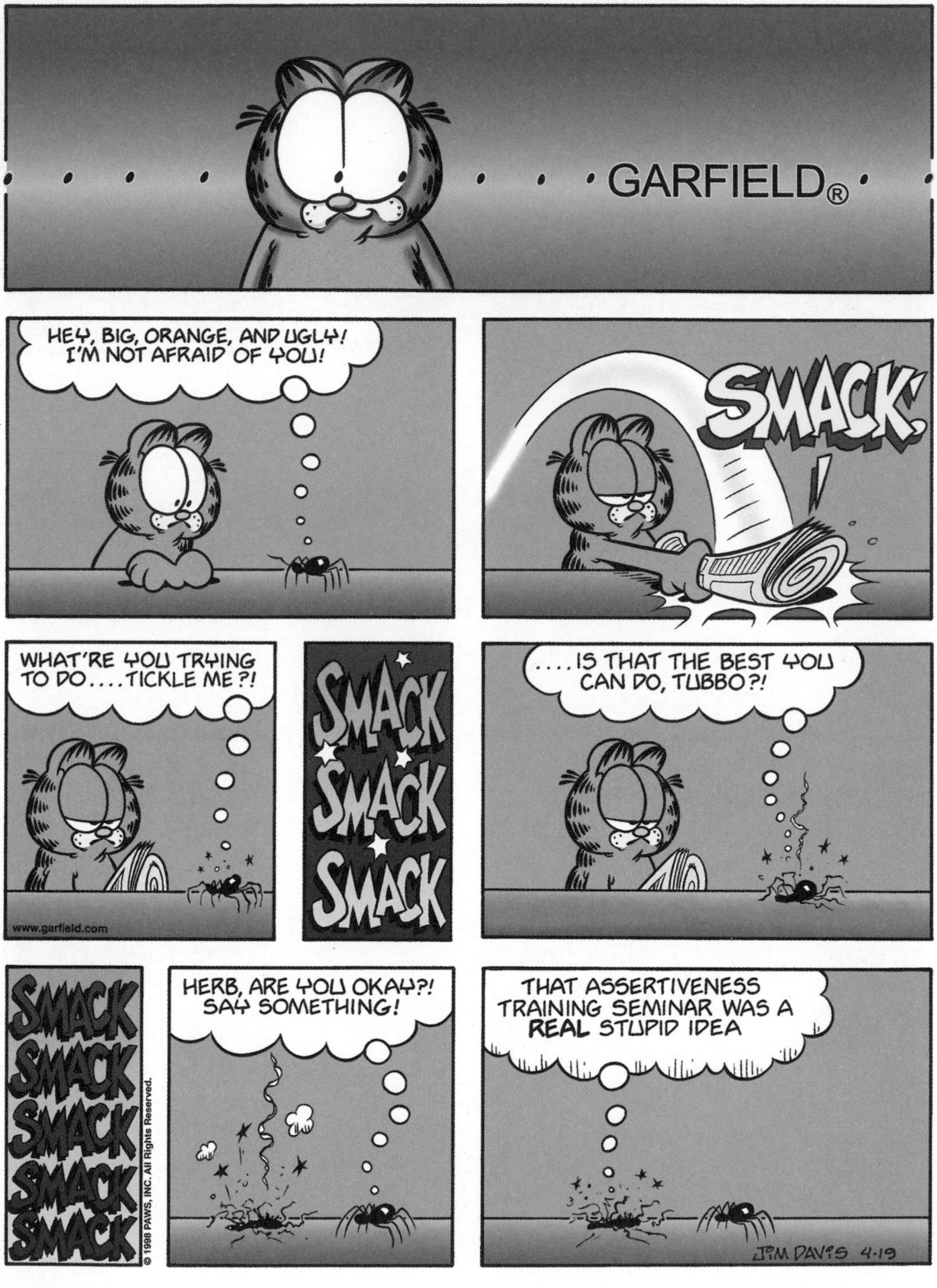
GARFIELD®
HEY, BIG, ORANGE, AND UGLY! I'M NOT AFRAID OF YOU!
SMACK!
WHAT'RE YOU TRYING TO DO.... TICKLE ME?!
www.garfield.com
SMACK
SMACK
SMACK
....IS THAT THE BEST YOU CAN DO, TUBBO?!
SMACK
SMACK
SMACK
SMACK
SMACK
© 1998 PAWS, INC. All Rights Reserved.
HERB, ARE YOU OKAY?! SAY SOMETHING!
THAT ASSERTIVENESS TRAINING SEMINAR WAS A **REAL** STUPID IDEA
JIM DAVIS 4-19

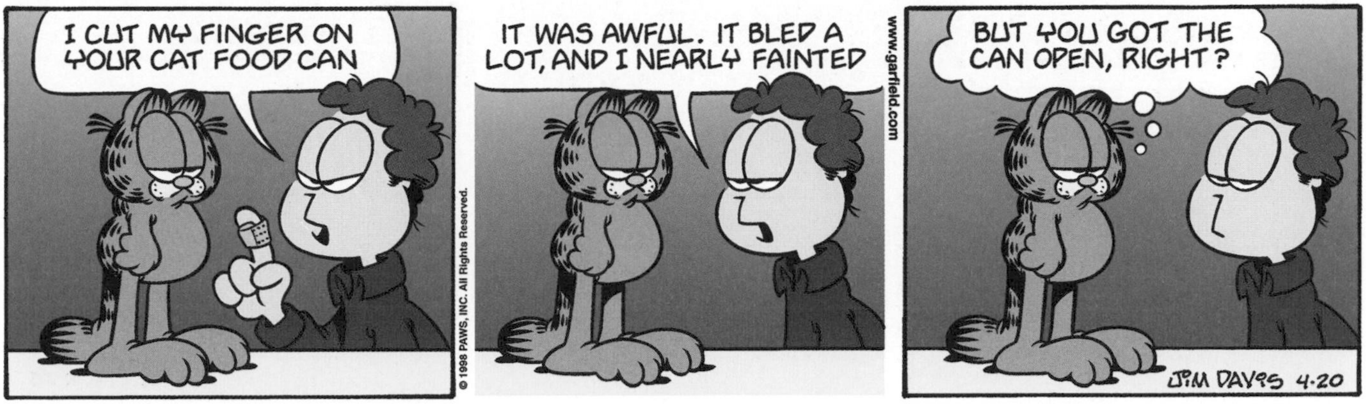
I CUT MY FINGER ON YOUR CAT FOOD CAN
© 1998 PAWS, INC. All Rights Reserved.
IT WAS AWFUL. IT BLED A LOT, AND I NEARLY FAINTED
www.garfield.com
BUT YOU GOT THE CAN OPEN, RIGHT?
JIM DAVIS 4·20

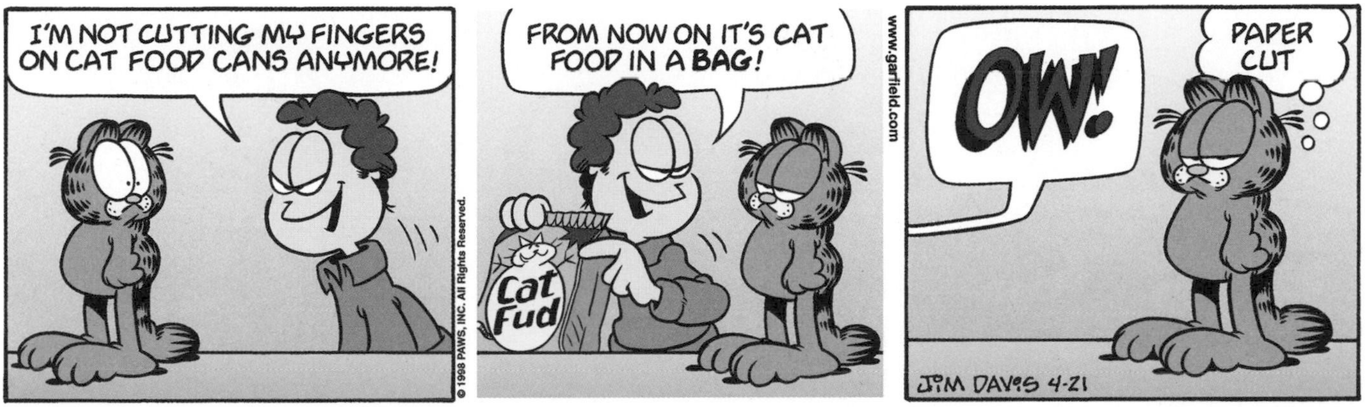
I'M NOT CUTTING MY FINGERS ON CAT FOOD CANS ANYMORE!
© 1998 PAWS, INC. All Rights Reserved.
FROM NOW ON IT'S CAT FOOD IN A **BAG**!
Cat Fud
www.garfield.com
OW!
PAPER CUT
JIM DAVIS 4·21

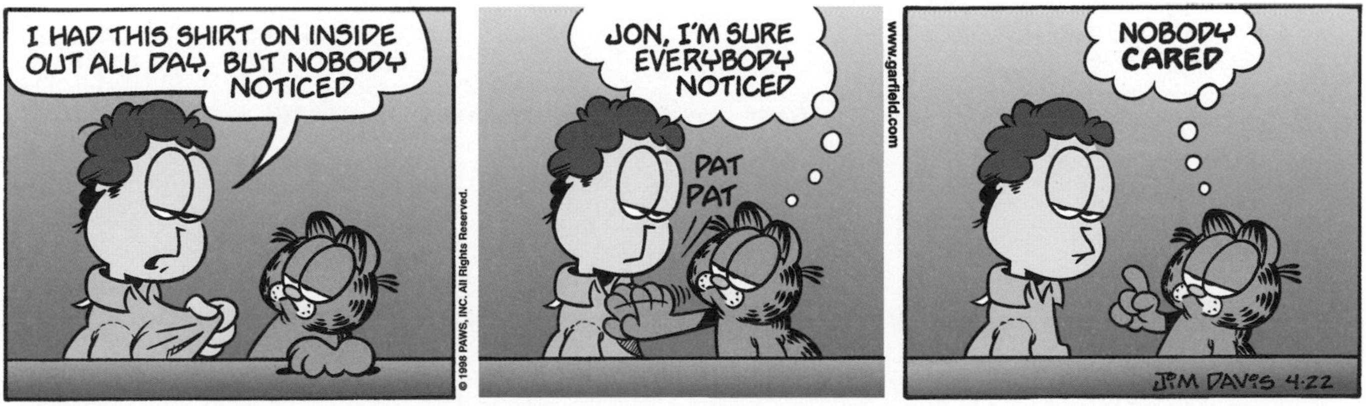
I HAD THIS SHIRT ON INSIDE OUT ALL DAY, BUT NOBODY NOTICED
© 1998 PAWS, INC. All Rights Reserved.
JON, I'M SURE EVERYBODY NOTICED
PAT PAT
www.garfield.com
NOBODY **CARED**
JIM DAVIS 4·22

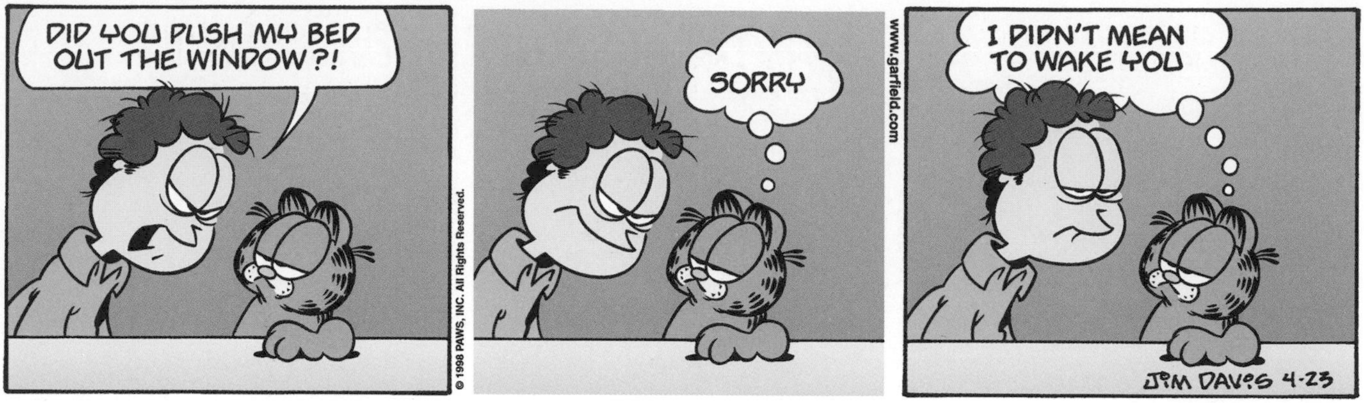
DID YOU PUSH MY BED OUT THE WINDOW?!
© 1998 PAWS, INC. All Rights Reserved.
SORRY
www.garfield.com
I DIDN'T MEAN TO WAKE YOU
JIM DAVIS 4-23

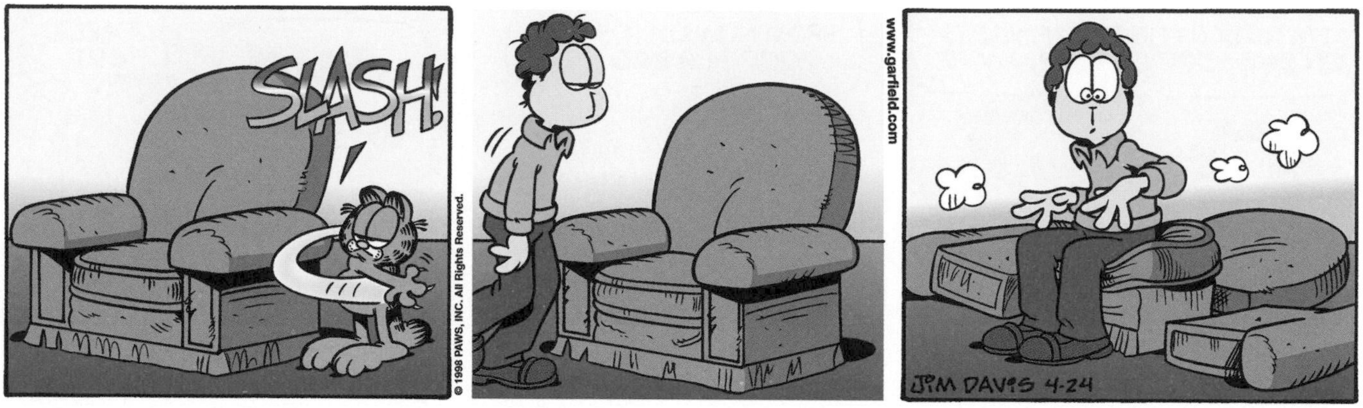
SLASH!
© 1998 PAWS, INC. All Rights Reserved.
www.garfield.com
JIM DAVIS 4-24

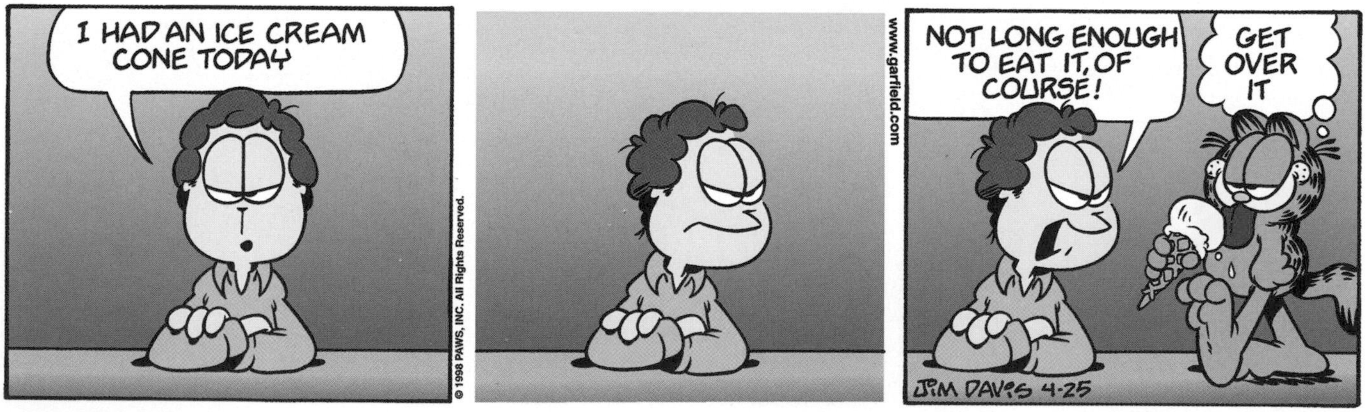
I HAD AN ICE CREAM CONE TODAY
© 1998 PAWS, INC. All Rights Reserved.
www.garfield.com
NOT LONG ENOUGH TO EAT IT, OF COURSE!
GET OVER IT
JIM DAVIS 4-25

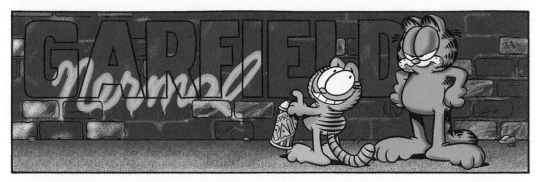

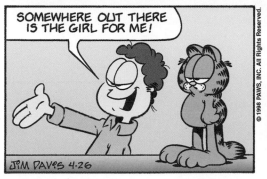

GARFIELD
Normal
SOMEWHERE OUT THERE IS THE GIRL FOR ME!
© 1998 PAWS, INC. All Rights Reserved.
JIM DAVIS 4·26
I GET THE POINT!

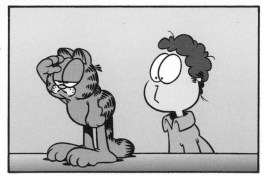

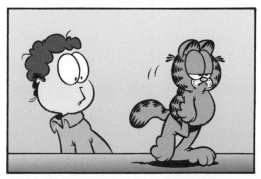

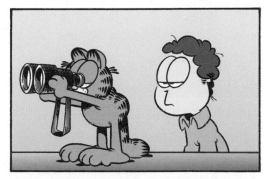

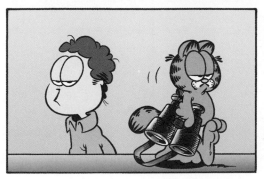

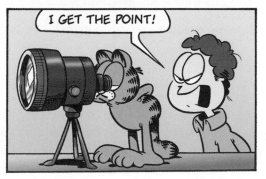

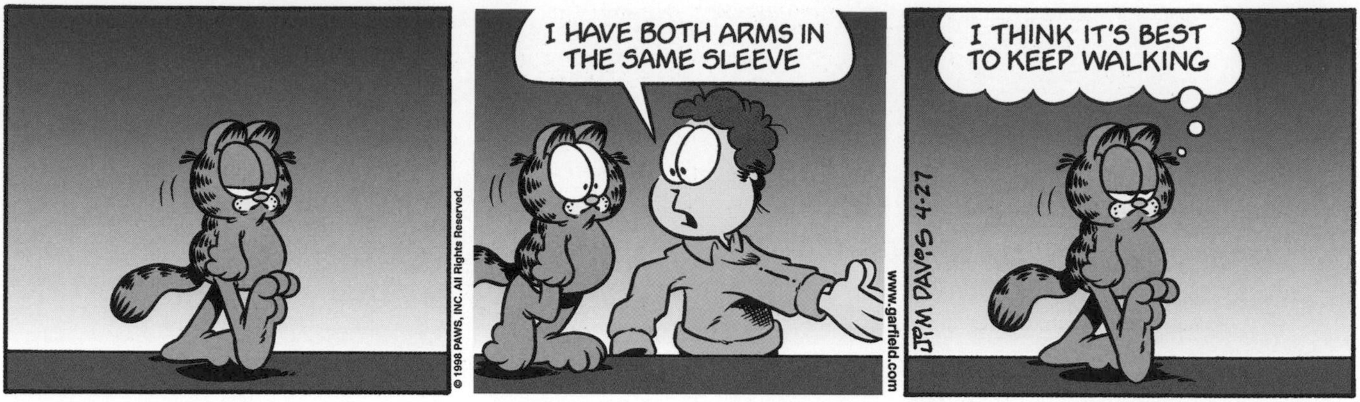
© 1998 PAWS, INC. All Rights Reserved.
I HAVE BOTH ARMS IN THE SAME SLEEVE
www.garfield.com
JIM DAVIS 4-27
I THINK IT'S BEST TO KEEP WALKING

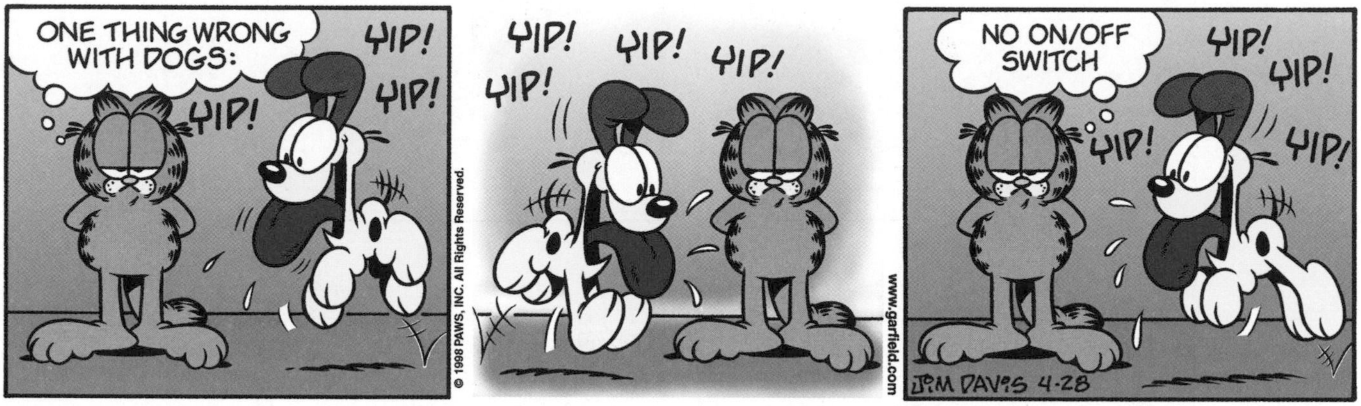
ONE THING WRONG WITH DOGS:
YIP!
YIP!
YIP!
© 1998 PAWS, INC. All Rights Reserved.
YIP!
YIP!
YIP!
YIP!
www.garfield.com
NO ON/OFF SWITCH
YIP!
YIP!
YIP!
YIP!
JIM DAVIS 4-28

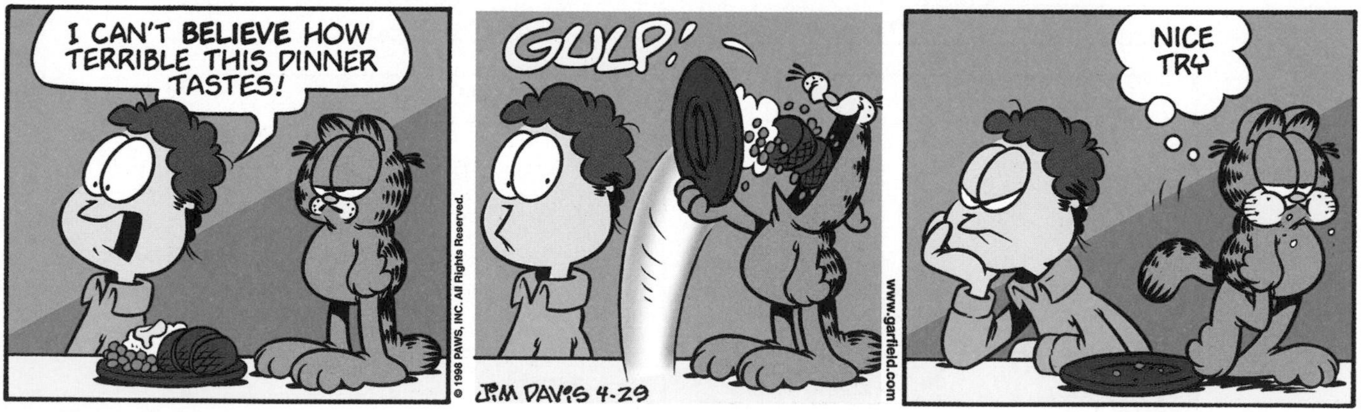
I CAN'T **BELIEVE** HOW TERRIBLE THIS DINNER TASTES!
© 1998 PAWS, INC. All Rights Reserved.
GULP!
JIM DAVIS 4-29
www.garfield.com
NICE TRY

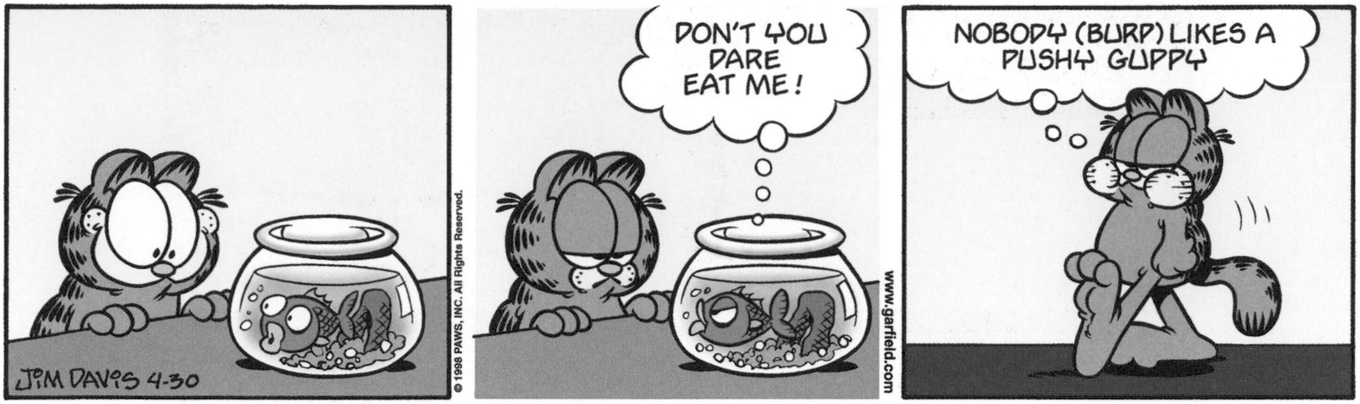
JIM DAVIS 4-30
© 1998 PAWS, INC. All Rights Reserved.
DON'T YOU DARE EAT ME!
www.garfield.com
NOBODY (BURP) LIKES A PUSHY GUPPY

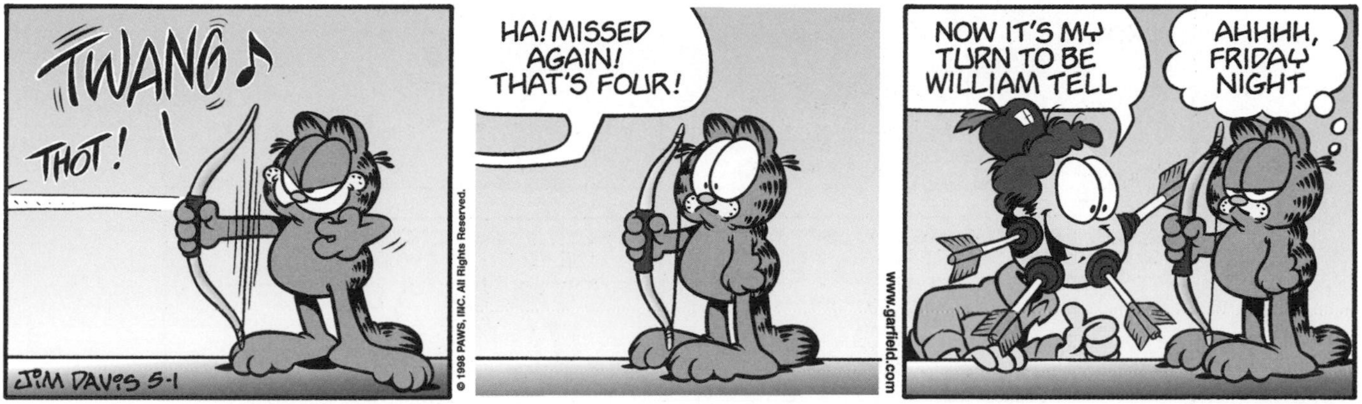
TWANG ♪
THOT!
JIM DAVIS 5-1
© 1998 PAWS, INC. All Rights Reserved.
HA! MISSED AGAIN! THAT'S FOUR!
www.garfield.com
NOW IT'S MY TURN TO BE WILLIAM TELL
AHHHH, FRIDAY NIGHT

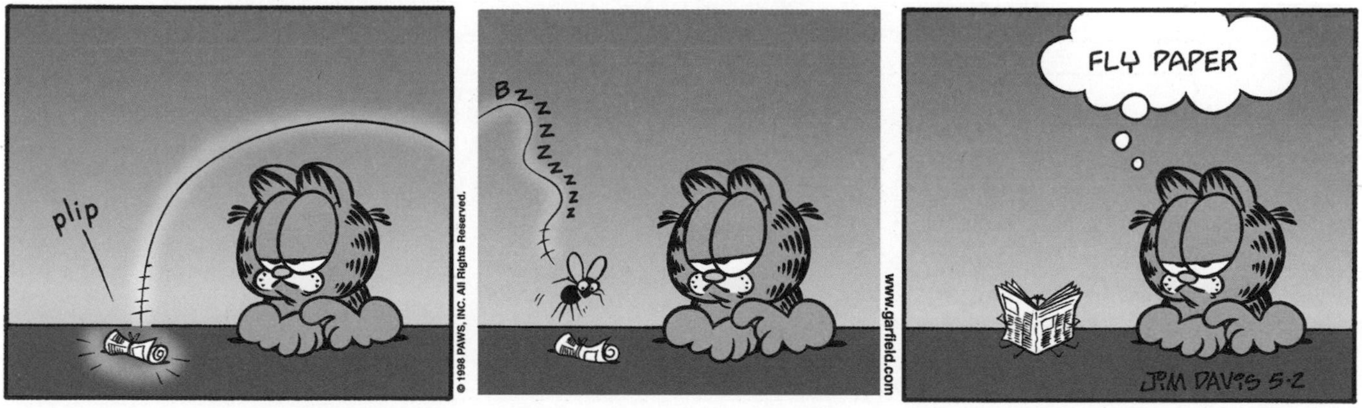
plip
© 1998 PAWS, INC. All Rights Reserved.
BZZZZZZZ
www.garfield.com
FLY PAPER
JIM DAVIS 5-2

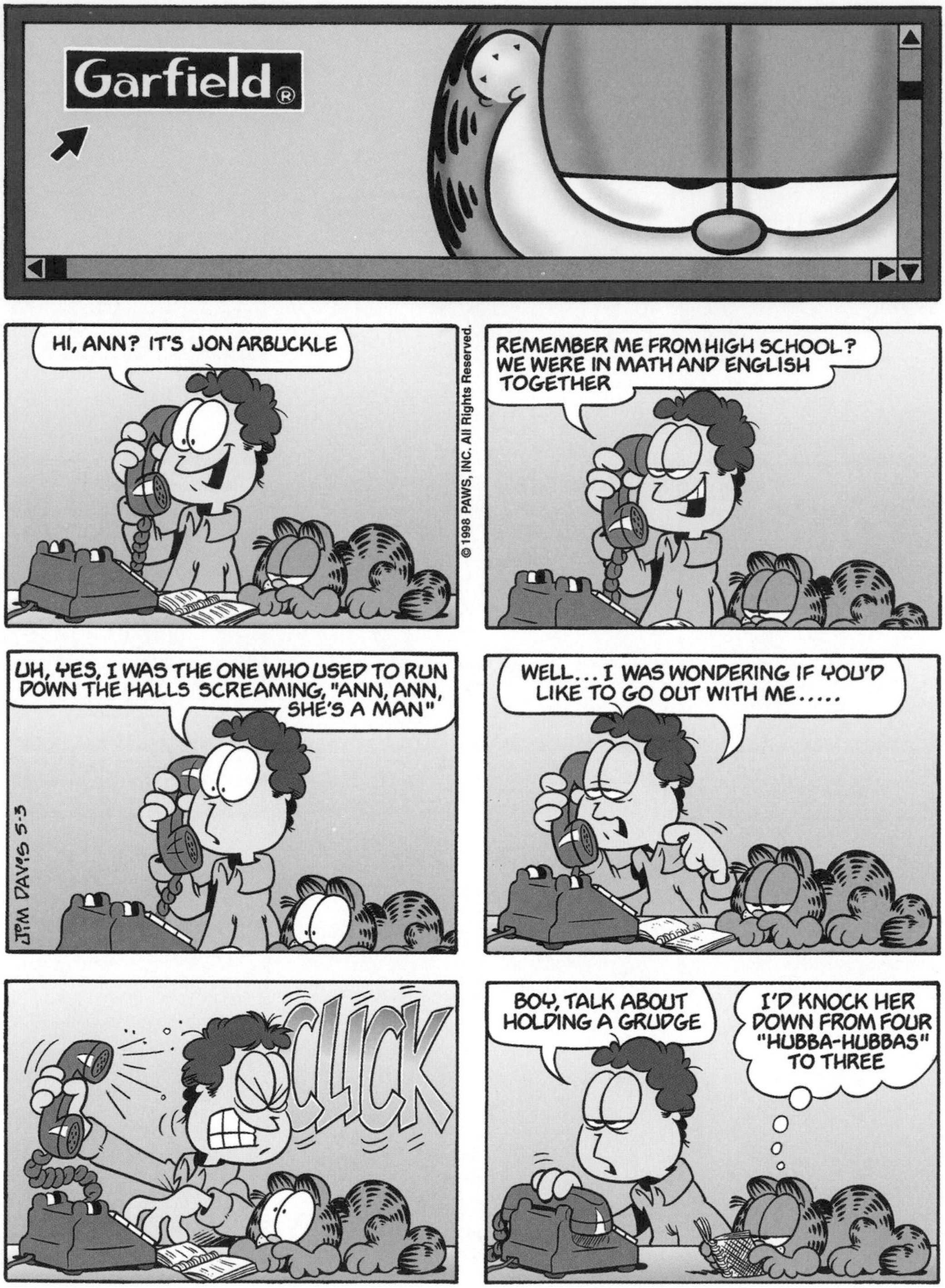
Garfield®
HI, ANN? IT'S JON ARBUCKLE
© 1998 PAWS, INC. All Rights Reserved.
REMEMBER ME FROM HIGH SCHOOL? WE WERE IN MATH AND ENGLISH TOGETHER
UH, YES, I WAS THE ONE WHO USED TO RUN DOWN THE HALLS SCREAMING, "ANN, ANN, SHE'S A MAN"
JPM DAVIS 5-3
WELL... I WAS WONDERING IF YOU'D LIKE TO GO OUT WITH ME.....
CLICK
BOY, TALK ABOUT HOLDING A GRUDGE
I'D KNOCK HER DOWN FROM FOUR "HUBBA-HUBBAS" TO THREE

THIS IS MY NEW COLLEGE INTERN, BIFF
www.garfield.com
© 1998 PAWS, INC. All Rights Reserved.
IS THERE SOMETHING I SHOULD BE DOING?
YOU'VE GOT A LOT TO LEARN ABOUT BEING A CAT, BIFF
JIM DAVIS 5-4

OKAY, COLLEGE INTERN BIFF, DO YOU KNOW WHAT A CAT IS SUPPOSED TO DO WITH A BALL OF YARN?
JIM DAVIS 5-5
www.garfield.com
KNIT A SWEATER AND SELL IT TO BUY FOOD?
© 1998 PAWS, INC. All Rights Reserved.
WOW, AND I WAS JUST GUESSING
I'M STARTING TO LIKE THIS KID

REMEMBER, BIFF, A CAT CAN'T DO TOO LITTLE
www.garfield.com
JIM DAVIS 5-6
© 1998 PAWS, INC. All Rights Reserved.
I'M SORRY. I WASN'T LISTENING
ATTABOY

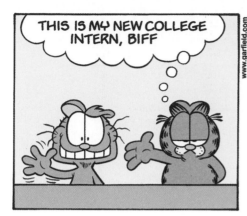

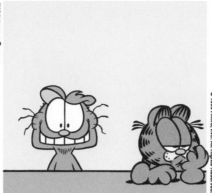

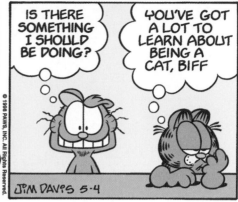

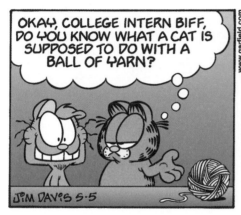

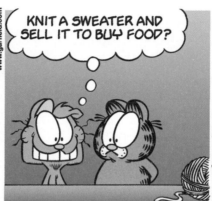

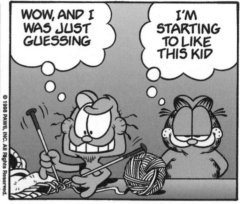

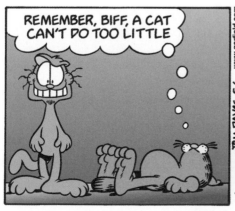

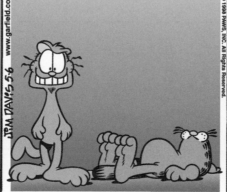

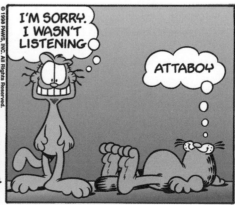

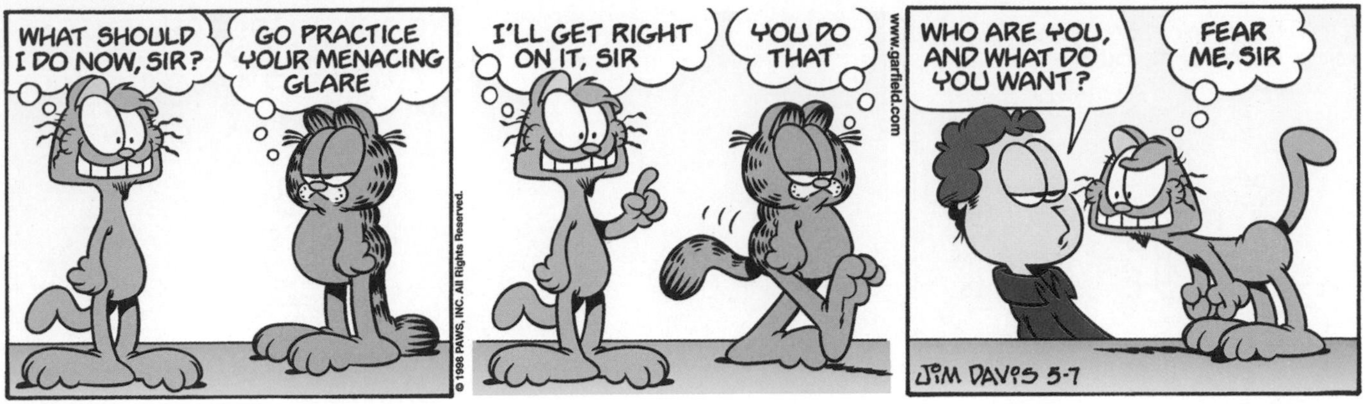
WHAT SHOULD I DO NOW, SIR?
GO PRACTICE YOUR MENACING GLARE
© 1998 PAWS, INC. All Rights Reserved.
I'LL GET RIGHT ON IT, SIR
YOU DO THAT
www.garfield.com
WHO ARE YOU, AND WHAT DO YOU WANT?
FEAR ME, SIR
JIM DAVIS 5-7

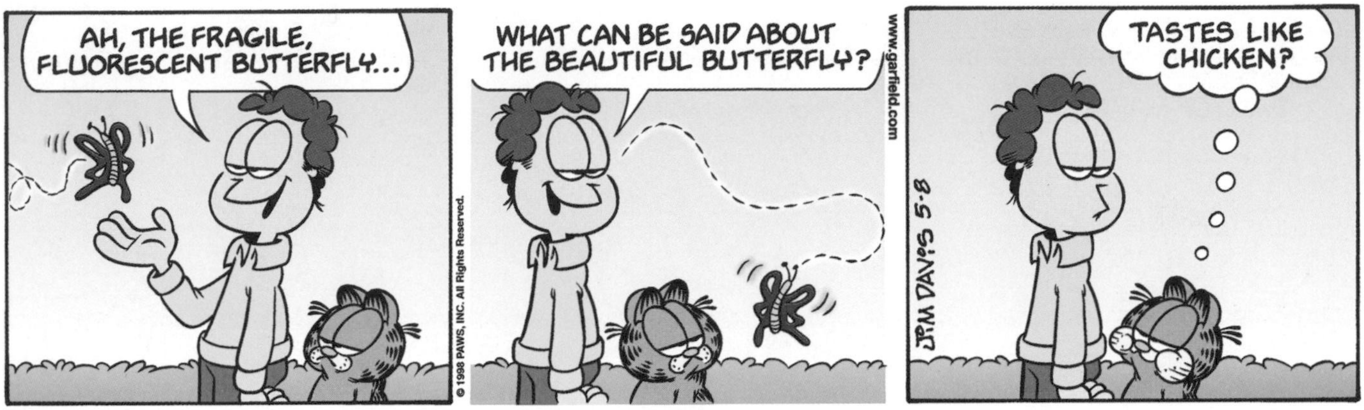
AH, THE FRAGILE, FLUORESCENT BUTTERFLY...
© 1998 PAWS, INC. All Rights Reserved.
WHAT CAN BE SAID ABOUT THE BEAUTIFUL BUTTERFLY?
www.garfield.com
JIM DAVIS 5-8
TASTES LIKE CHICKEN?

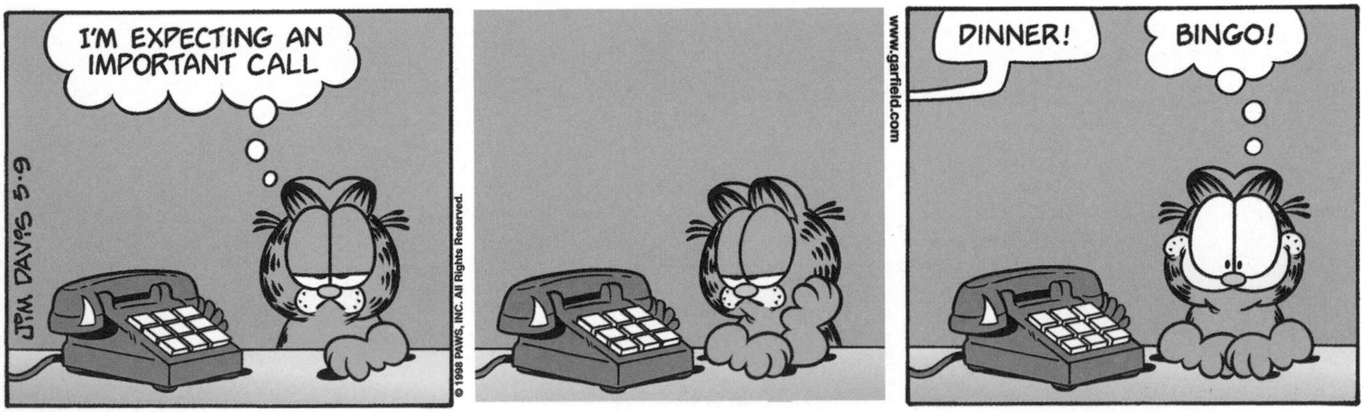
I'M EXPECTING AN IMPORTANT CALL
JIM DAVIS 5-9
© 1998 PAWS, INC. All Rights Reserved.
www.garfield.com
DINNER!
BINGO!

GARFIELD®
...AND THE DEALER TAKES ONE
I'LL BET TWO...
KLINK KLINK
CALL, AND RAISE
I'LL YELL AT HIM AFTER HE STOPS WINNING
JIM DAVIS 5-10
© 1998 PAWS, INC. All Rights Reserved.

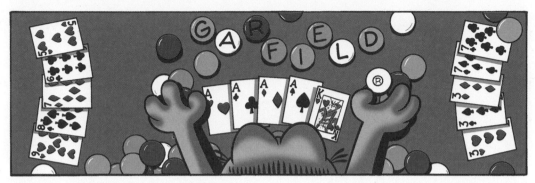

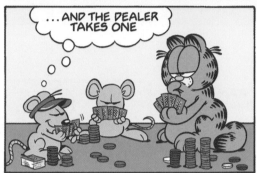

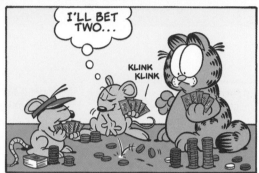

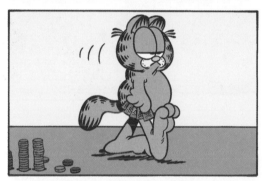

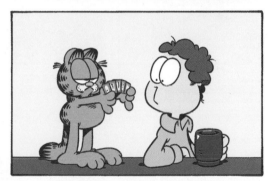

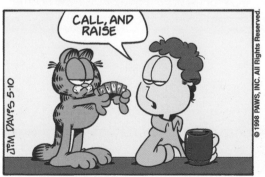

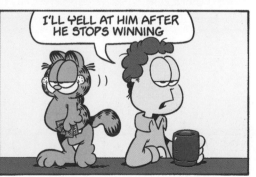

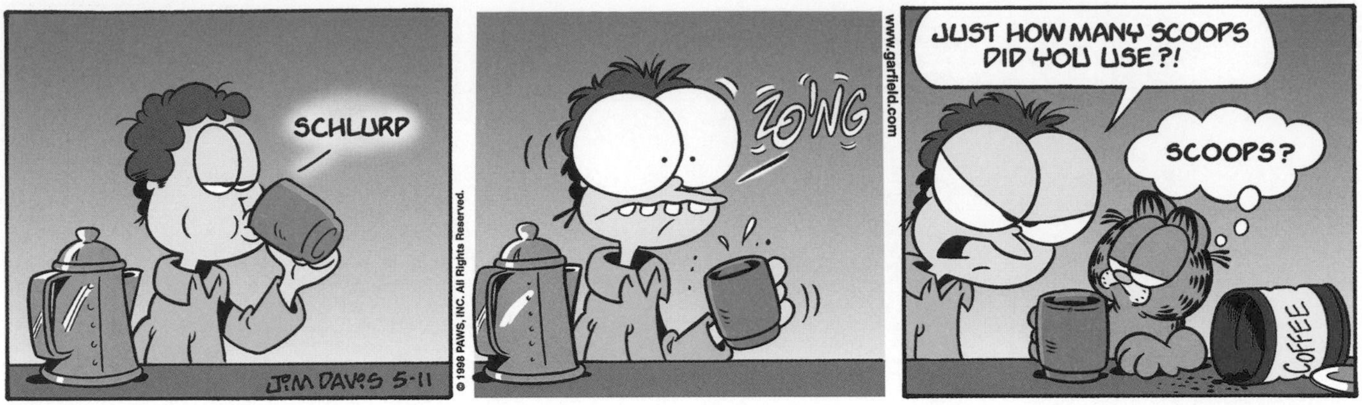
SCHLURP
JIM DAVIS 5-11
© 1998 PAWS, INC. All Rights Reserved.
ZOING
www.garfield.com
JUST HOW MANY SCOOPS DID YOU USE?!
SCOOPS?
COFFEE

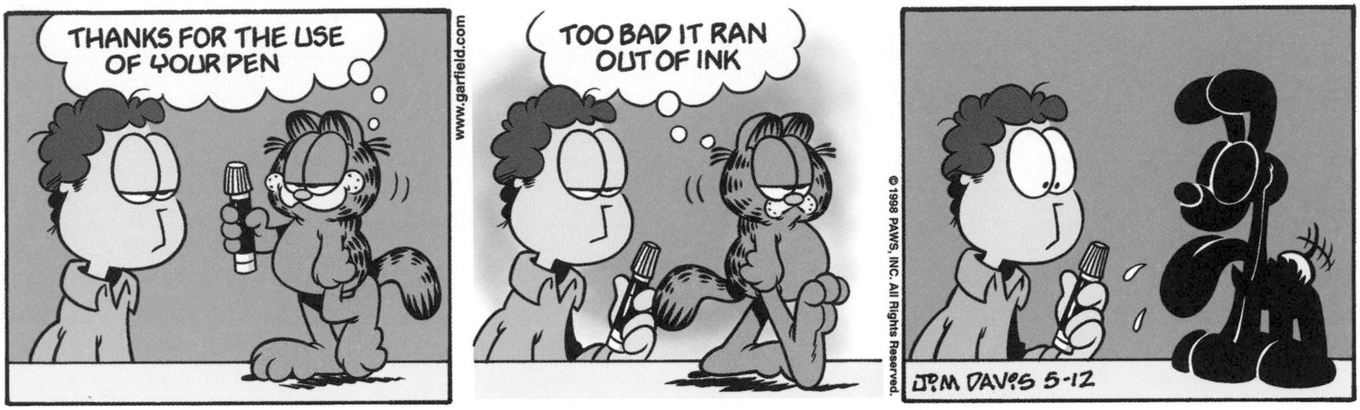
THANKS FOR THE USE OF YOUR PEN
www.garfield.com
TOO BAD IT RAN OUT OF INK
© 1998 PAWS, INC. All Rights Reserved.
JIM DAVIS 5-12

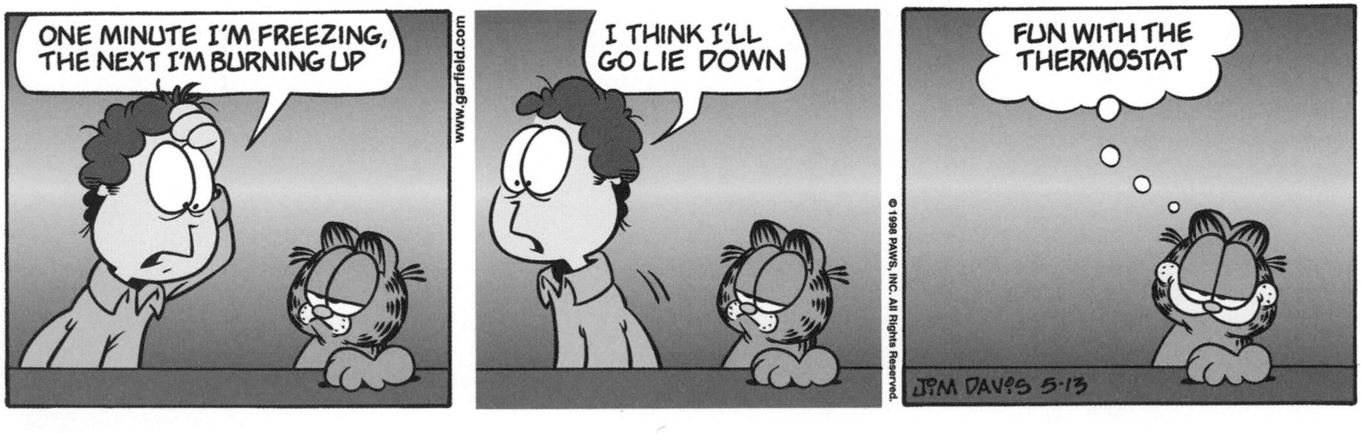
ONE MINUTE I'M FREEZING, THE NEXT I'M BURNING UP
www.garfield.com
I THINK I'LL GO LIE DOWN
© 1998 PAWS, INC. All Rights Reserved.
FUN WITH THE THERMOSTAT
JIM DAVIS 5-13

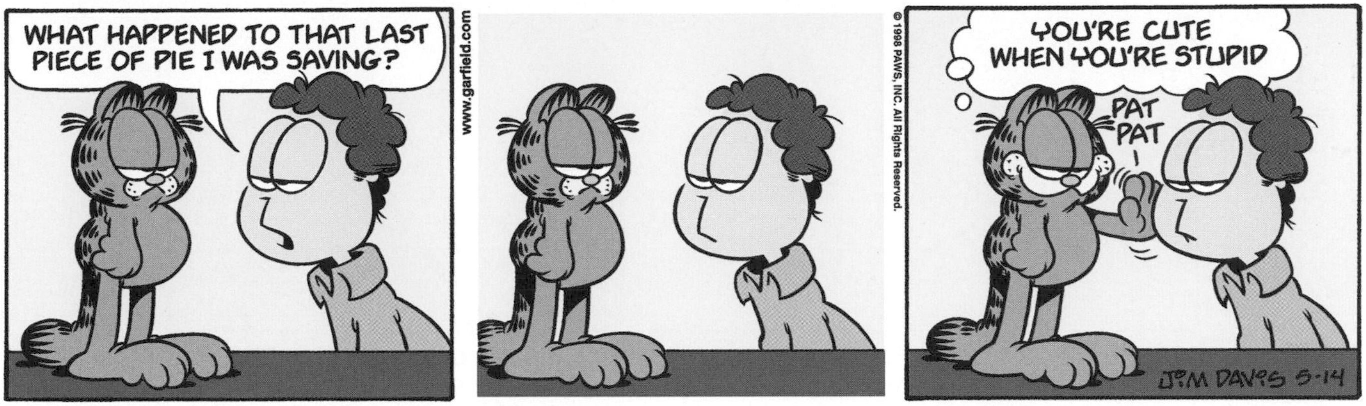
WHAT HAPPENED TO THAT LAST PIECE OF PIE I WAS SAVING?
www.garfield.com
© 1998 PAWS, INC. All Rights Reserved.
YOU'RE CUTE WHEN YOU'RE STUPID
PAT PAT
JIM DAVIS 5-14

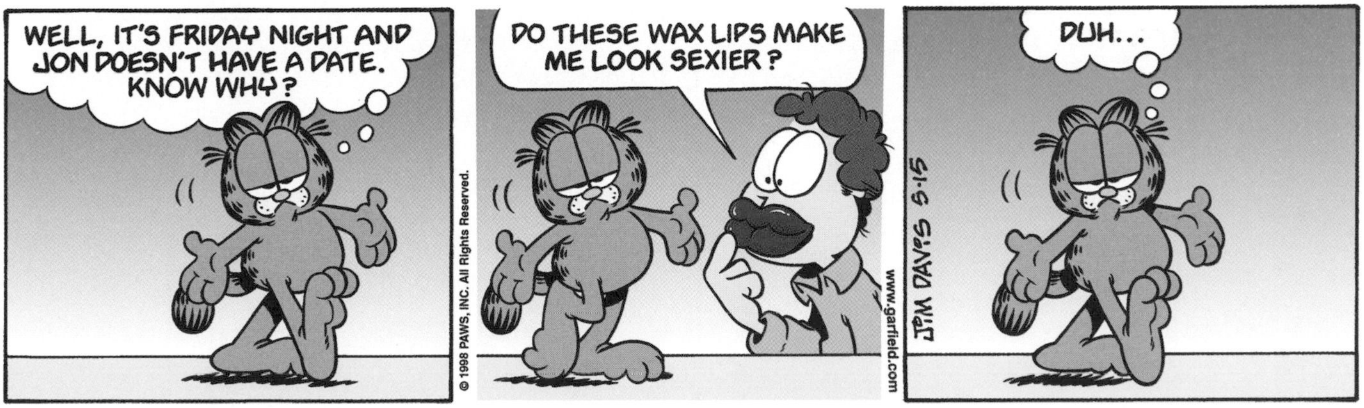
WELL, IT'S FRIDAY NIGHT AND JON DOESN'T HAVE A DATE. KNOW WHY?
© 1998 PAWS, INC. All Rights Reserved.
DO THESE WAX LIPS MAKE ME LOOK SEXIER?
www.garfield.com
JIM DAVIS 5-15
DUH...

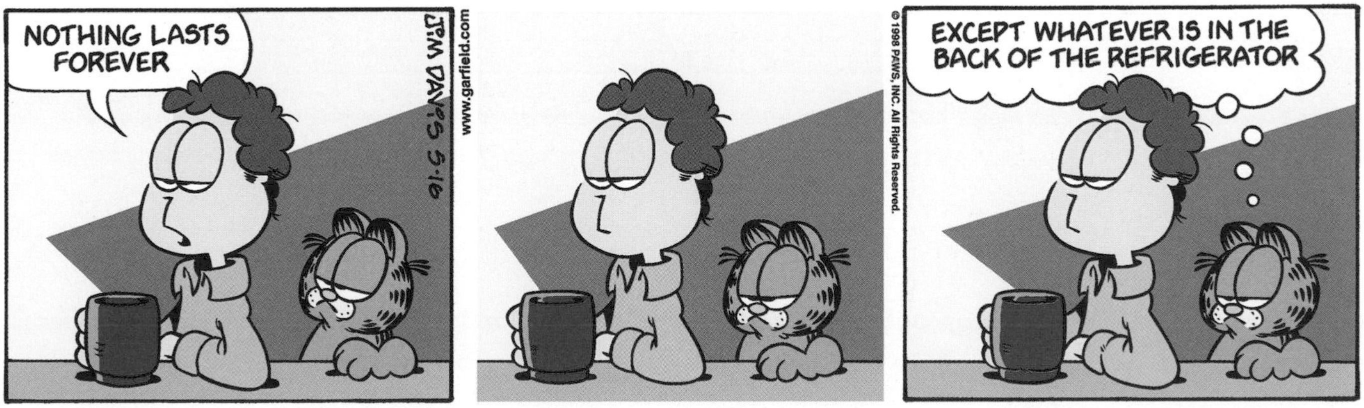
NOTHING LASTS FOREVER
JIM DAVIS 5-16
www.garfield.com
© 1998 PAWS, INC. All Rights Reserved.
EXCEPT WHATEVER IS IN THE BACK OF THE REFRIGERATOR

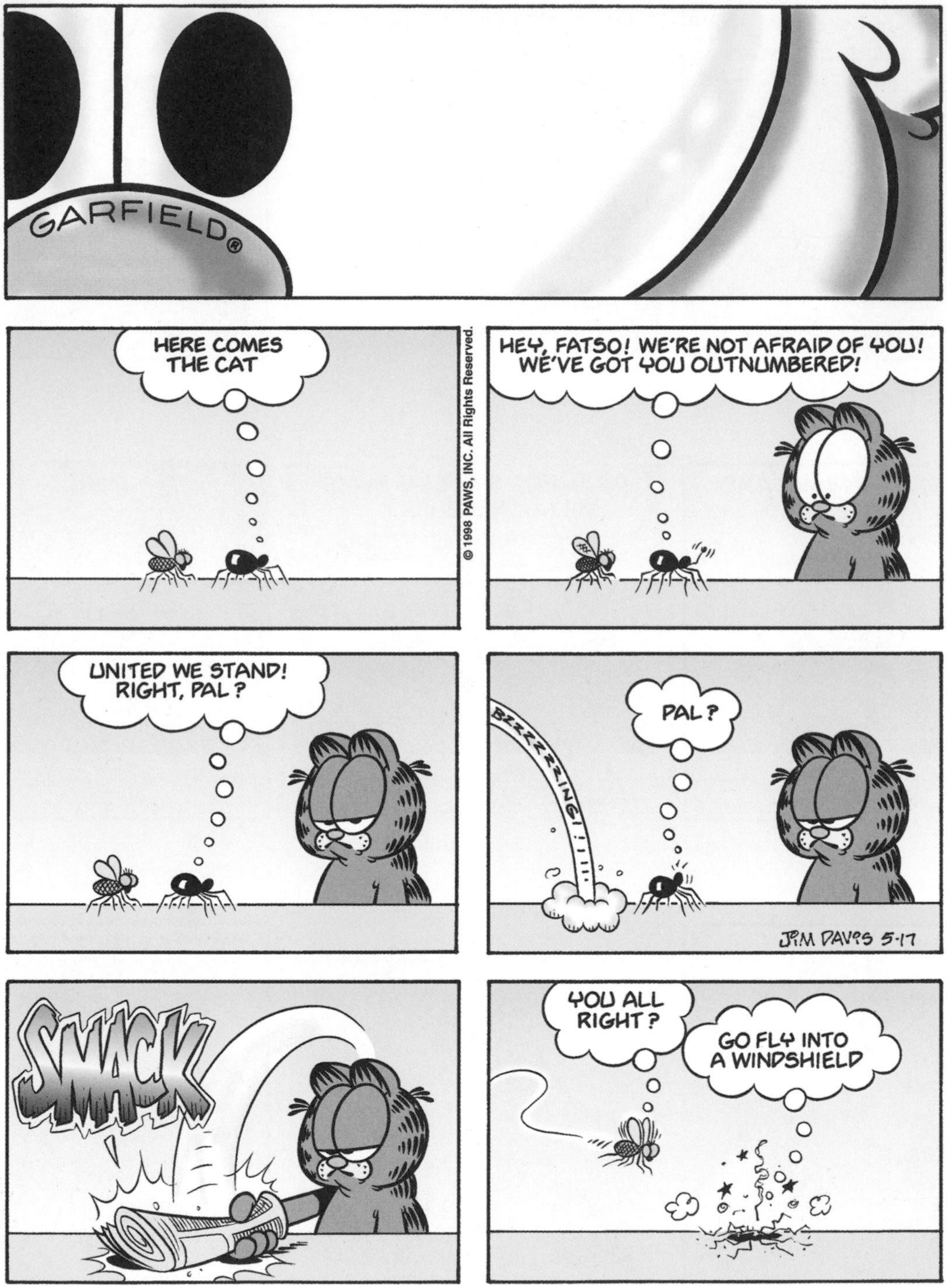
GARFIELD®
HERE COMES THE CAT
© 1998 PAWS, INC. All Rights Reserved.
HEY, FATSO! WE'RE NOT AFRAID OF YOU! WE'VE GOT YOU OUTNUMBERED!
UNITED WE STAND! RIGHT, PAL?
BZZZZRING!
PAL?
JIM DAVIS 5-17
SMACK
YOU ALL RIGHT?
GO FLY INTO A WINDSHIELD

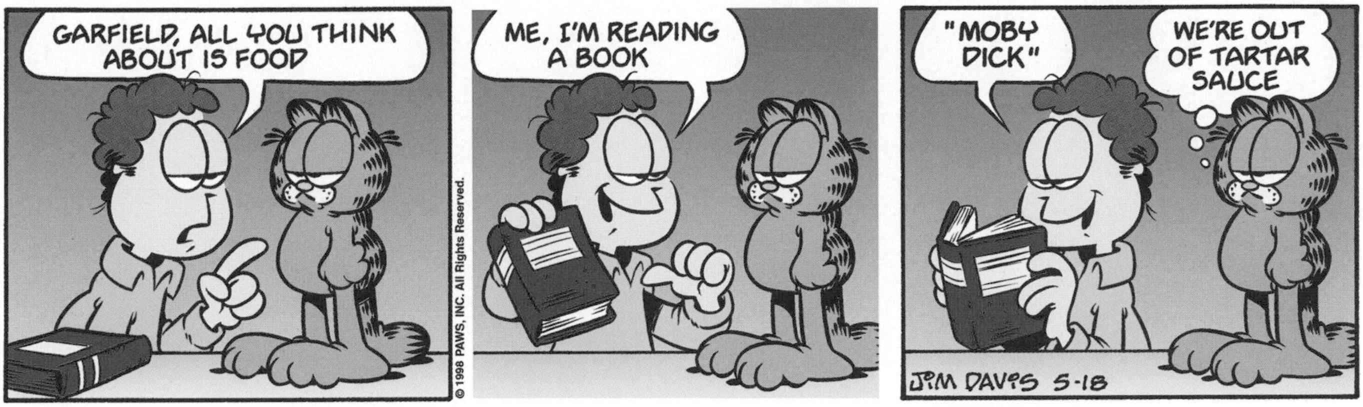
GARFIELD, ALL YOU THINK ABOUT IS FOOD
© 1998 PAWS, INC. All Rights Reserved.
ME, I'M READING A BOOK
"MOBY DICK"
WE'RE OUT OF TARTAR SAUCE
JIM DAVIS 5-18

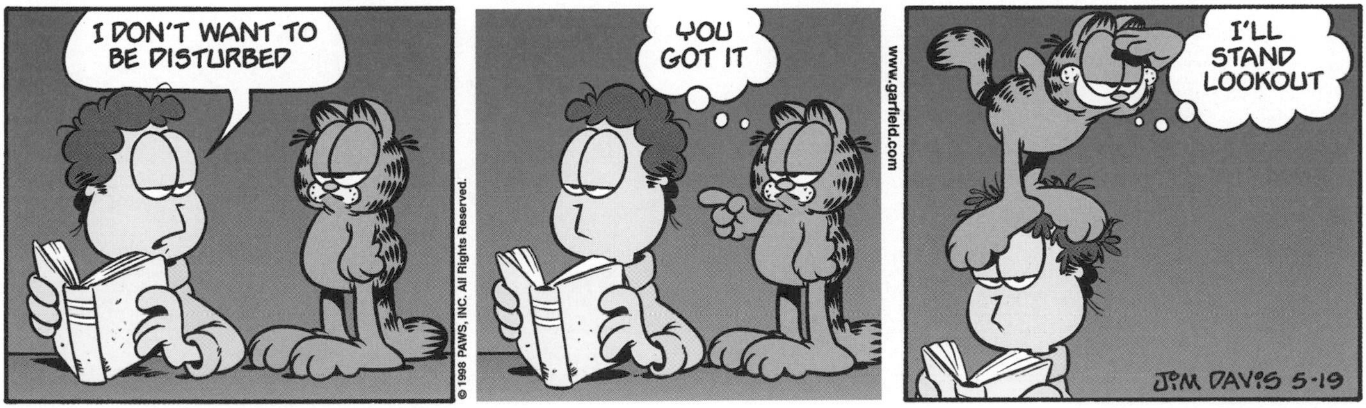
I DON'T WANT TO BE DISTURBED
© 1998 PAWS, INC. All Rights Reserved.
YOU GOT IT
www.garfield.com
I'LL STAND LOOKOUT
JIM DAVIS 5-19

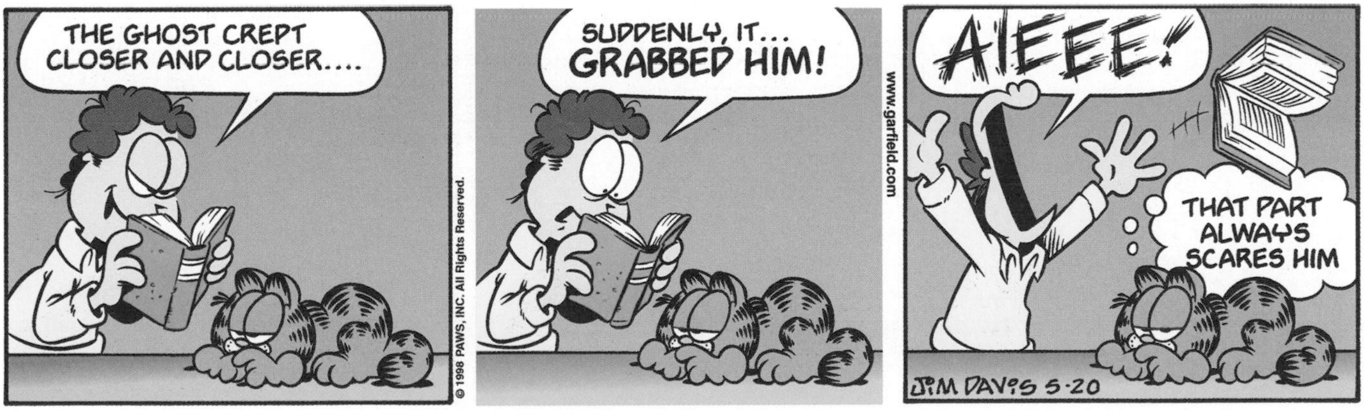
THE GHOST CREPT CLOSER AND CLOSER....
© 1998 PAWS, INC. All Rights Reserved.
SUDDENLY, IT... GRABBED HIM!
www.garfield.com
AIEEE!
THAT PART ALWAYS SCARES HIM
JIM DAVIS 5-20

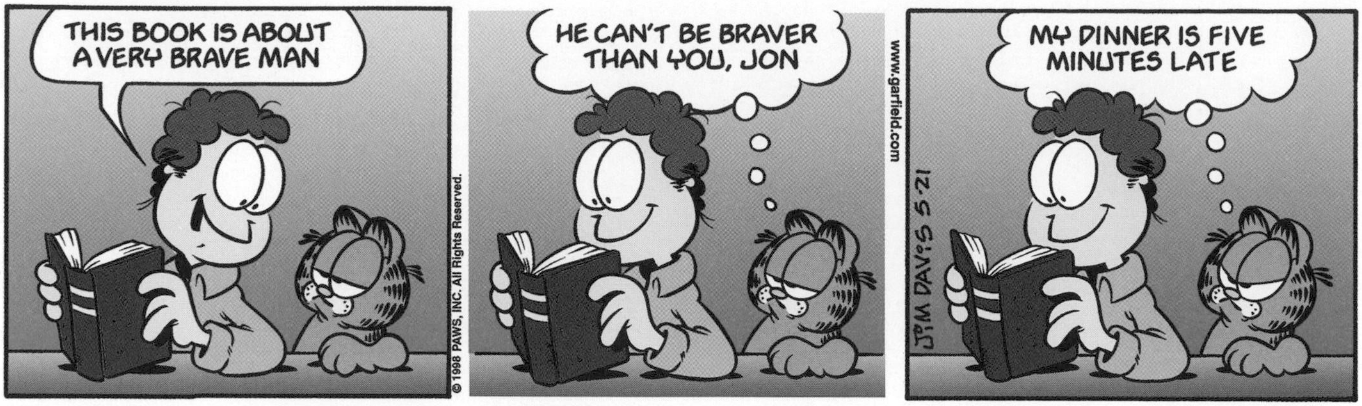
THIS BOOK IS ABOUT A VERY BRAVE MAN
HE CAN'T BE BRAVER THAN YOU, JON
MY DINNER IS FIVE MINUTES LATE
JIM DAVIS 5-21
© 1998 PAWS, INC. All Rights Reserved.
www.garfield.com

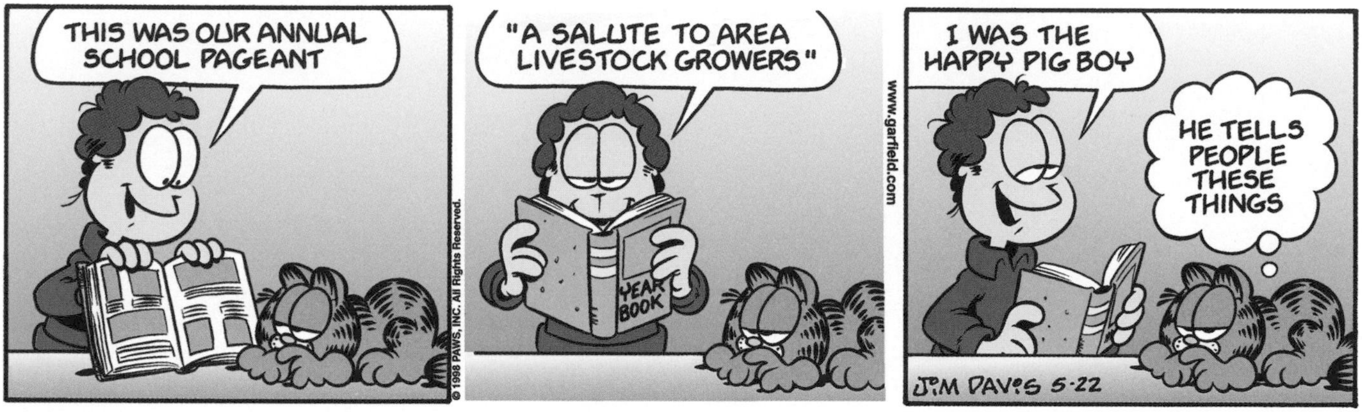
THIS WAS OUR ANNUAL SCHOOL PAGEANT
"A SALUTE TO AREA LIVESTOCK GROWERS"
YEAR BOOK
I WAS THE HAPPY PIG BOY
HE TELLS PEOPLE THESE THINGS
JIM DAVIS 5-22
© 1998 PAWS, INC. All Rights Reserved.
www.garfield.com

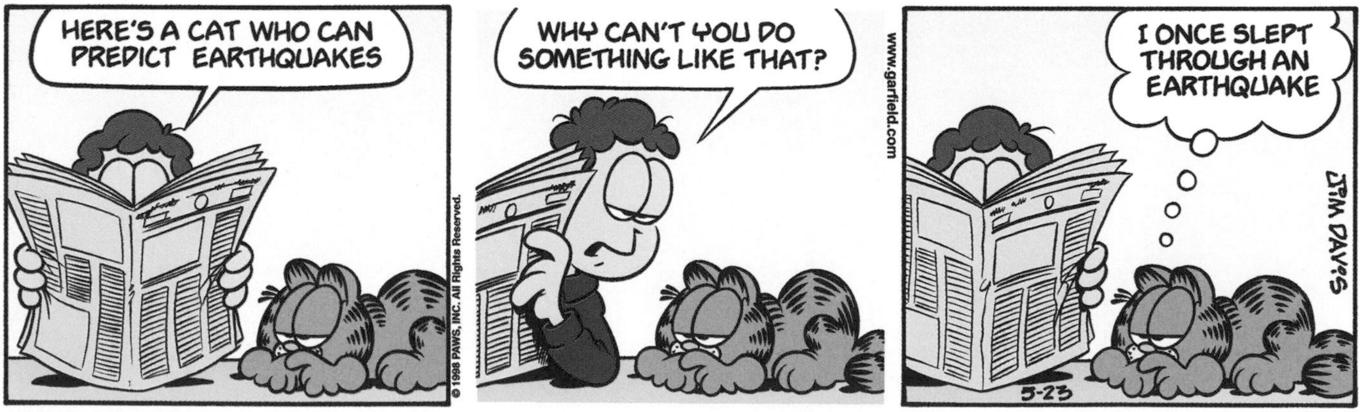
HERE'S A CAT WHO CAN PREDICT EARTHQUAKES
WHY CAN'T YOU DO SOMETHING LIKE THAT?
I ONCE SLEPT THROUGH AN EARTHQUAKE
JIM DAVIS
5-23
© 1998 PAWS, INC. All Rights Reserved.
www.garfield.com

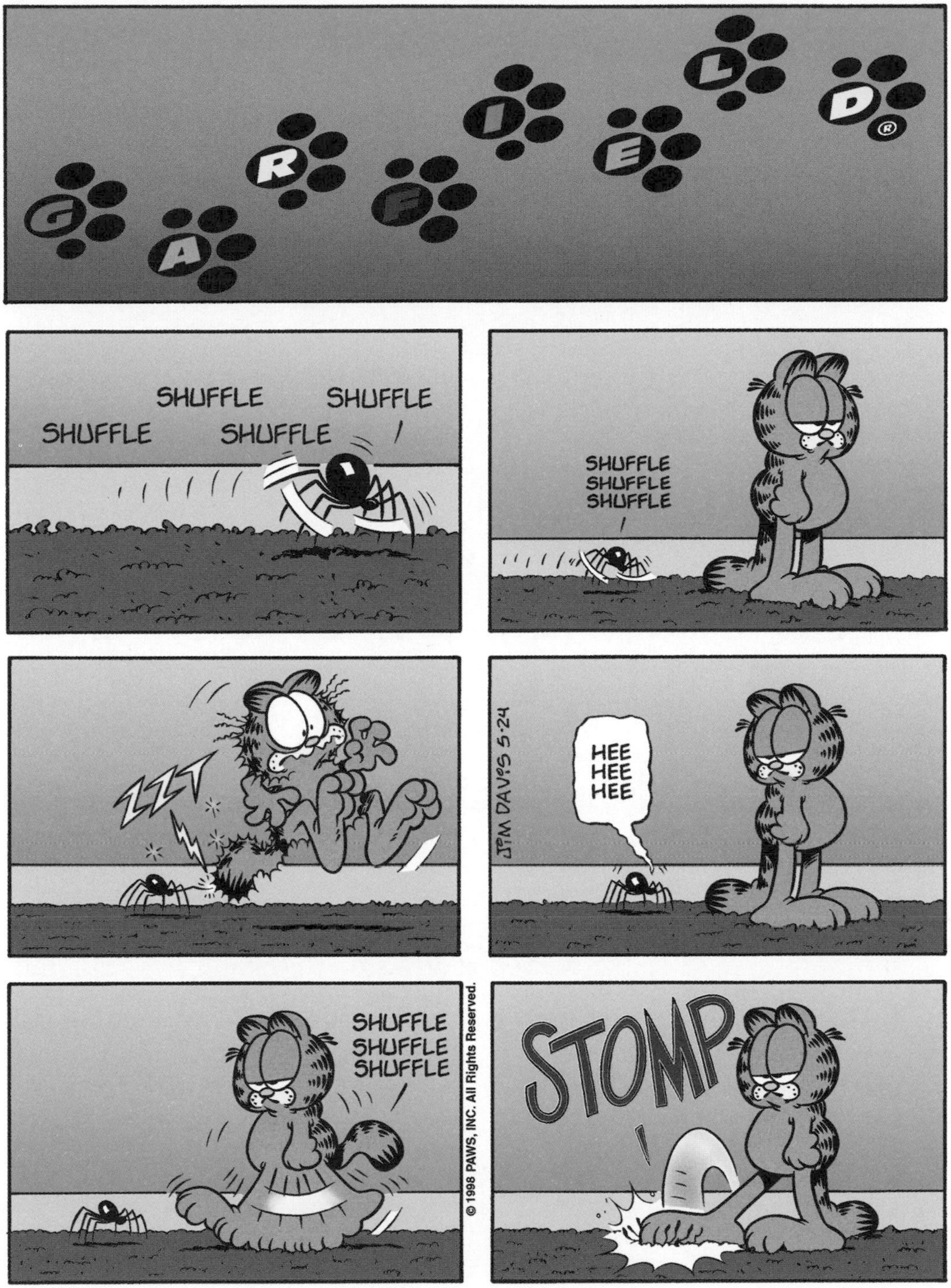
GARFIELD®
SHUFFLE
SHUFFLE
SHUFFLE
SHUFFLE
SHUFFLE
SHUFFLE
SHUFFLE
ZZZT
JIM DAVIS 5·24
HEE
HEE
HEE
SHUFFLE
SHUFFLE
SHUFFLE
STOMP

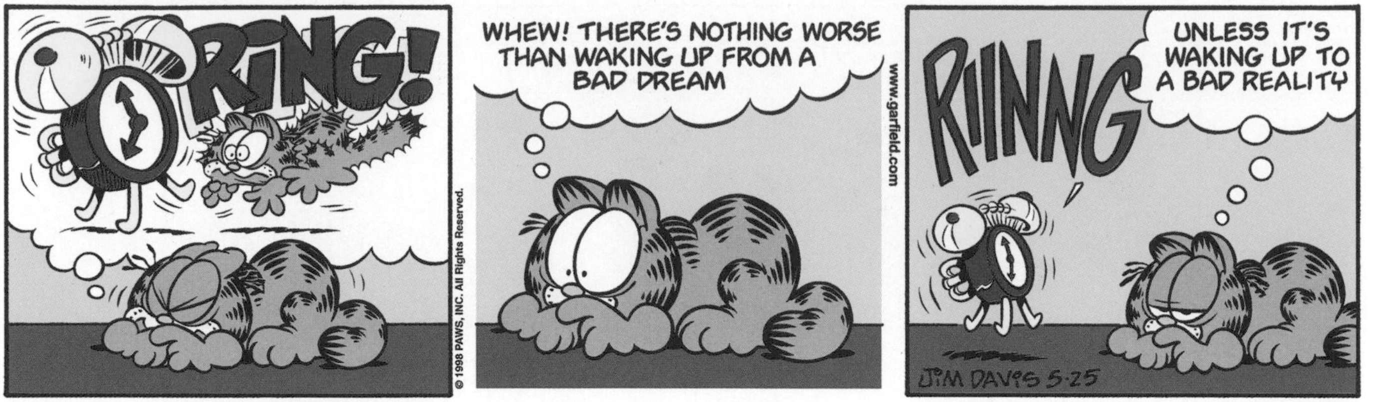
RING!
WHEW! THERE'S NOTHING WORSE THAN WAKING UP FROM A BAD DREAM
RIINNG
UNLESS IT'S WAKING UP TO A BAD REALITY
JIM DAVIS 5-25
© 1998 PAWS, INC. All Rights Reserved.
www.garfield.com

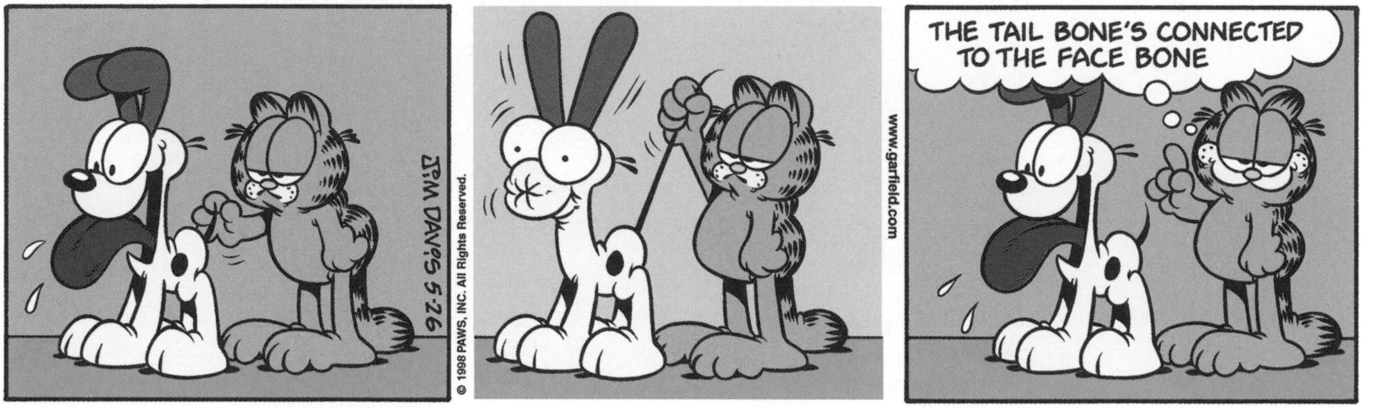
JIM DAVIS 5-26
THE TAIL BONE'S CONNECTED TO THE FACE BONE
© 1998 PAWS, INC. All Rights Reserved.
www.garfield.com

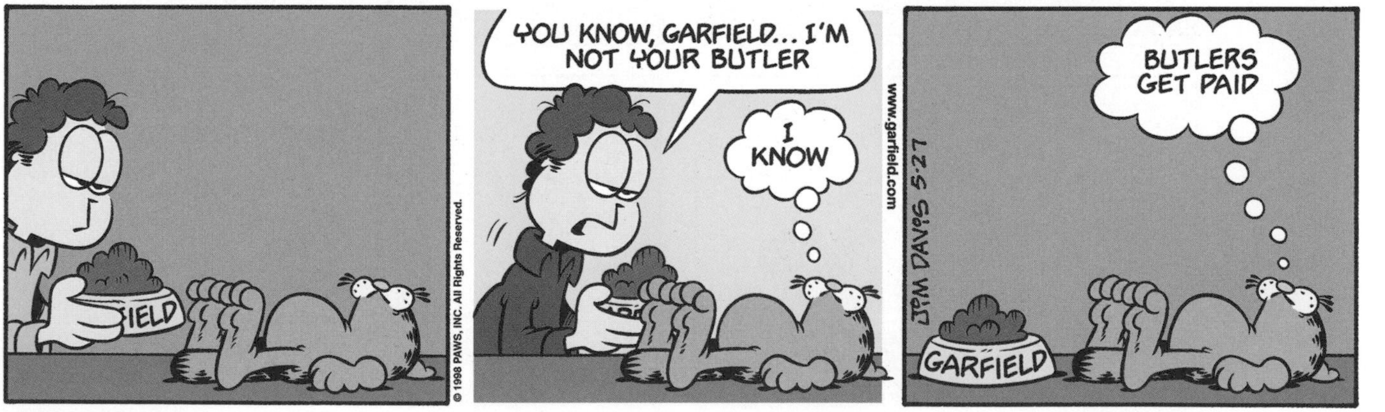
IELD
YOU KNOW, GARFIELD... I'M NOT YOUR BUTLER
I KNOW
JIM DAVIS 5-27
BUTLERS GET PAID
GARFIELD
© 1998 PAWS, INC. All Rights Reserved.
www.garfield.com

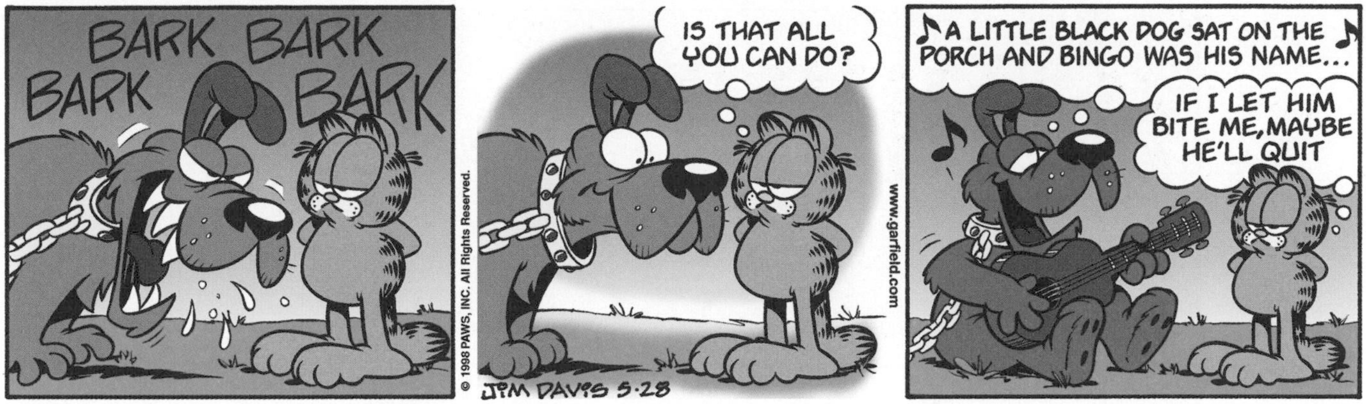
BARK BARK BARK BARK
IS THAT ALL YOU CAN DO?
♪A LITTLE BLACK DOG SAT ON THE PORCH AND BINGO WAS HIS NAME...♪
IF I LET HIM BITE ME, MAYBE HE'LL QUIT
© 1998 PAWS, INC. All Rights Reserved.
www.garfield.com
JIM DAVIS 5-28

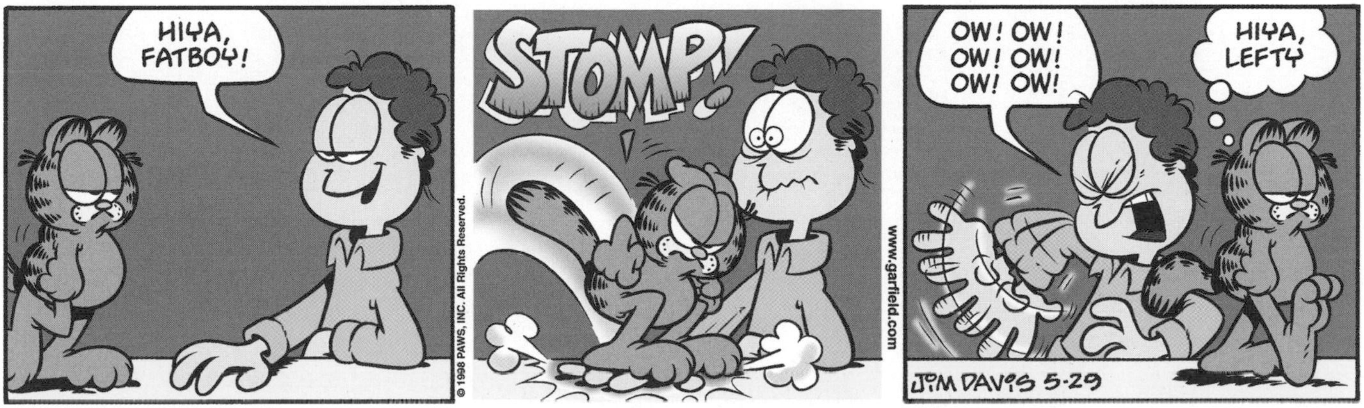
HIYA, FATBOY!
STOMP!
OW! OW! OW! OW! OW! OW!
HIYA, LEFTY
© 1998 PAWS, INC. All Rights Reserved.
www.garfield.com
JIM DAVIS 5-29

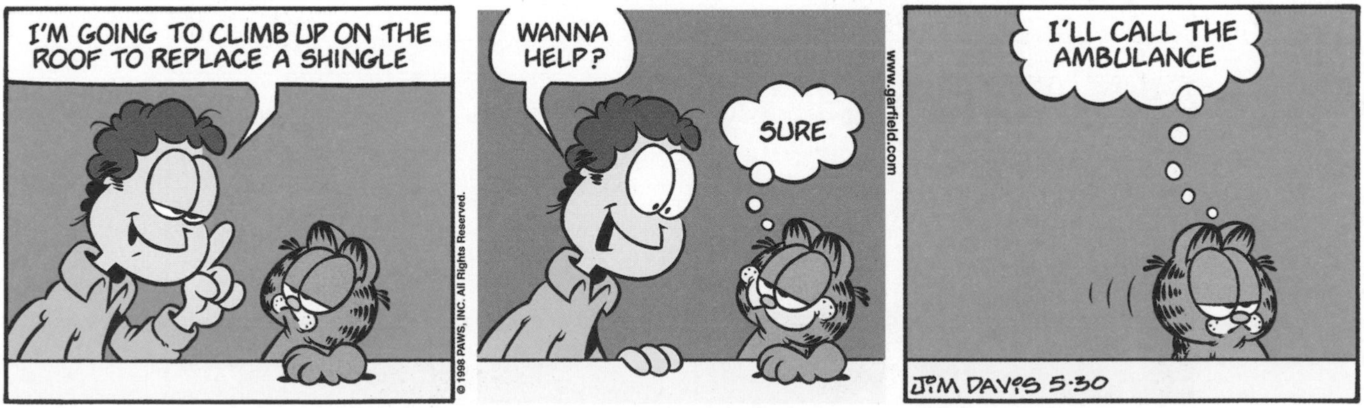
I'M GOING TO CLIMB UP ON THE ROOF TO REPLACE A SHINGLE
WANNA HELP?
SURE
I'LL CALL THE AMBULANCE
© 1998 PAWS, INC. All Rights Reserved.
www.garfield.com
JIM DAVIS 5-30

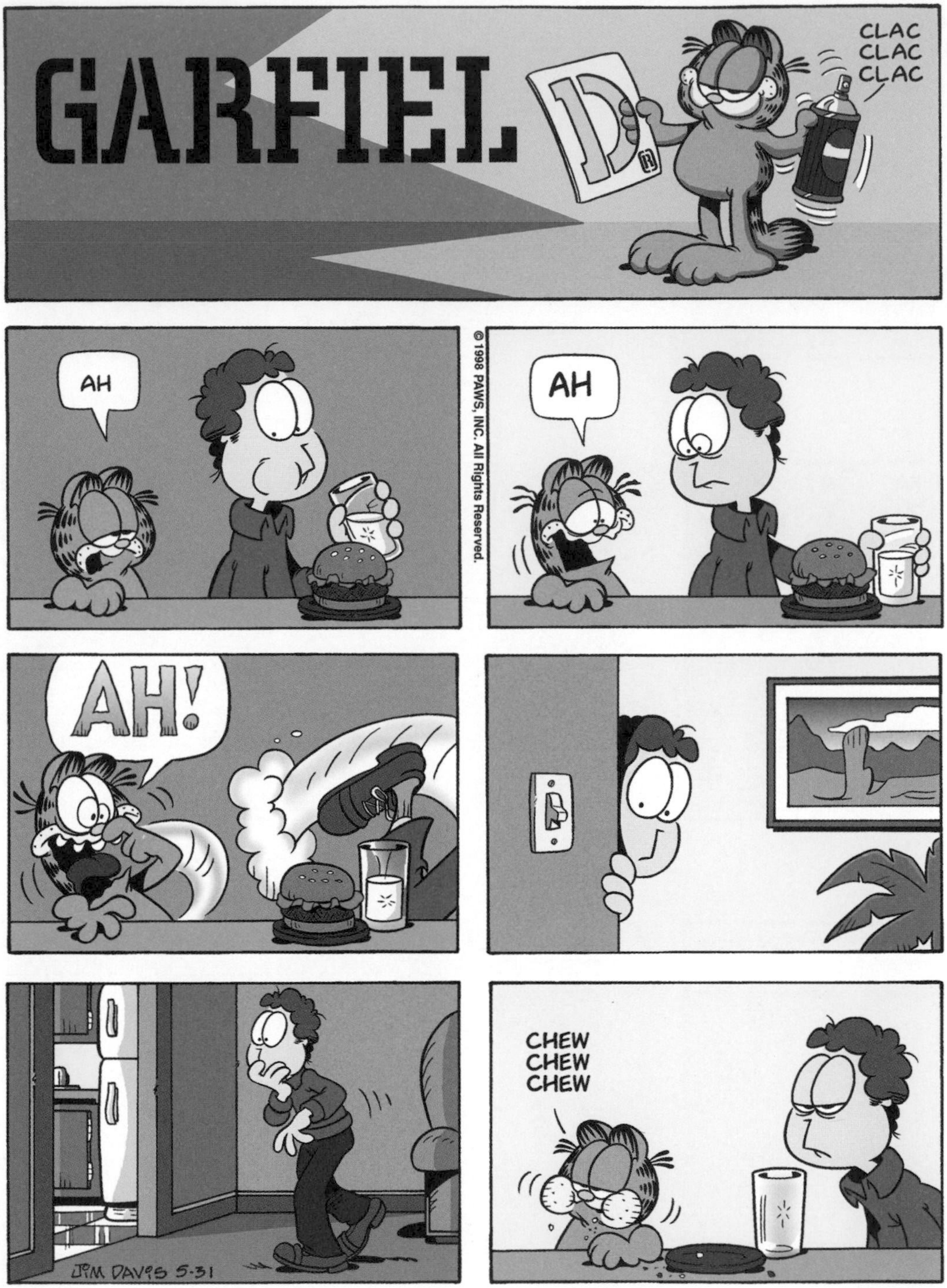
GARFIEL D
CLAC
CLAC
CLAC
AH
AH
AH!
JIM DAVIS 5-31
CHEW
CHEW
CHEW

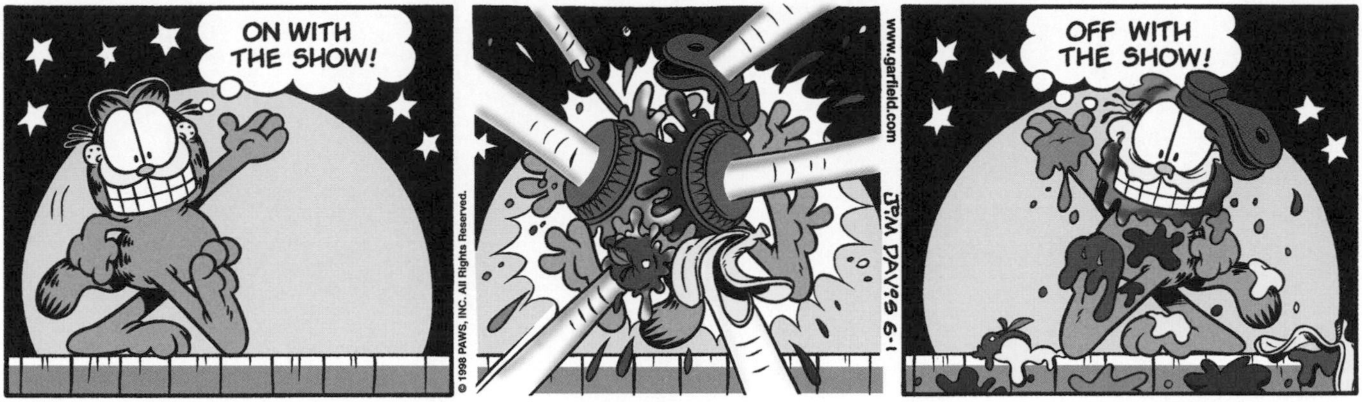
ON WITH THE SHOW!
OFF WITH THE SHOW!
© 1998 PAWS, INC. All Rights Reserved.
www.garfield.com
JPM DAVPS 6-1

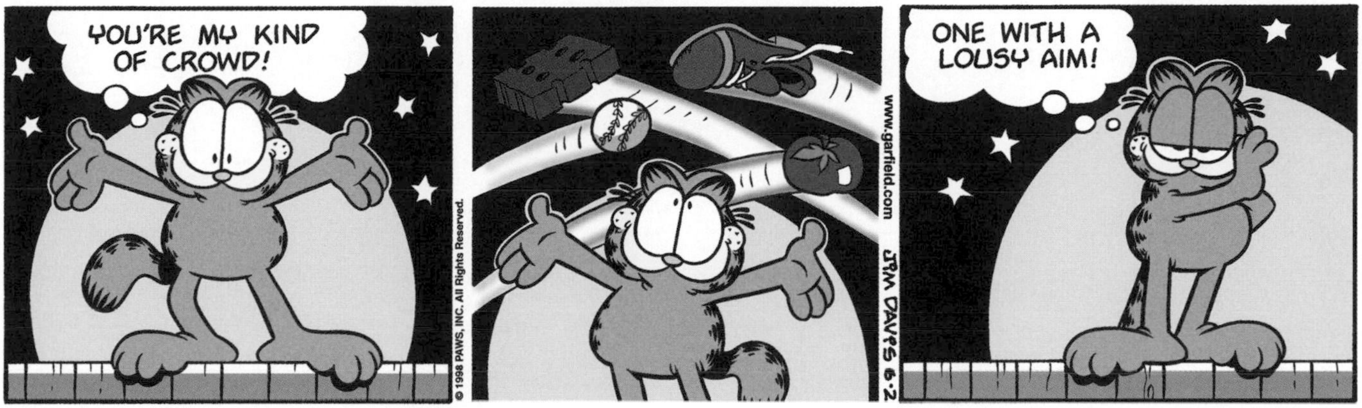
YOU'RE MY KIND OF CROWD!
ONE WITH A LOUSY AIM!
© 1998 PAWS, INC. All Rights Reserved.
www.garfield.com
JPM DAVPS 6-2

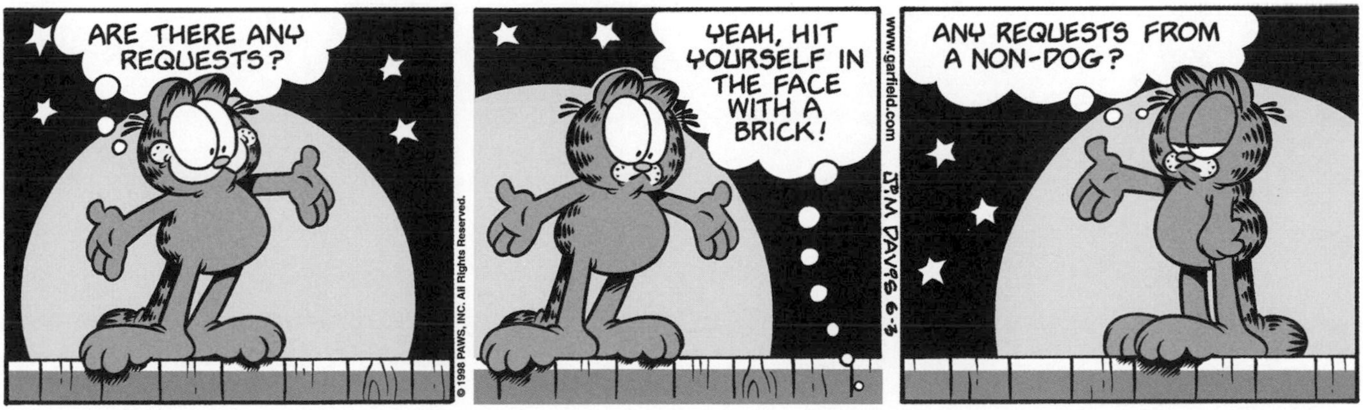
ARE THERE ANY REQUESTS?
YEAH, HIT YOURSELF IN THE FACE WITH A BRICK!
ANY REQUESTS FROM A NON-DOG?
© 1998 PAWS, INC. All Rights Reserved.
www.garfield.com
JPM DAVPS 6-3

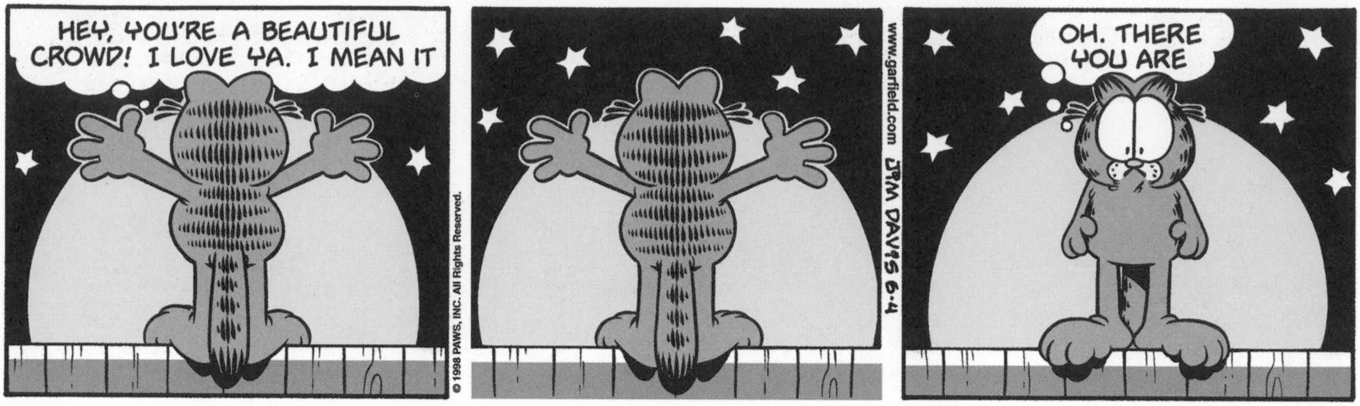
HEY, YOU'RE A BEAUTIFUL CROWD! I LOVE YA. I MEAN IT
OH. THERE YOU ARE
© 1998 PAWS, INC. All Rights Reserved.
www.garfield.com
JIM DAVIS 6-4

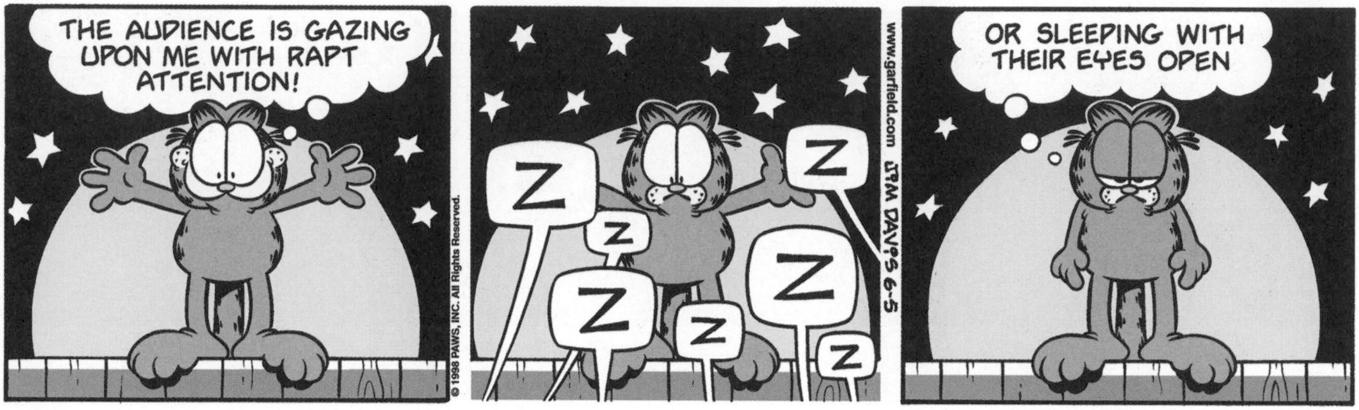
THE AUDIENCE IS GAZING UPON ME WITH RAPT ATTENTION!
Z
Z
Z
Z
Z
Z
Z
OR SLEEPING WITH THEIR EYES OPEN
© 1998 PAWS, INC. All Rights Reserved.
www.garfield.com
JIM DAVIS 6-5

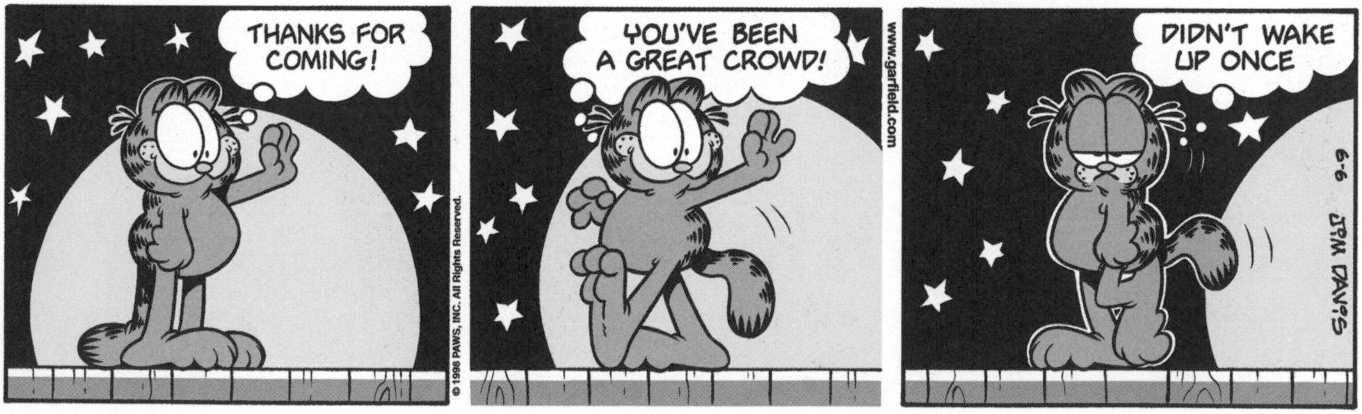
THANKS FOR COMING!
YOU'VE BEEN A GREAT CROWD!
DIDN'T WAKE UP ONCE
© 1998 PAWS, INC. All Rights Reserved.
www.garfield.com
JIM DAVIS 6-6

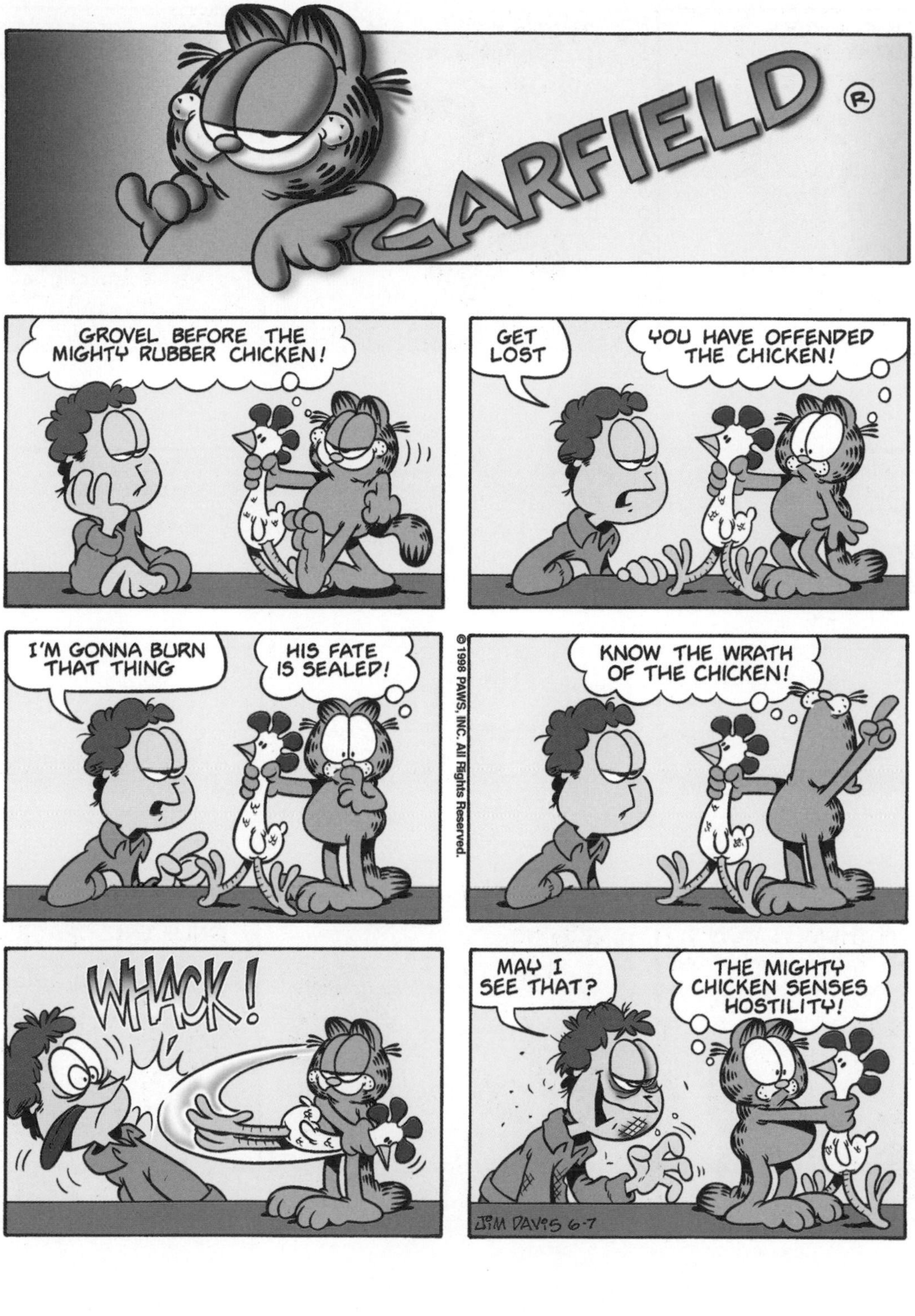
GARFIELD®
GROVEL BEFORE THE MIGHTY RUBBER CHICKEN!
GET LOST
YOU HAVE OFFENDED THE CHICKEN!
I'M GONNA BURN THAT THING
HIS FATE IS SEALED!
© 1998 PAWS, INC. All Rights Reserved.
KNOW THE WRATH OF THE CHICKEN!
WHACK!
MAY I SEE THAT?
THE MIGHTY CHICKEN SENSES HOSTILITY!
JIM DAVIS 6-7

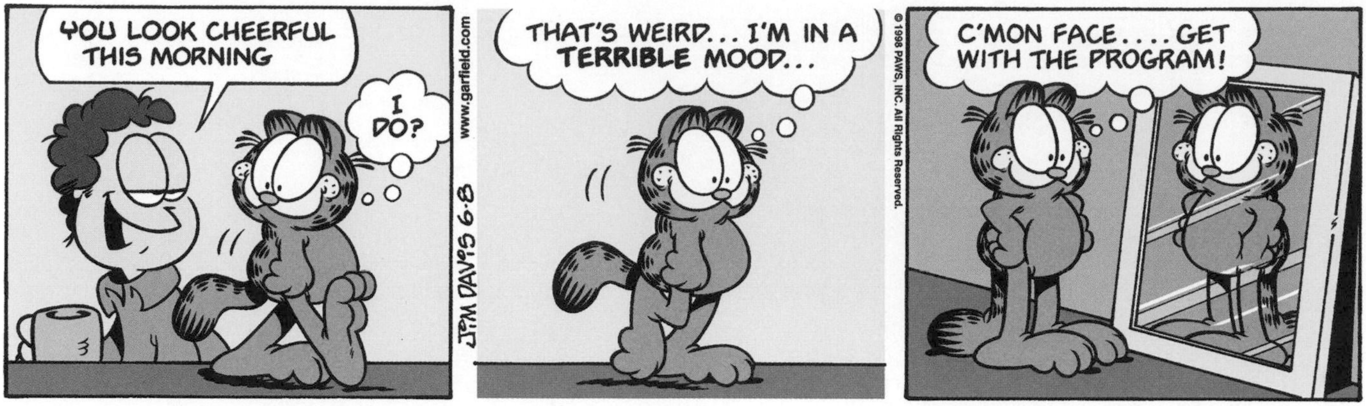
YOU LOOK CHEERFUL THIS MORNING
I DO?
THAT'S WEIRD... I'M IN A TERRIBLE MOOD...
C'MON FACE.... GET WITH THE PROGRAM!

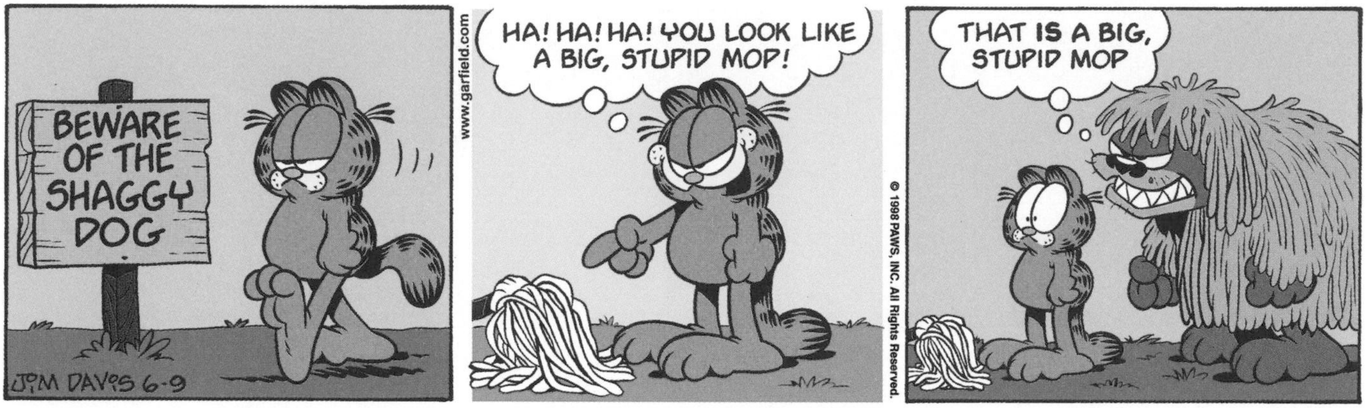
BEWARE OF THE SHAGGY DOG
HA! HA! HA! YOU LOOK LIKE A BIG, STUPID MOP!
THAT IS A BIG, STUPID MOP

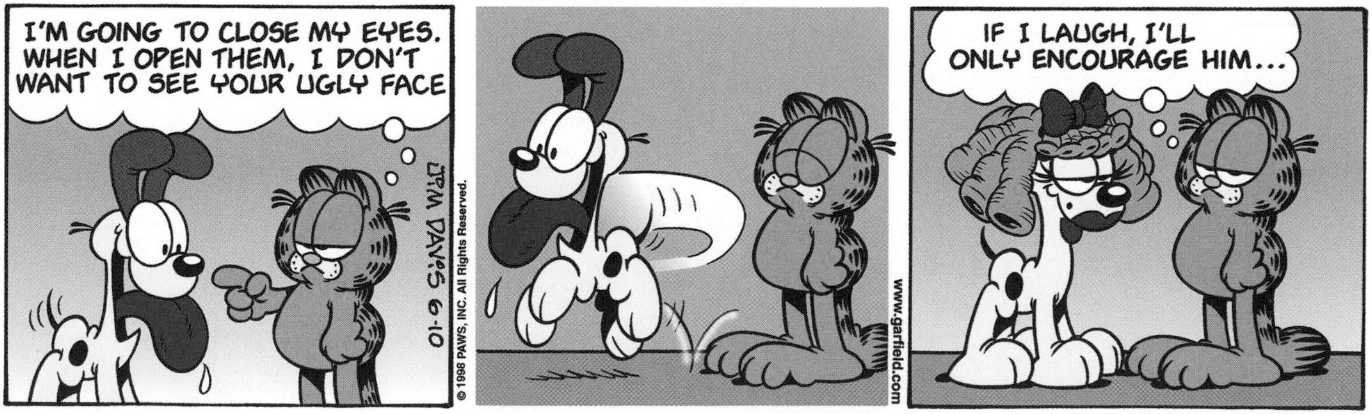
I'M GOING TO CLOSE MY EYES. WHEN I OPEN THEM, I DON'T WANT TO SEE YOUR UGLY FACE
IF I LAUGH, I'LL ONLY ENCOURAGE HIM...

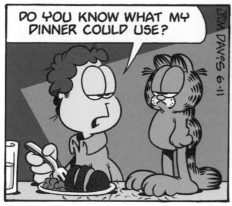

DO YOU KNOW WHAT MY DINNER COULD USE?
JIM DAVIS 6-11
www.garfield.com
MORE CAT HAIR?
© 1998 PAWS, INC. All Rights Reserved.
LESS CAT HAIR!
I FIGURED IT WAS ONE OR THE OTHER

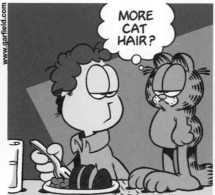

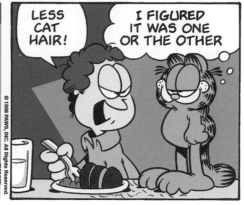

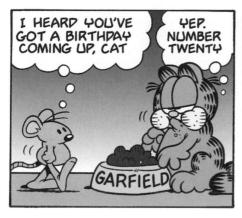

I HEARD YOU'VE GOT A BIRTHDAY COMING UP, CAT
YEP. NUMBER TWENTY
GARFIELD
GARFIELD
© 1998 PAWS, INC. All Rights Reserved.
WANT ME TO CUT THAT UP FOR YOU?
GARFIELD
JIM DAVIS 6-12

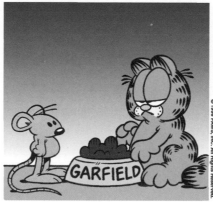

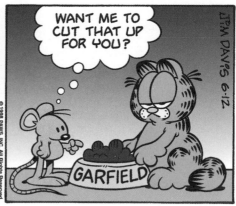

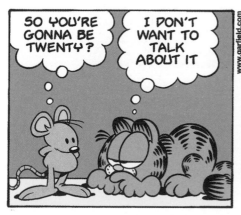

SO YOU'RE GONNA BE TWENTY?
I DON'T WANT TO TALK ABOUT IT
www.garfield.com
HAVE YOU TRIED DENIAL?
WHAT'S SO GREAT ABOUT DENIAL?
© 1998 PAWS, INC. All Rights Reserved.
CHEAPER THAN WRINKLE CREAM, PAL
GO AWAY
JIM DAVIS 6-13

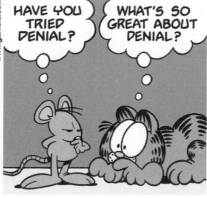

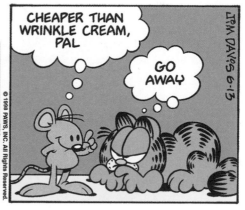

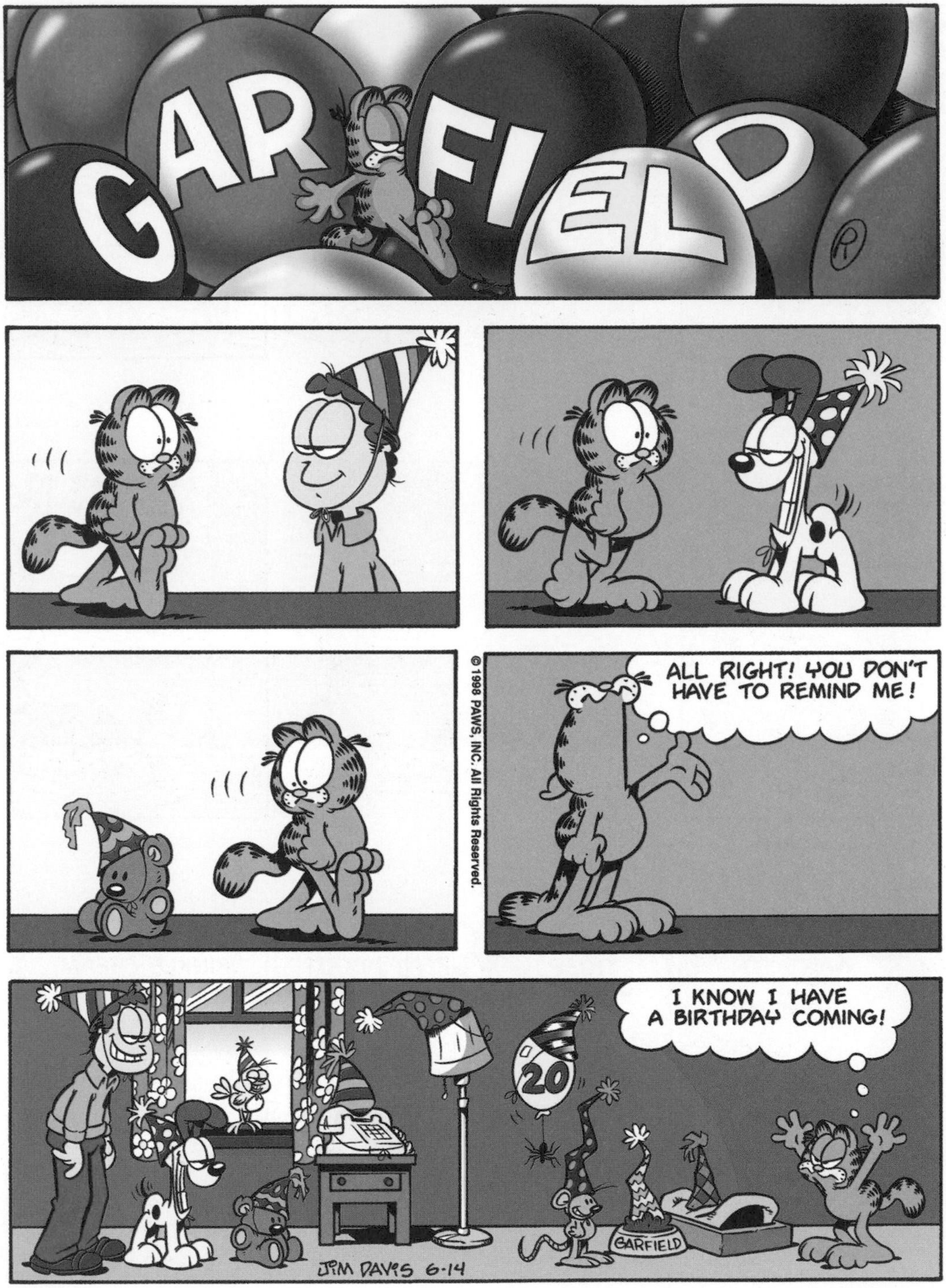
GARFIELD
ALL RIGHT! YOU DON'T HAVE TO REMIND ME!
I KNOW I HAVE A BIRTHDAY COMING!
20
GARFIELD
JIM DAVIS 6-14

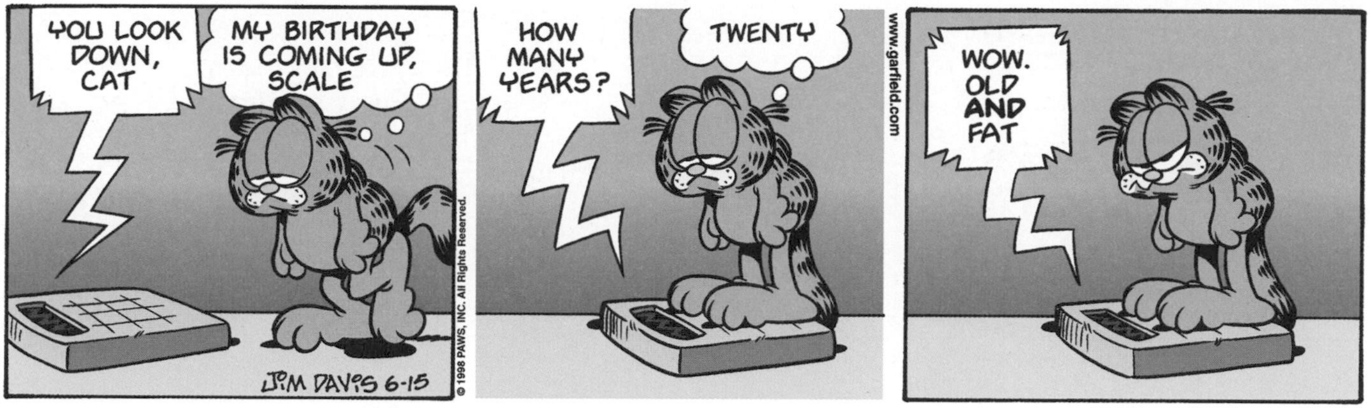
YOU LOOK DOWN, CAT
MY BIRTHDAY IS COMING UP, SCALE
JIM DAVIS 6-15
© 1998 PAWS, INC. All Rights Reserved.
HOW MANY YEARS?
TWENTY
www.garfield.com
WOW. OLD AND FAT

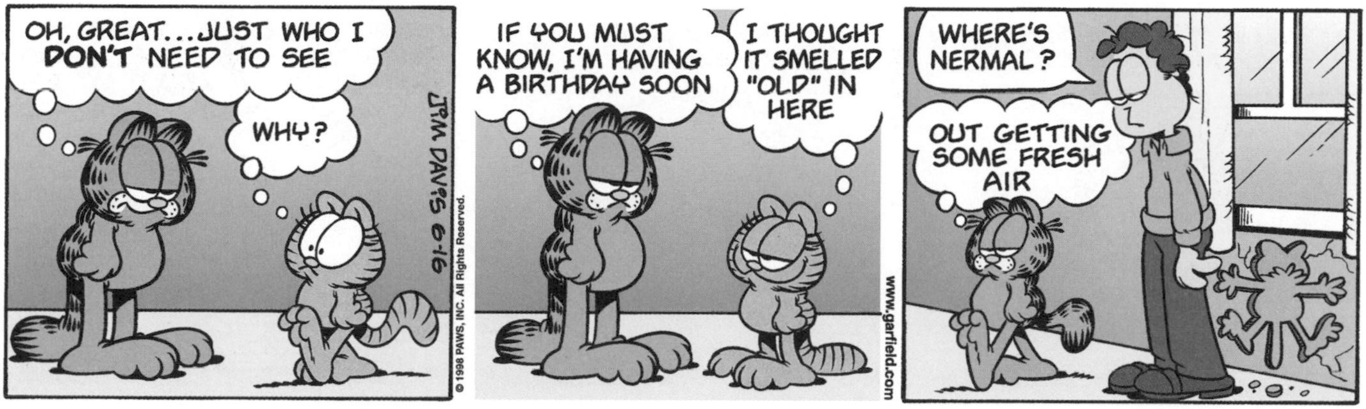
OH, GREAT...JUST WHO I DON'T NEED TO SEE
WHY?
JIM DAVIS 6-16
© 1998 PAWS, INC. All Rights Reserved.
IF YOU MUST KNOW, I'M HAVING A BIRTHDAY SOON
I THOUGHT IT SMELLED "OLD" IN HERE
www.garfield.com
WHERE'S NERMAL?
OUT GETTING SOME FRESH AIR

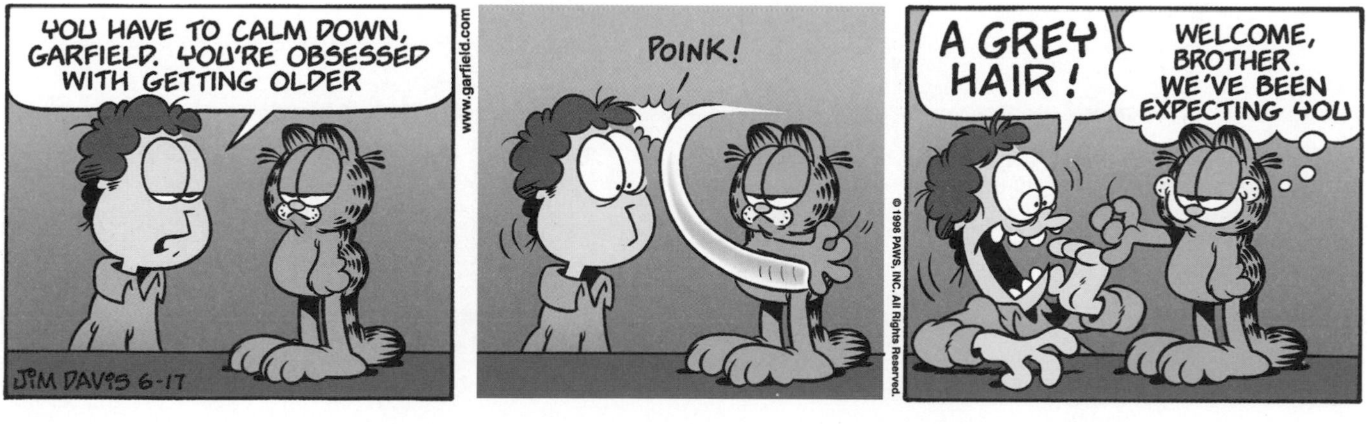
YOU HAVE TO CALM DOWN, GARFIELD. YOU'RE OBSESSED WITH GETTING OLDER
JIM DAVIS 6-17
www.garfield.com
POINK!
A GREY HAIR!
WELCOME, BROTHER. WE'VE BEEN EXPECTING YOU
© 1998 PAWS, INC. All Rights Reserved.

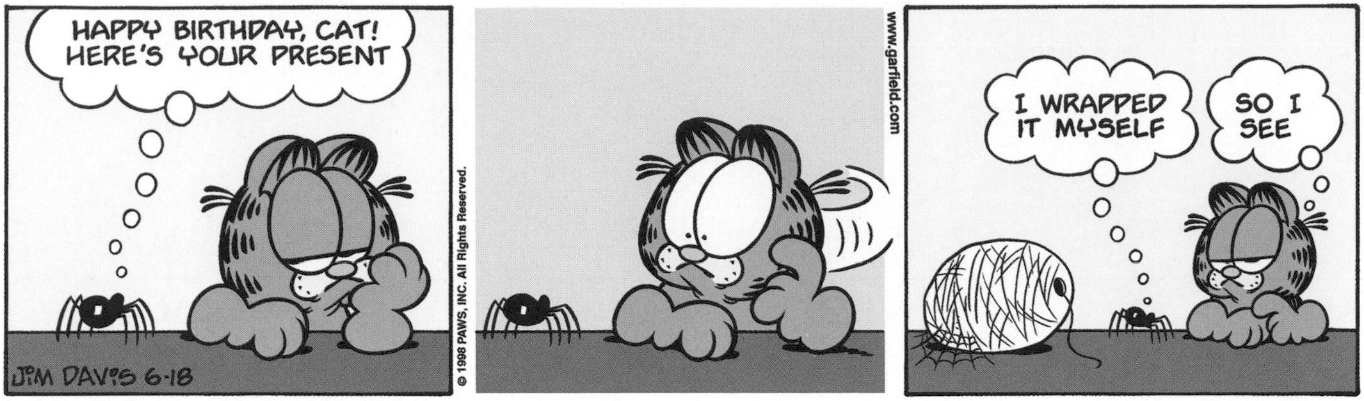
HAPPY BIRTHDAY, CAT! HERE'S YOUR PRESENT
JIM DAVIS 6-18
© 1998 PAWS, INC. All Rights Reserved.
www.garfield.com
I WRAPPED IT MYSELF
SO I SEE

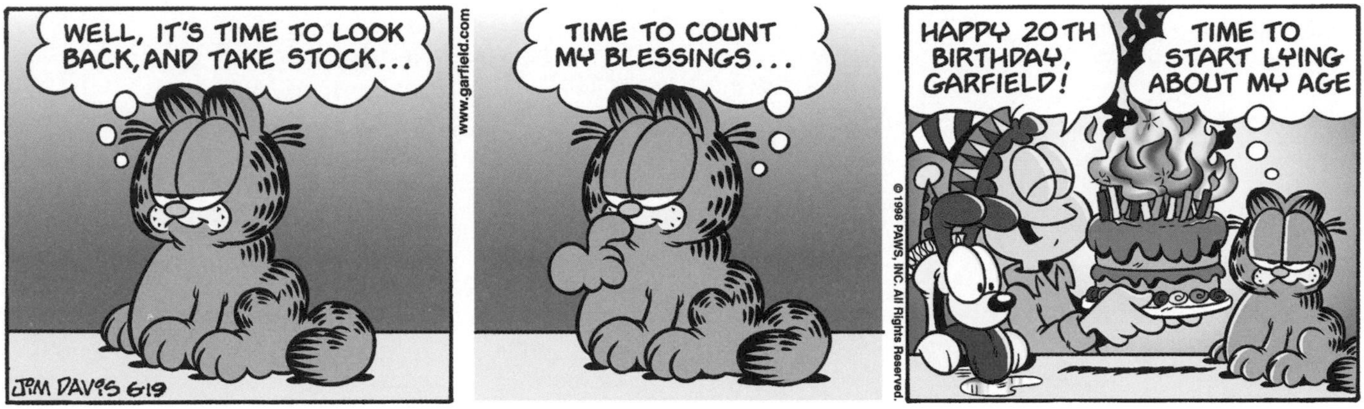
WELL, IT'S TIME TO LOOK BACK, AND TAKE STOCK...
JIM DAVIS 6-19
www.garfield.com
TIME TO COUNT MY BLESSINGS...
HAPPY 20TH BIRTHDAY, GARFIELD!
TIME TO START LYING ABOUT MY AGE
© 1998 PAWS, INC. All Rights Reserved.

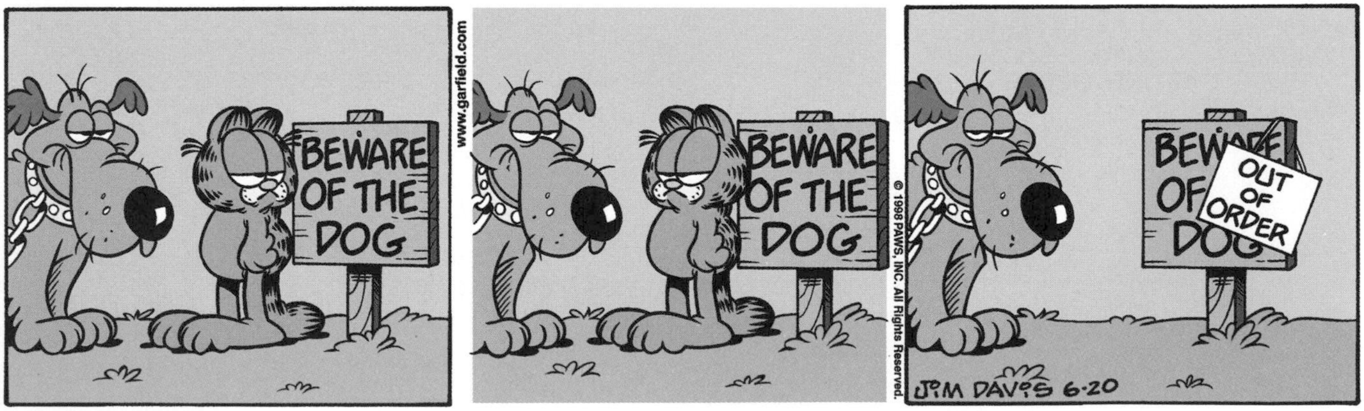
BEWARE OF THE DOG
www.garfield.com
BEWARE OF THE DOG
© 1998 PAWS, INC. All Rights Reserved.
OUT OF ORDER
JIM DAVIS 6-20

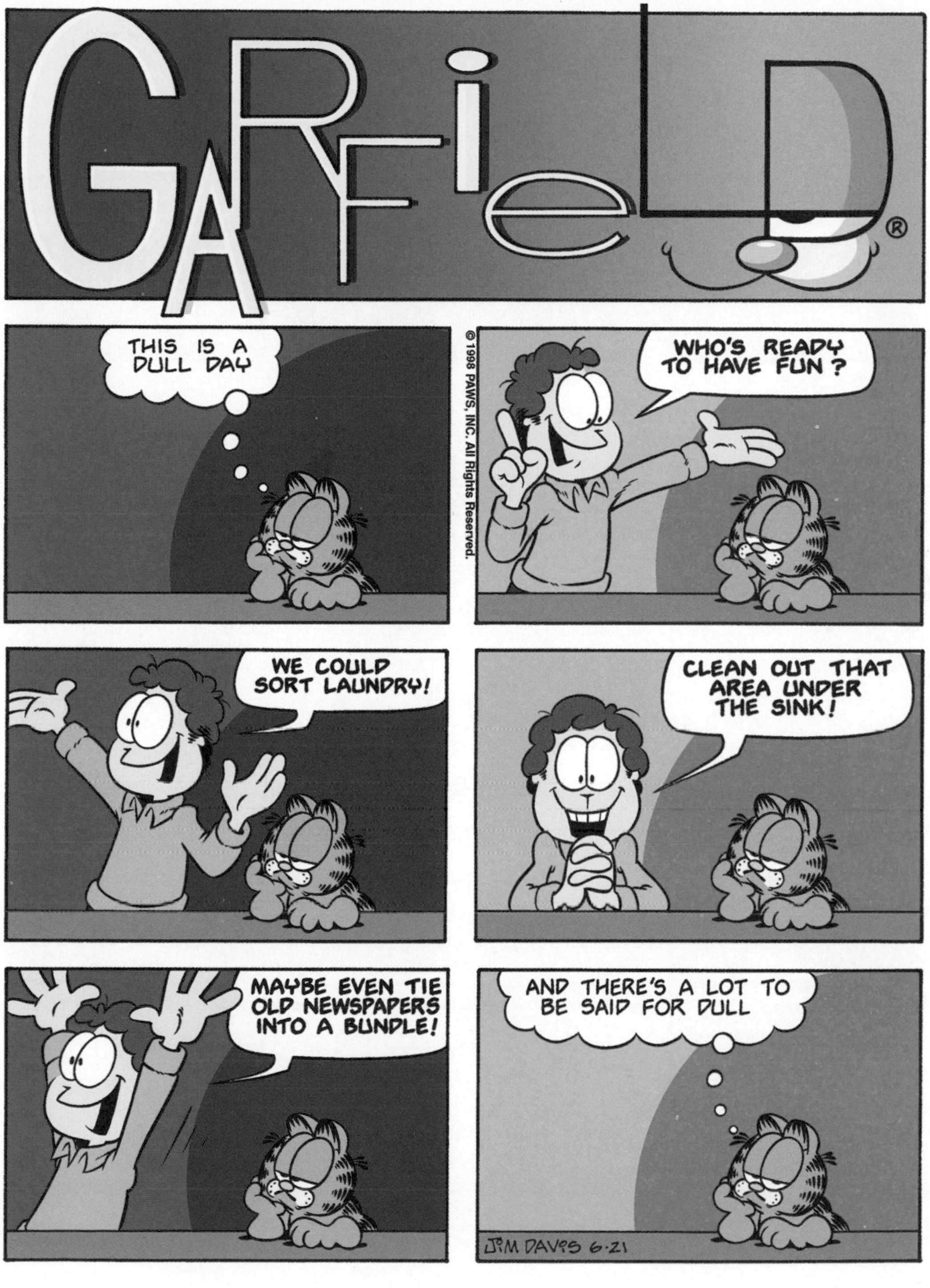
GARFIELD®
THIS IS A DULL DAY
© 1998 PAWS, INC. All Rights Reserved.
WHO'S READY TO HAVE FUN?
WE COULD SORT LAUNDRY!
CLEAN OUT THAT AREA UNDER THE SINK!
MAYBE EVEN TIE OLD NEWSPAPERS INTO A BUNDLE!
AND THERE'S A LOT TO BE SAID FOR DULL
JIM DAVIS 6-21

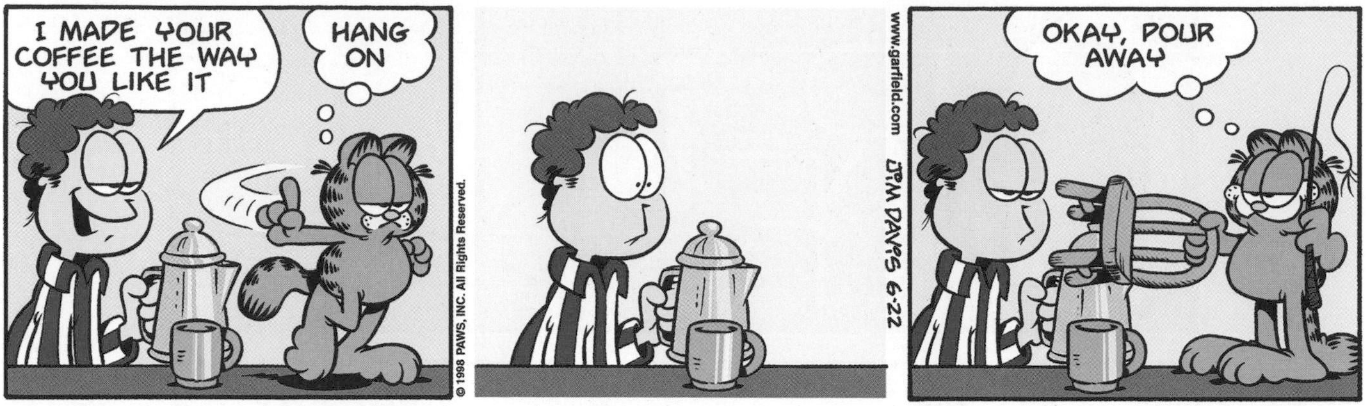
I MADE YOUR COFFEE THE WAY YOU LIKE IT
HANG ON
© 1998 PAWS, INC. All Rights Reserved.
www.garfield.com
JIM DAVIS 6-22
OKAY, POUR AWAY

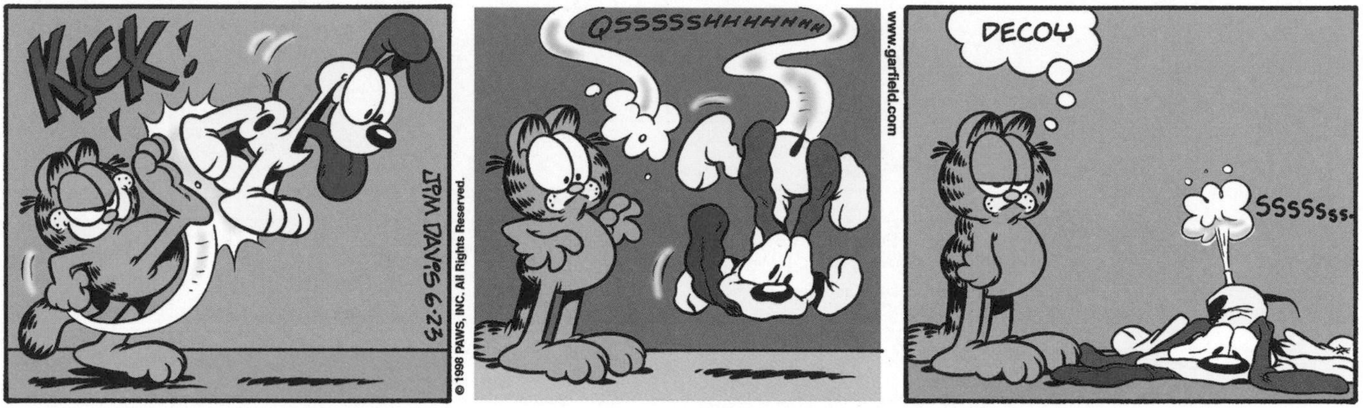
KICK!
JIM DAVIS 6-23
© 1998 PAWS, INC. All Rights Reserved.
QSSSSSSHHHHHHH
www.garfield.com
DECOY
SSSSSss.

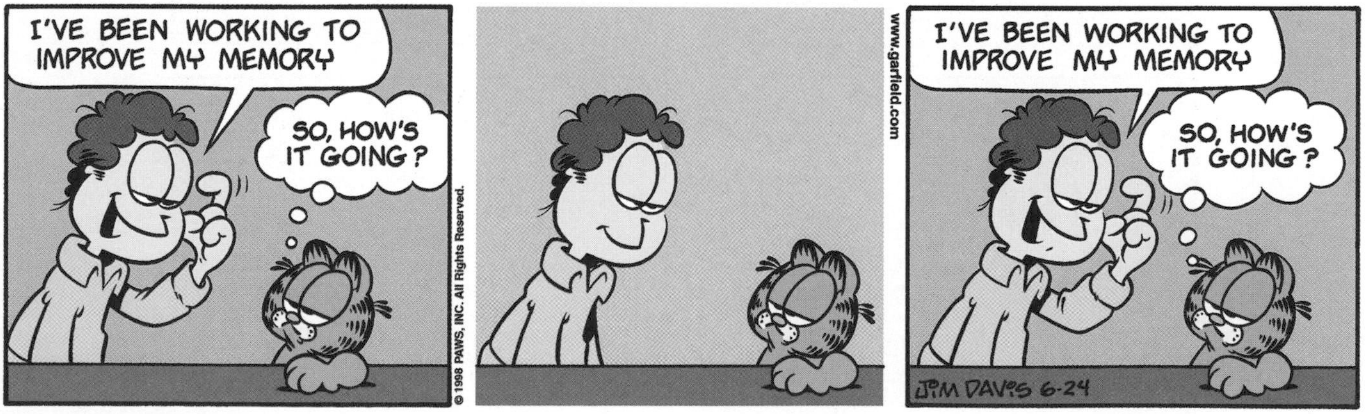
I'VE BEEN WORKING TO IMPROVE MY MEMORY
SO, HOW'S IT GOING?
© 1998 PAWS, INC. All Rights Reserved.
www.garfield.com
I'VE BEEN WORKING TO IMPROVE MY MEMORY
SO, HOW'S IT GOING?
JIM DAVIS 6-24

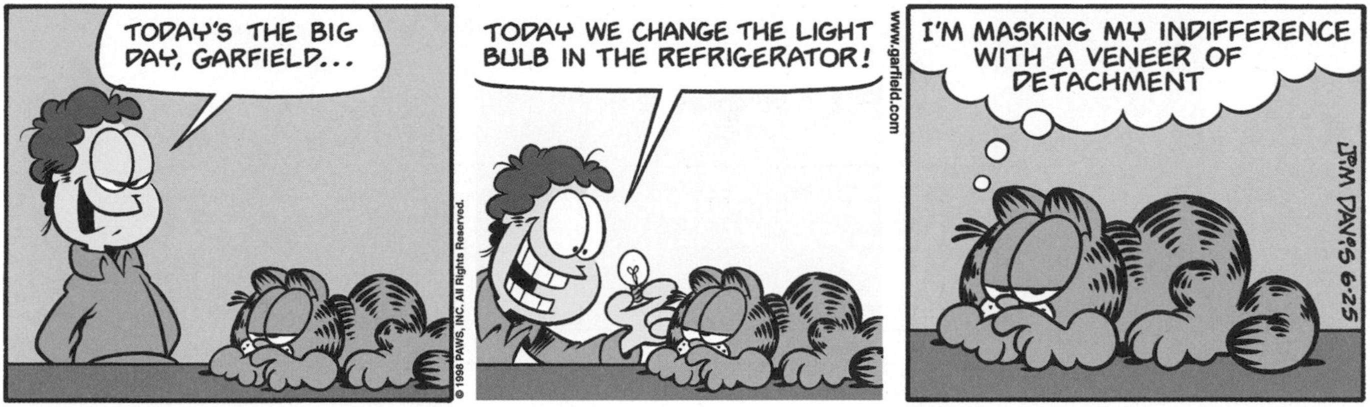
TODAY'S THE BIG DAY, GARFIELD...
TODAY WE CHANGE THE LIGHT BULB IN THE REFRIGERATOR!
I'M MASKING MY INDIFFERENCE WITH A VENEER OF DETACHMENT
JIM DAVIS 6-25
© 1998 PAWS, INC. All Rights Reserved.
www.garfield.com

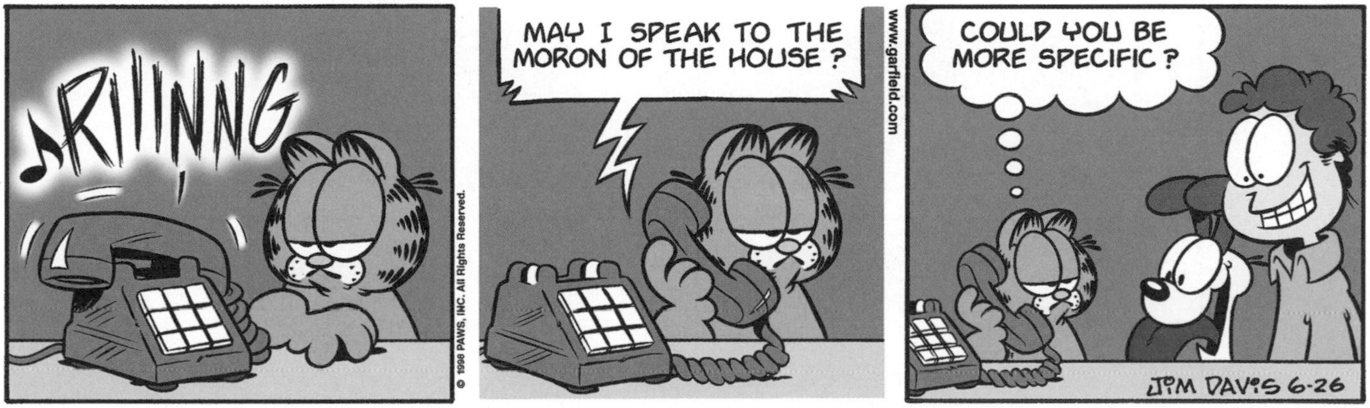
RIIINNG
MAY I SPEAK TO THE MORON OF THE HOUSE?
COULD YOU BE MORE SPECIFIC?
JIM DAVIS 6-26
© 1998 PAWS, INC. All Rights Reserved.
www.garfield.com

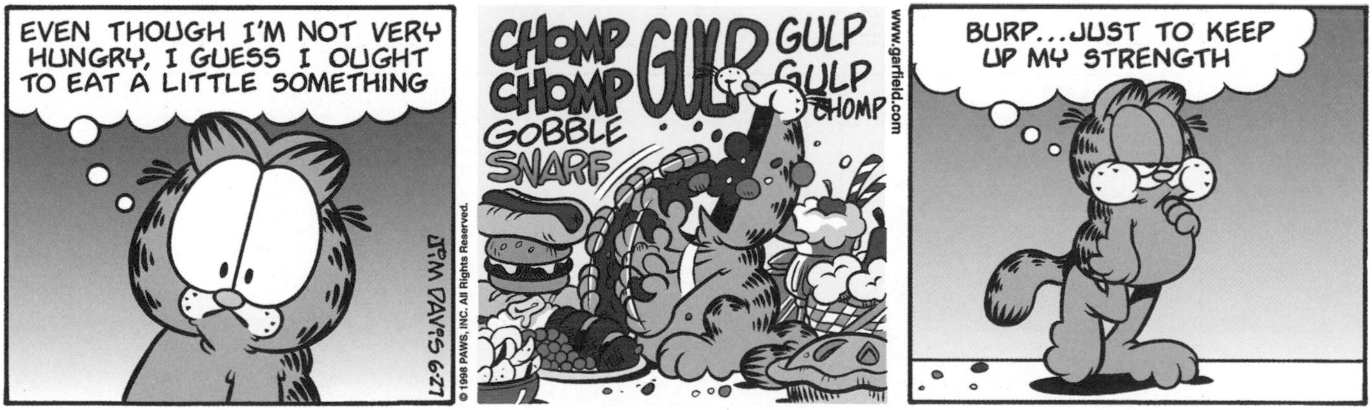
EVEN THOUGH I'M NOT VERY HUNGRY, I GUESS I OUGHT TO EAT A LITTLE SOMETHING
JIM DAVIS 6-27
CHOMP CHOMP GOBBLE SNARF GULP GULP GULP CHOMP
BURP...JUST TO KEEP UP MY STRENGTH
© 1998 PAWS, INC. All Rights Reserved.
www.garfield.com

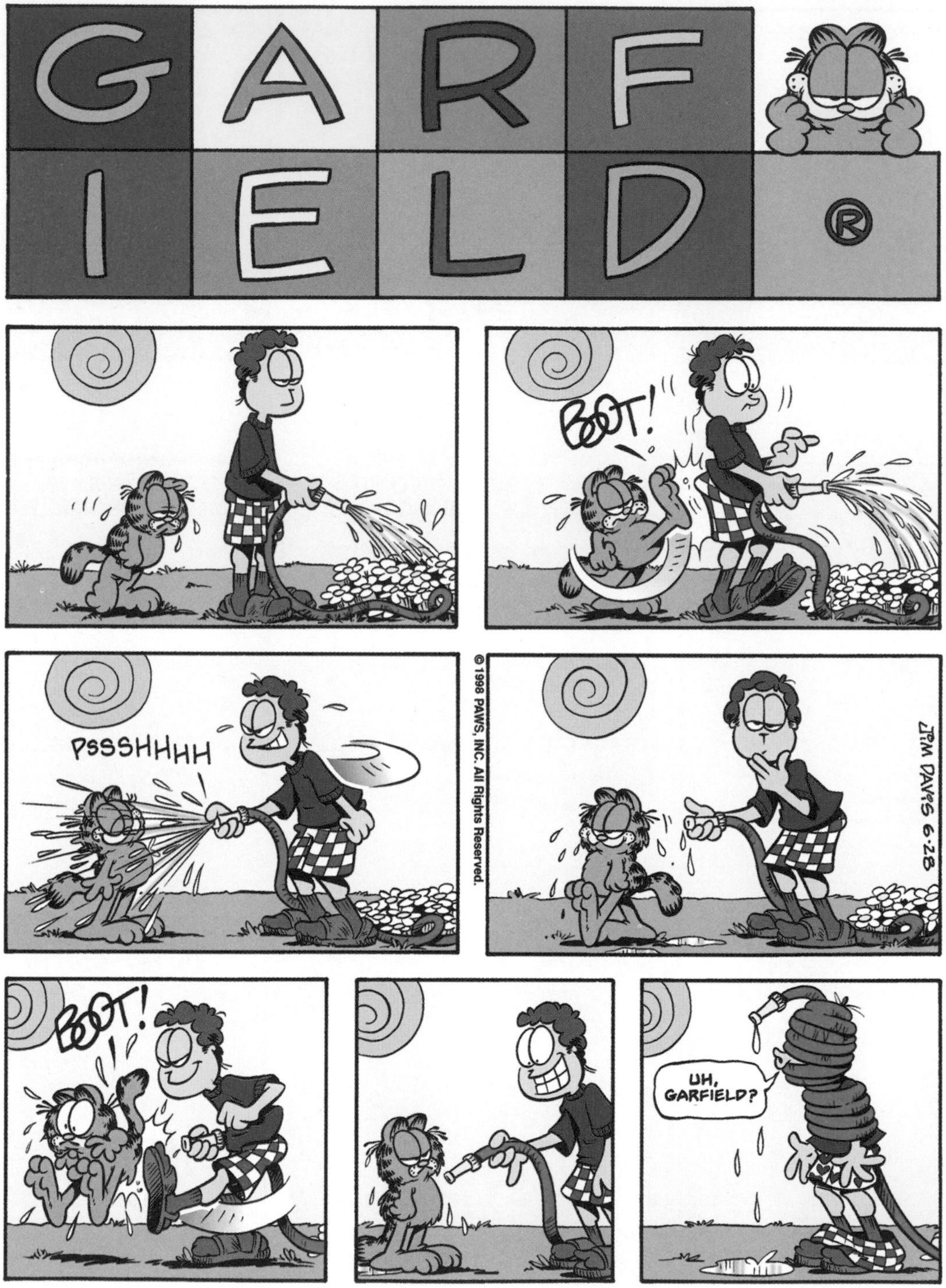
GARFIELD®
BOOT!
PSSSHHHH
© 1998 PAWS, INC. All Rights Reserved.
JIM DAVIS 6-28
BOOT!
UH, GARFIELD?

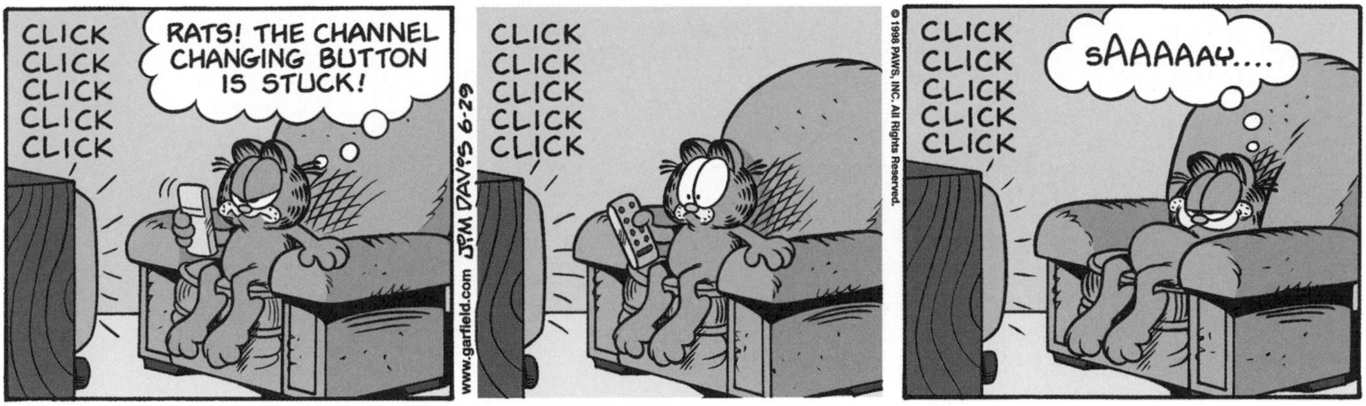
CLICK CLICK CLICK CLICK CLICK
RATS! THE CHANNEL CHANGING BUTTON IS STUCK!
JIM DAVIS 6-29
www.garfield.com
CLICK CLICK CLICK CLICK CLICK
© 1998 PAWS, INC. All Rights Reserved.
CLICK CLICK CLICK CLICK CLICK
sAAAAAY....

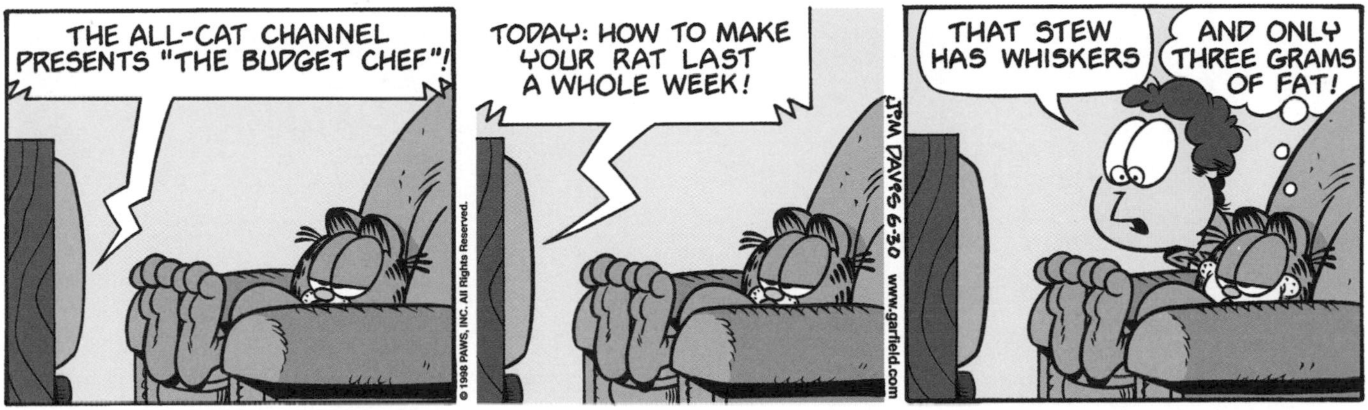
THE ALL-CAT CHANNEL PRESENTS "THE BUDGET CHEF"!
© 1998 PAWS, INC. All Rights Reserved.
TODAY: HOW TO MAKE YOUR RAT LAST A WHOLE WEEK!
JIM DAVIS 6-30
www.garfield.com
THAT STEW HAS WHISKERS
AND ONLY THREE GRAMS OF FAT!

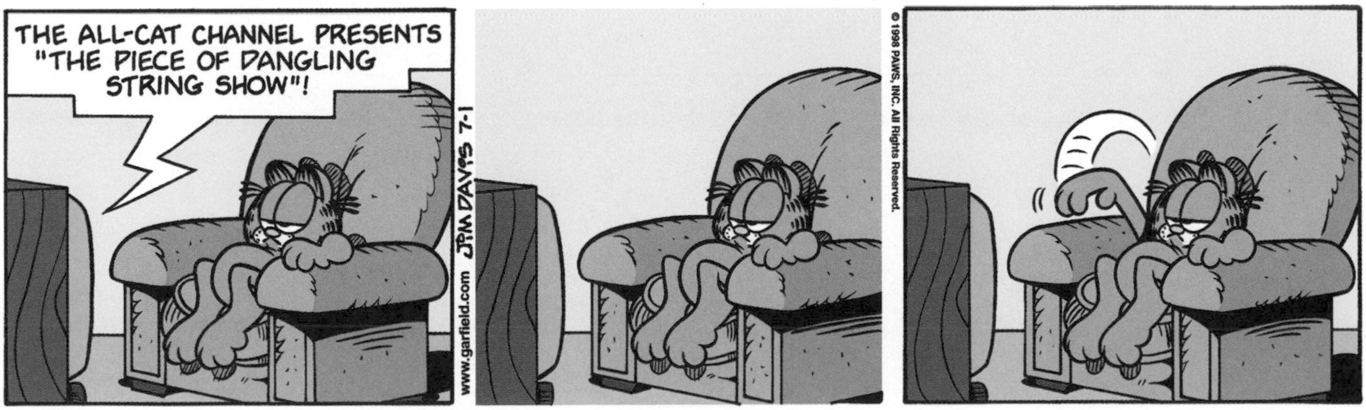
THE ALL-CAT CHANNEL PRESENTS "THE PIECE OF DANGLING STRING SHOW"!
JIM DAVIS 7-1
www.garfield.com
© 1998 PAWS, INC. All Rights Reserved.

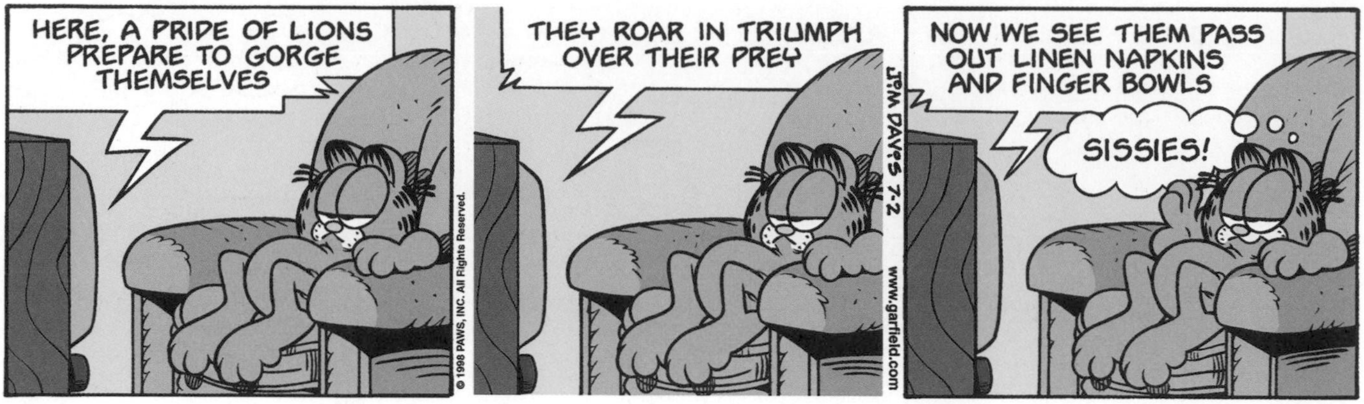
HERE, A PRIDE OF LIONS PREPARE TO GORGE THEMSELVES
© 1998 PAWS, INC. All Rights Reserved.
THEY ROAR IN TRIUMPH OVER THEIR PREY
JIM DAVIS 7-2
www.garfield.com
NOW WE SEE THEM PASS OUT LINEN NAPKINS AND FINGER BOWLS
SISSIES!

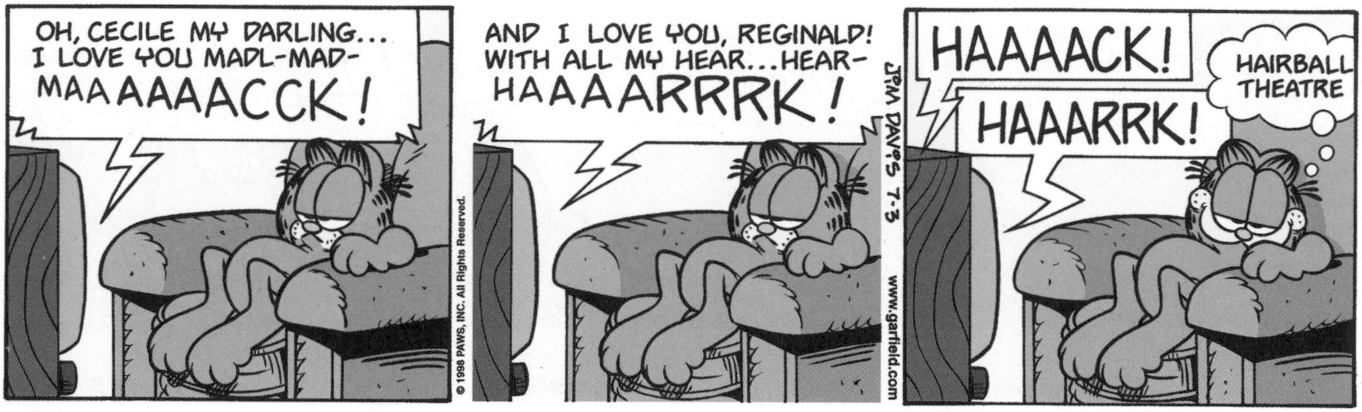
OH, CECILE MY DARLING... I LOVE YOU MADL-MAD-MAAAAAACCK!
© 1998 PAWS, INC. All Rights Reserved.
AND I LOVE YOU, REGINALD! WITH ALL MY HEAR...HEAR-HAAAARRRK!
JIM DAVIS 7-3
www.garfield.com
HAAAACK!
HAAARRK!
HAIRBALL THEATRE

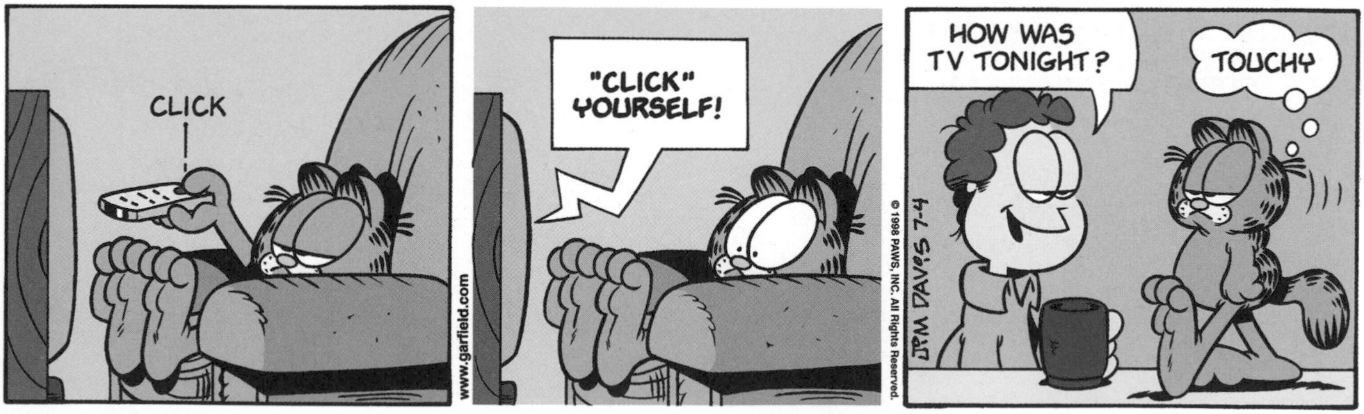
CLICK
www.garfield.com
"CLICK" YOURSELF!
© 1998 PAWS, INC. All Rights Reserved.
JIM DAVIS 7-4
HOW WAS TV TONIGHT?
TOUCHY

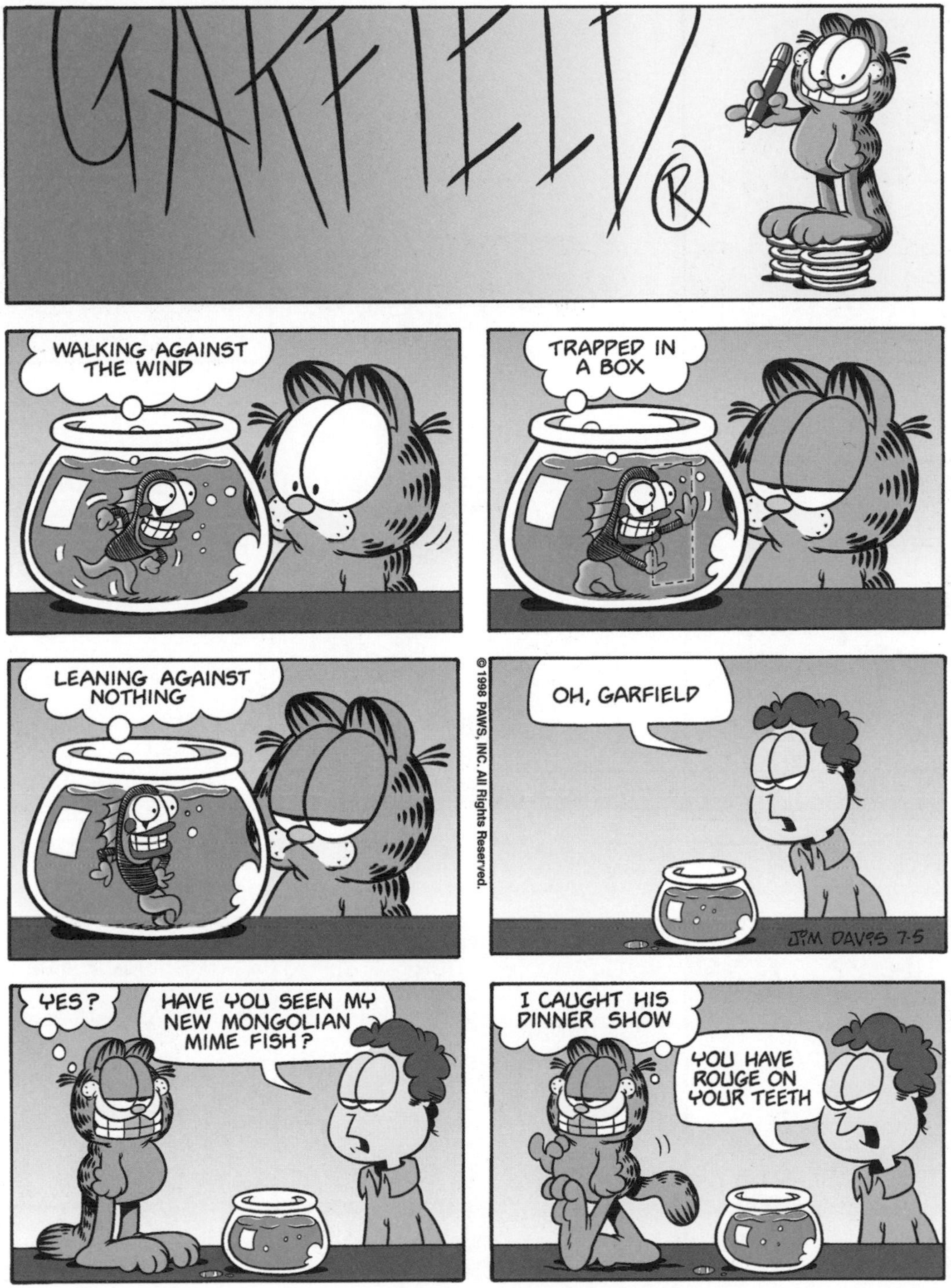
GARFIELD ®
WALKING AGAINST THE WIND
TRAPPED IN A BOX
LEANING AGAINST NOTHING
OH, GARFIELD
JIM DAVIS 7-5
YES?
HAVE YOU SEEN MY NEW MONGOLIAN MIME FISH?
I CAUGHT HIS DINNER SHOW
YOU HAVE ROUGE ON YOUR TEETH

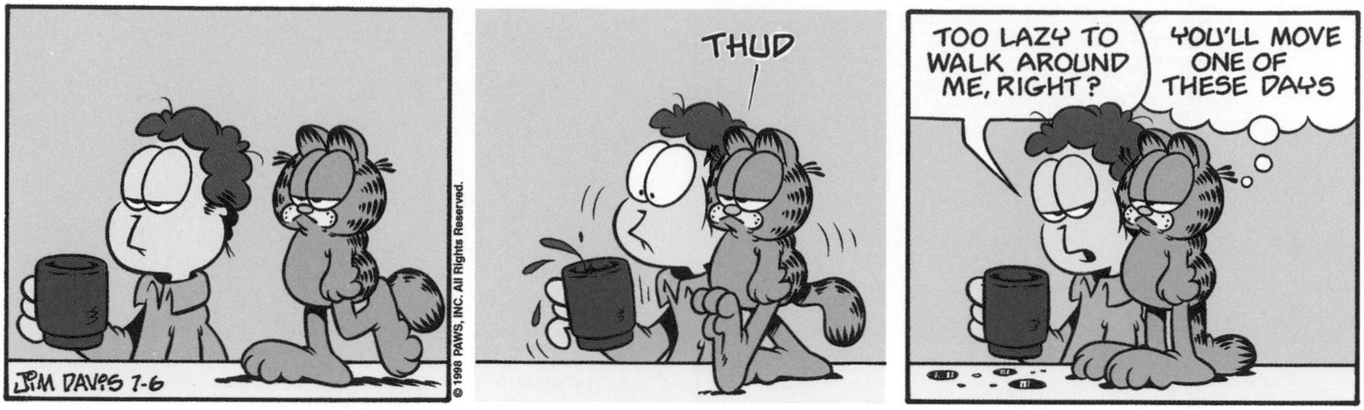
JIM DAVIS 7-6
© 1998 PAWS, INC. All Rights Reserved.
THUD
TOO LAZY TO WALK AROUND ME, RIGHT?
YOU'LL MOVE ONE OF THESE DAYS

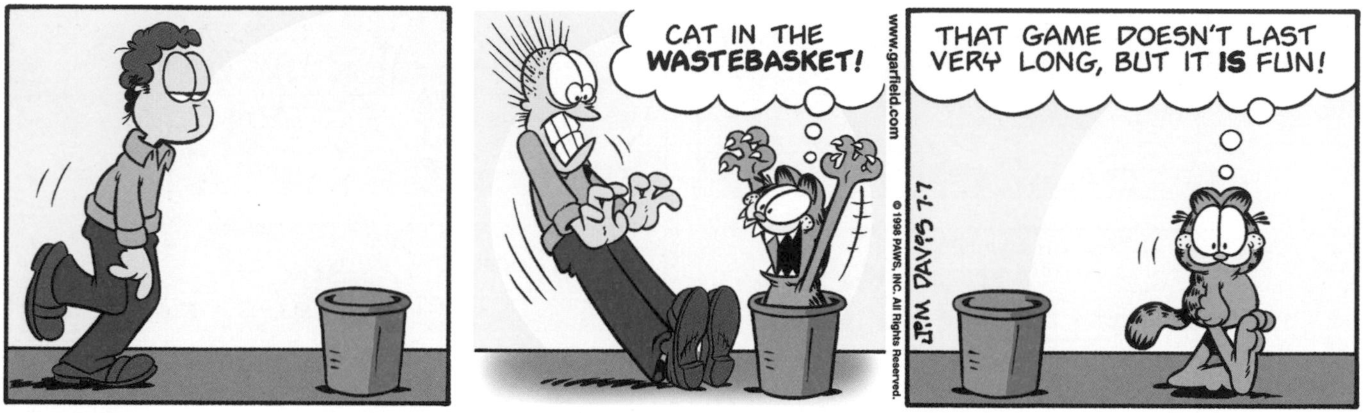
CAT IN THE **WASTEBASKET**!
www.garfield.com
© 1998 PAWS, INC. All Rights Reserved.
JIM DAVIS 7-7
THAT GAME DOESN'T LAST VERY LONG, BUT IT **IS** FUN!

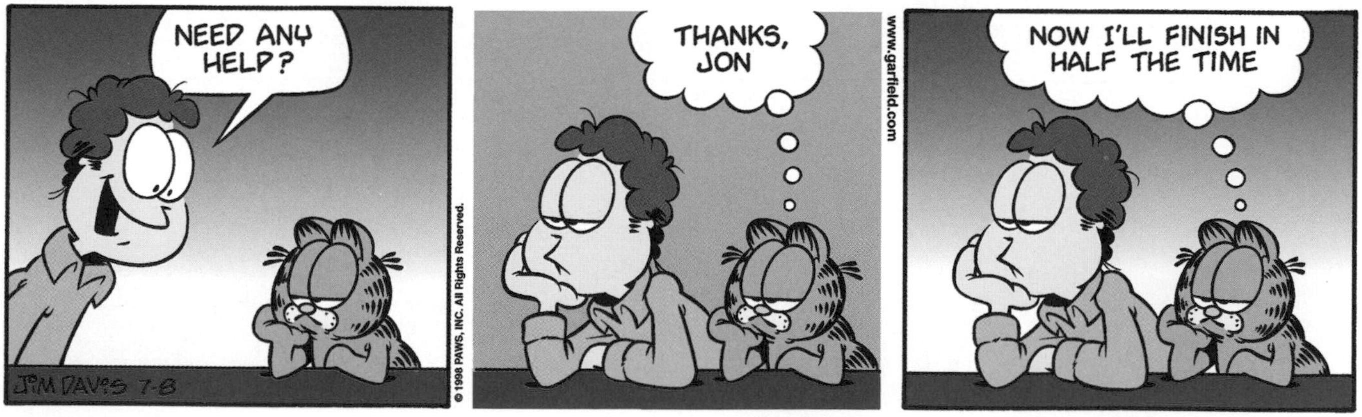
NEED ANY HELP?
JIM DAVIS 7-8
© 1998 PAWS, INC. All Rights Reserved.
THANKS, JON
www.garfield.com
NOW I'LL FINISH IN HALF THE TIME

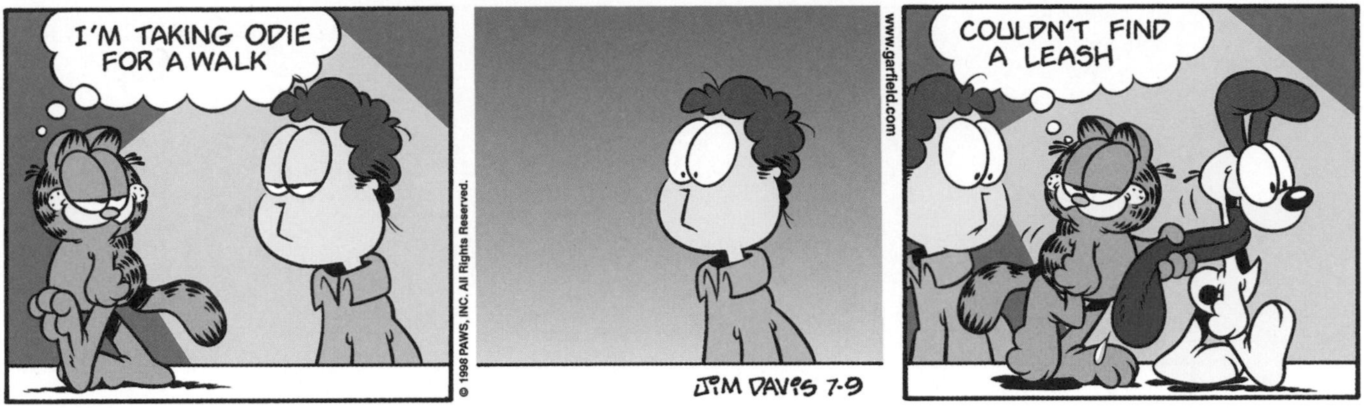
I'M TAKING ODIE FOR A WALK
© 1998 PAWS, INC. All Rights Reserved.
JIM DAVIS 7-9
www.garfield.com
COULDN'T FIND A LEASH

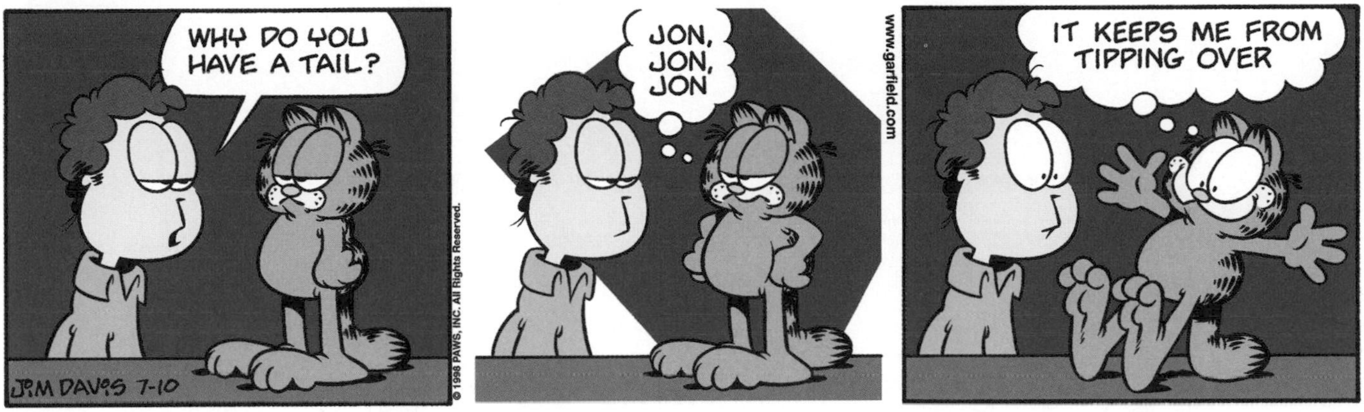
WHY DO YOU HAVE A TAIL?
JIM DAVIS 7-10
© 1998 PAWS, INC. All Rights Reserved.
JON, JON, JON
www.garfield.com
IT KEEPS ME FROM TIPPING OVER

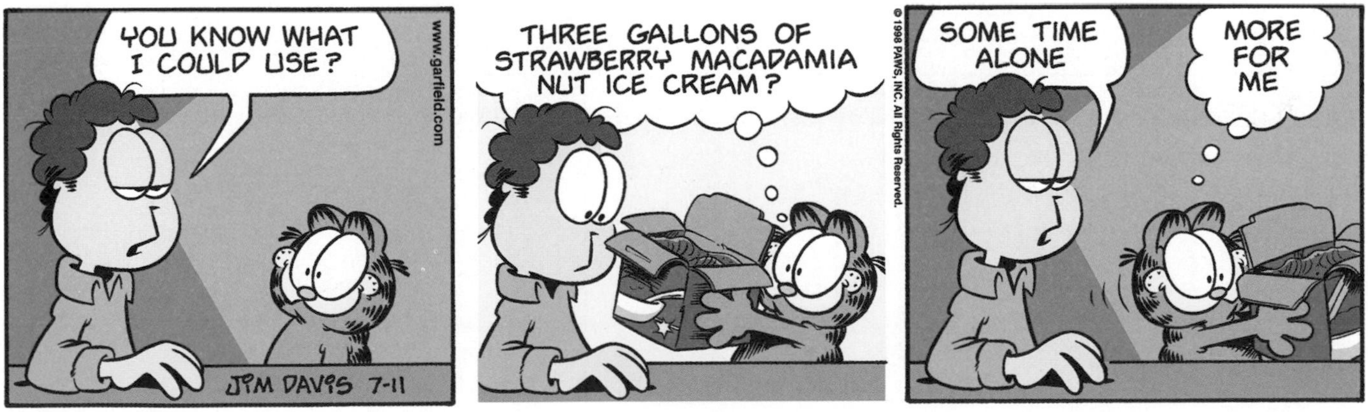
YOU KNOW WHAT I COULD USE?
JIM DAVIS 7-11
www.garfield.com
THREE GALLONS OF STRAWBERRY MACADAMIA NUT ICE CREAM?
© 1998 PAWS, INC. All Rights Reserved.
SOME TIME ALONE
MORE FOR ME

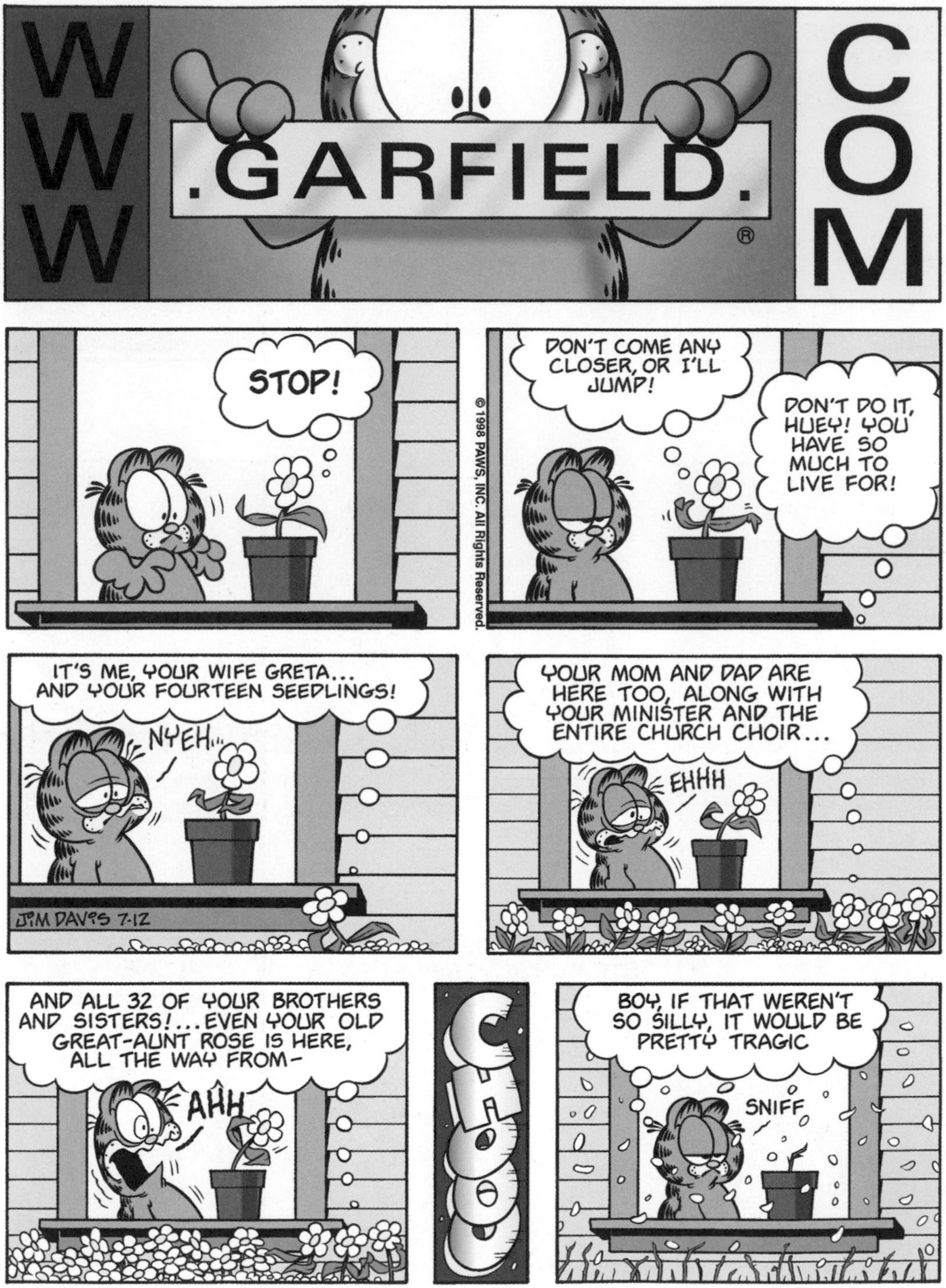
WWW.GARFIELD.COM
STOP!
DON'T COME ANY CLOSER, OR I'LL JUMP!
DON'T DO IT, HUEY! YOU HAVE SO MUCH TO LIVE FOR!
© 1998 PAWS, INC. All Rights Reserved.
IT'S ME, YOUR WIFE GRETA... AND YOUR FOURTEEN SEEDLINGS!
NYEH
JIM DAVIS 7-12
YOUR MOM AND DAD ARE HERE TOO, ALONG WITH YOUR MINISTER AND THE ENTIRE CHURCH CHOIR...
EHHH
AND ALL 32 OF YOUR BROTHERS AND SISTERS!... EVEN YOUR OLD GREAT-AUNT ROSE IS HERE, ALL THE WAY FROM—
AHH
CHOOO
BOY, IF THAT WEREN'T SO SILLY, IT WOULD BE PRETTY TRAGIC
SNIFF

LIFE HAS ITS UPS AND DOWNS
© 1998 PAWS, INC. All Rights Reserved.
www.garfield.com
I HAVE UPS!
I DIDN'T SAY ANYTHING
JIM DAVIS 7-13

JIM DAVIS 7-14
CHEW
CHEW
CHEW
CHEW
CHEW
GARFIELD
© 1998 PAWS, INC. All Rights Reserved.
CHEW CHEW
CHEW
CHEW
CHEW CHEW
GARFIELD
www.garfield.com
WILL YOU SWALLOW?!
ONLY IF THERE'S MORE FOOD
CHEW
CHEW
CHEW
CHEW
CHEW
GARFIELD

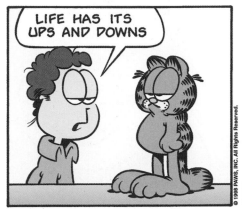

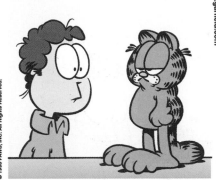

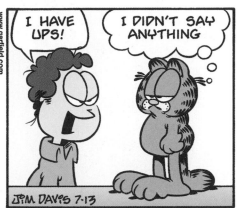

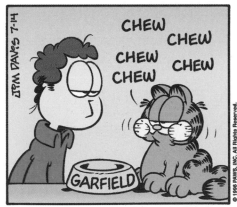

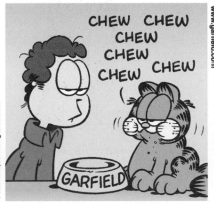

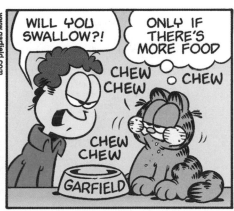

JON'S SCARIEST DATES

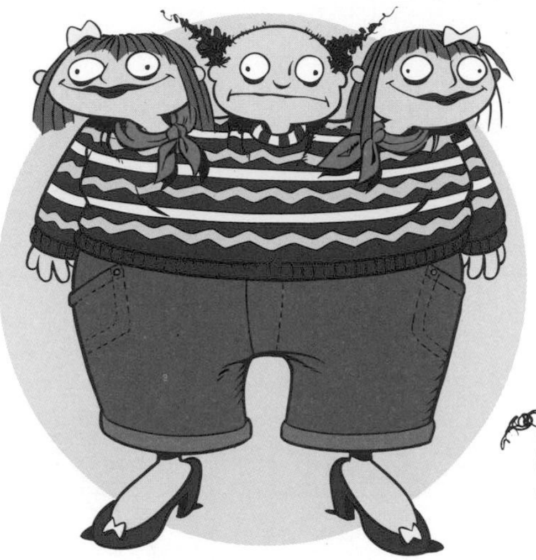

Gertie, Greta, and Bob, Siamese Triplets

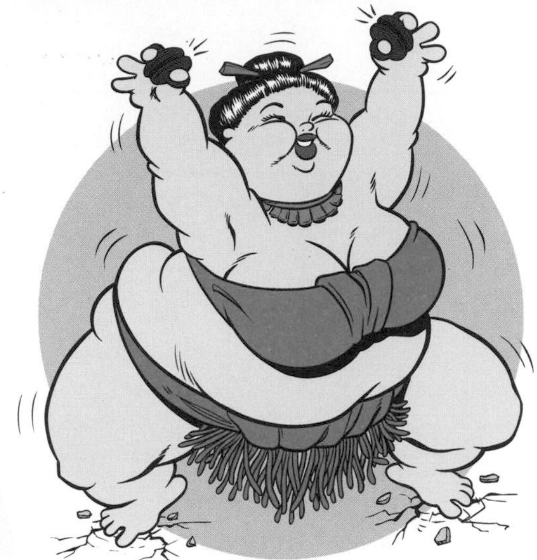

Suki the Sumo Belly Dancer

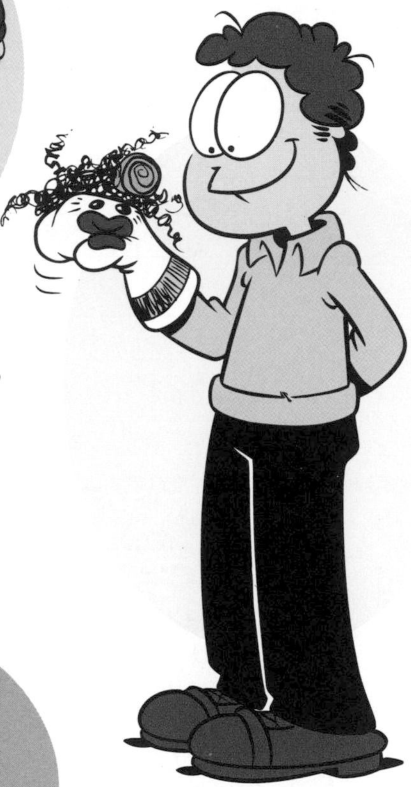

"Señorita Del Fuego"

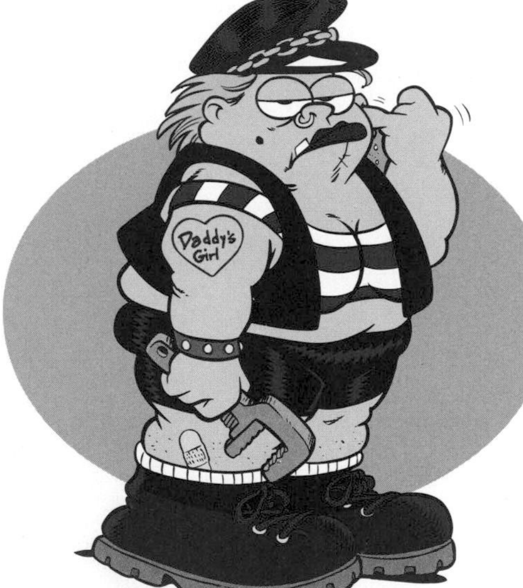

Annie Axelrod, Harley mechanic

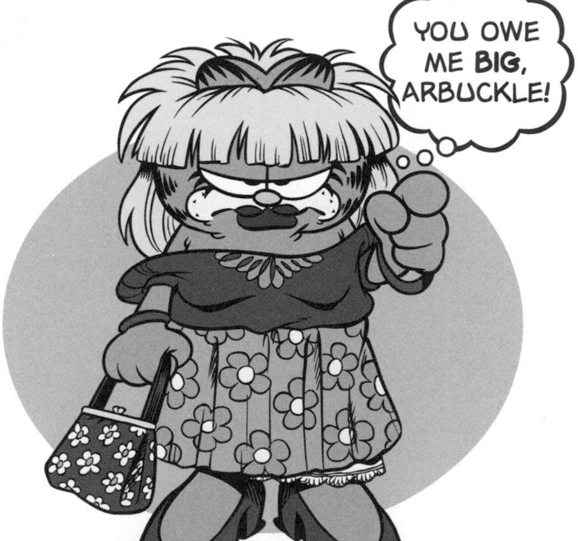
YOU OWE ME BIG, ARBUCKLE!

Garfield